The Reformation

McMaster Divinity College Press
McMaster General Studies Series, Volume 13

The Reformation

Past Voices, Current Implications

edited by
STEVEN M. STUDEBAKER AND GORDON L. HEATH

PICKWICK *Publications* · Eugene, Oregon

THE REFORMATION
Past Voices, Current Implications

McMaster General Studies Series, Volume 13
McMaster Divinity College Press

Copyright © 2021 Wipf and Stock Publishers. All rights reserved. Except for brief quotations in critical publications or reviews, no part of this book may be reproduced in any manner without prior written permission from the publisher. Write: Permissions, Wipf and Stock Publishers, 199 W. 8th Ave., Suite 3, Eugene, OR 97401.

Pickwick Publications	McMaster Divinity College Press
An Imprint of Wipf and Stock Publishers	1280 Main Street West
199 W. 8th Ave., Suite 3	Hamilton, ON, Canada L8S 4K1
Eugene, OR 97401	

www.wipfandstock.com

PAPERBACK ISBN: 978-1-7252-8707-5
HARDCOVER ISBN: 978-1-7252-8708-2
EBOOK ISBN: 978-1-7252-8709-9

Cataloguing-in-Publication data:

Names: Studebaker, Steven M., editor. | Heath, Gordon L., editor.

Title: The Reformation : past voices, current implications / edited by Steven M. Studebaker and Gordon L. Heath

Description: Eugene, OR: Pickwick Publications, 2021. | McMaster General Studies Series 13. | Includes bibliographical references and index.

Identifiers: ISBN 978-1-7252-8707-5 (paperback). | ISBN 978-1-7252-8708-2 (hardcover) | ISBN 978-1-7252-8709-9 (ebook).

Subjects: LCSH: Reformation. | Theology—16th Century.

Classification: BR303.5 R45 2021 (print). | BR303.5 (ebook).

Manufactured in the U.S.A.   04/14/21

Contents

Contributors | vii

1 Introduction | 1

2 Martin Luther and the Origins of the Reformation
   —*Victor A. Shepherd* | 11

3 Luther, the Ninety-Five Theses, and Ecumenism:
   That They May be One in 2017 —*James Keller* | 29

4 Thomas Cranmer, Roger Martyn, and the Transformation
   of Worship in the English Reformation
   —*Gwenfair Walters Adams* | 58

5 Calvin, the Anabaptists, and Tradition —*W. David Buschart* | 82

6 Anti-Semitism in the Reformation Era
   —*Victor A. Shepherd* | 102

7 Appropriating Reformation Tradition(s) Today:
   Should We Put the Past Behind Us?
   —*W. David Buschart* | 115

8 More "Unintended Consequences": How the Reformation
   (Mis)Shaped the Church for Mission in North America
   —*David Fitch* | 135

9   William Byrd and the Musical Reshaping of Liturgy
    in Reformation England: Insights for Worship
    in a Post-Christian Context —*Wendy J. Porter* | 152

10 Imperishable Seed: A Sermon for the 500th Anniversary
    of the Reformation —*Jennifer Powell McNutt* | 183

Index of Names | 197
Index of Subjects | 201

Contributors

EDITORS

Steven M. Studebaker (PhD, Marquette University) is the Howard and Shirley Bentall Chair in Evangelical Thought and Professor of Systematic and Historical Theology at McMaster Divinity College. He is the author of *A Pentecostal Political Theology for American Renewal* (Palgrave, 2016), *From Pentecost to the Triune God* (Eerdmans, 2012), and several other books on Jonathan Edwards' Trinitarian theology and Pentecostal theology.

Gordon L. Heath (PhD, St. Michael's College), FRHistS, is Professor of Christian History and Centenary Chair in World Christianity at McMaster Divinity College, Hamilton, Ontario. He also serves as Director of the Canadian Baptist Archives. His publications include *The British Nation is Our Nation: The BACSANZ Baptist Press and the South African War, 1899–1902* (Paternoster, 2017) and *A War with a Silver Lining: Canadian Protestant Churches and the South African War, 1899–1902* (MQUP, 2009).

CONTRIBUTORS

Gwenfair Walters Adams (PhD, Cambridge University) is Professor of Church History at Gordon-Conwell Theological Seminary. She is the author of *Visions in Late Medieval England* and the editor of the *Romans 1–8* volume of the Reformation Commentary on Scripture series (InterVarsity Press).

W. David Buschart is Professor of Theology and Historical Studies at Denver Seminary. His research and writing has focused on the nature and function of tradition and traditions within Protestantism, comparative Protestant theologies, and theologies of retrieval. He is currently studying the theological frameworks guiding evangelical work in creation care, social justice, and faith and work.

David Fitch (PhD, Northwestern University) is B. R. Lindner Chair of Evangelical Theology at Northern Seminary, Chicago. He works and writes within the fields of Neo-Anabaptist theology, missiology, culture studies, and political theory. He is an ordained pastor in the Christian and Missionary Alliance and currently co-pastors the Peace of Christ Church of Westmont IL, USA.

James Keller is Pastor of Historic St Paul's Lutheran Church in Kitchener, ON. A former pharmacist, Keller is a graduate of Concordia Lutheran Theological Seminary in St. Catharines, ON, and received his PhD in Christian Theology from McMaster Divinity College. He is married and has a daughter.

Wendy J. Porter is Associate Professor of Music and Worship at McMaster Divinity College. She teaches courses in Ministry Studies in areas of worship studies, liturgy, spiritual discernment, and theological reflection on the intersection of faith, work, and worship, and she plans and leads chapels throughout the academic year with a team of talented and committed graduate students.

Jennifer Powell McNutt is the Franklin S. Dyrness Associate Professor of Biblical & Theological Studies at Wheaton College. She has received awards for her teaching and scholarship including the Frank S. and Elizabeth D. Brewer Prize by the American Society of Church History for her monograph, *Calvin Meets Voltaire: The Clergy of Geneva in the Age of Enlightenment, 1685–1798* (Ashgate, 2014). She is a Fellow in the Royal Historical Society as well as an ordained minister in the Presbyterian Church (USA).

Victor Shepherd, a minister of the Presbyterian Church in Canada, is Professor Emeritus at Tyndale University, Professorial Fellow (Core Faculty) at Wycliffe College (University of Toronto), and *Professor Ordinarius* at University of Oxford, UK. A specialist in Reformation Theology and History, he has addressed audiences in Canada, the USA, and Great Britain. As a student of Christian Anti-Semitism he is a frequent speaker in synagogues, churches, and high schools. He is married to Maureen McGuigan. They have two children and five grandchildren.

1

Introduction

THE GERMAN MONK MARTIN Luther's nailing of the *Ninety-Five Theses* on the church door at Wittenberg was a pivotal moment in the birth of what would become known as the Reformation(s).[1] Five hundred years later, in 2017, numerous quincentennial celebrations at universities, seminaries, denominations, historical societies, and local churches around the world marked that iconic event. So, too, did the publication of a plethora of books.[2] The Centre for Post-Christendom Studies at McMaster Divinity College was one such organization that hosted a conference commemorating the event; however, while the conference did provide attendees with the necessary history and theology of the movement in the sixteenth century, its focus was to think about how the message and praxis of the reformers could be translated into a post-Christendom West.

The reforms birthed, denominations founded, and trajectories established by Luther and others eventually moved far afield from Germany

---

1. Those who refer to it as Reformation emphasize the unity of the event, whereas those who call it Reformations emphasis its diversity.

2. For historical, biographical, and theological works, see Balserak, *Calvinism*; DeRusha, *Katharina and Martin Luther*; Elwood, *A Brief Introduction to John Calvin*; Gregory, *Rebel in the Ranks*; Kaufmann, *A Short Life of Martin Luther*; Kittelson and Wiersma, *Luther the Reformer*; Kolb, *Martin Luther and the Enduring Word of God*; Lutzer, *Rescuing the Gospel*; Marty, *October 31, 1517*; Paulson, *A Brief Introduction to Martin Luther*; Roper, *Martin Luther*; Schilling, *Martin Luther*; Sunshine, *A Brief Introduction to the Reformation*. For a generally positive analysis of the impact of the Reformation, see Van Neste and Garrett, eds., *Reformation 500*. For works related to appropriating the Reformation for today, see Vanhoozer, *Biblical Authority after Babel*; Crisp, *Saving Calvinism*; García and Nunes, *Wittenberg Meets the World*. For two very different perspectives on the relevancy and future of Protestantism, see Walls and Collins, *Why I Am Not Roman Catholic*; Leithart, *End of Protestantism*.

and the Holy Roman Empire to become a global Protestant movement of over eight hundred million followers in the twenty-first century. Many of those Protestants live in the global south and are experiencing the incredible growth of the church. As Philip Jenkins and others have noted, one of the most remarkable events of the post-world war era has been the demographic explosion of the church in sub-Saharan Africa, Latin America, and parts of Asia. Churches in those regions face their own unique pressures, but the trajectories are, in many cases, towards the "Next-Christendom."[3] In the West, however, the telos is not so positive. Christianity is still the majority religion in terms of census results, but rapid secularization, a decrease in church attendance, a rise of "nones" (those with no religious affiliation), and, perhaps most alarming for many, a move from being powerful shapers of culture in the gilded halls of power to being on the margins (just one religious voice among many) has churches reeling. For centuries, churches relied on some sort of Christendom to bolster their privileged position, but those days seem over. It is a different world, with many old assumptions crumbling and new realities beginning to shape a post-Christendom West.

To be more precise, there have been two post-Christendoms in the West since the Reformation, and Luther—as the iconic reformer (or ringleader, in the eyes of his opponents)—has been blamed for both. The first post-Christendom was the permanent breakup of a unified medieval Christendom. Despite the divisions and dissenters of the medieval period, for roughly five-hundred years before Luther, Western Europe identified itself as a Christian civilization under the authority of the Catholic Church. There were attempts at solving the Reformation era theological controversies, but after the Council of Trent (1545–1563), Spanish Armada (1588), and Thirty Years War (1618–1648), it was clear that the division of European Christianity was permanent. Christendom, in terms of a structural, cultural, and spiritual unity, had been "destroyed."[4] For centuries that followed, Christianity remained powerful and central to culture and national identity, but the choice became allegiance to competing Christian confessions. The second post-Christendom is now, with the move of churches to the margins and away from power. Of course, its origins can be traced to a number of factors such as the Enlightenment, industrialization, urbanization, migration, and post-war angst, but the trajectories established by the Reformation had unintended consequences. As Brad S. Gregory has argued

---

3. Jenkins, *The Next Christendom*.
4. Greengrass, *Christendom Destroyed*.

INTRODUCTION

in *The Unintended Reformation*, "ideological and institutional shifts that occurred five or more centuries ago remain substantively necessary to an explanation of why the Western world today is as it is."[5] Stated simply, the religious revolutions of the sixteenth century charted a course to today's Western secularism and pluralism.

With the complicity of the Reformation in the plight of decline of Christendom, one may wonder what Luther and the other reformers have to say to churches today. The Centre for Post-Christendom Studies' conference sought to address that very issue by inviting various scholars to make links between the past and the present, with the purpose of drawing on the rich heritage of the sixteen and seventeenth-century reforms to equip Christians today. The expression *ecclesia semper reformanda* (the church must always be reformed), usually associated with Reformed (Calvinist) churches, may be generally appropriated to this theological and pastoral enterprise of re-imagining and re-applying the Reformation to a radically new cultural climate. The authors who contributed to this book acknowledge that the world of Luther, Ulrich Zwingli, John Calvin, and others is long gone, but they are also committed to the task of bringing their message to the modern world.

The chapters in this volume each originated as a presentation at the conference.[6] A number of others were published in *Post-Christendom Studies*, the journal of the Centre for Post-Christendom Studies.[7] The hope, of course, is that such publications nudge the discussion forward, and help churches today get a sense not only of their heritage (both good and bad), but the rich theological resources that could help shape their church's ministry in a world that Luther would never have recognized.

Victor Shepherd's first chapter introduces Luther and the religious ferment of the early-sixteenth century. He provides a sense of Luther's angst over his alienation from God, and how his solution to his spiritual crisis was rooted in an "utterly gratuitous, sheer gift of God" rather than a hunkering down and working even harder at earning salvation. He details the intense opposition to his reforms, his courage in the face of such hostility

---

5. Gregory, *Unintended Reformation*, 7.

6. Jennifer Powell McNutt chose not to include her plenary address in this volume or the journal.

7. They were printed as follows: Harris, "The Power of the Word of God," 5–19; Payton, Jr., "Reformation Ecumenism Reframed," 20–41; Knowles, "Preaching Before Posting," 42–66; Walker, "Ninety-Five Tweets," 67–86; and Heath, "Two Kingdoms for Today," 87–108.

(in contrast to Erasmus), and how the issue of indulgences was the catalyst for his *Ninety-Five Theses*. He also clarifies what the "Freedom of a Christian" is; "Christians, *freed* by Christ for their true nature—*bound* to Christ by faith and *bound* to the neighbor by love—live henceforth in radical self-forgetfulness." The implications of Luther's message were far reaching, and undermined much of accepted piety and theology; views on indulgences, saints, clergy, grace, faith, marriage, and sacraments were all re-cast to reflect Luther's biblical vision. The lesson from his life, Shepherd concludes, is "for the church in a post-Christian context . . . to believe and proclaim that same message."

James Keller seeks to explore the ecumenical content and value of the *Ninety-Five Theses* from three perspectives. First, he places the document in context, arguing that "Luther's vision at the time of the *Theses* did not stray beyond the theological parameters of what at the time would be considered standard procedure." Second, the *Theses* predate the Reformation, and were written to stimulate and inform a theological debate (sadly, one that never materialized). Third, the *Theses* themselves were "intended as an ecumenical mechanism for reform, not reformation." Luther had no idea of what the future held, but he did intend to seek the renewal of the church through—in this case—theological debate. Rather than see him as a man on a mission to be a great reformer, Keller argues, Luther's actions in Wittenberg in those early years are better understood as efforts to reform. He was, Keller writes, before being excommunicated, a "proto-ecumenist . . . who reflected on his ecclesial age with genuine gospel concern for all Christendom." Luther's early ecumenical vision, he concludes, is a way forward for both Catholics and Protestants.

Gwenfair Walters Adams provides a window into the way the struggle for the Reformation of the English churches played out at the national and local levels. The Church of the Holy Trinity, Long Melford, Suffolk and Roger Martyn's role in this church tells the story at the local level. Thomas Cranmer's reform initiatives provide the larger national narrative. First, the church at Long Melford of Roger Martyn's experience of the Reformation was built by the wealthy merchant families of the Martyns and Cloptons in the late fifteenth century on its earlier Saxon foundations. Adams provides an intimate portrait of the church's pre-reformation practices, architecture, chapels, seven altars, poem-bedecked walls, vestments, and stained-glass windows. Protestant policies would lead to the destruction and defacing of most of these ornamentations. Under Queen Mary and

INTRODUCTION

later monarchs Martyn restored elements of Catholic worship to Long Melford, but the richness of its pre-Reformation worship was gone forever. Adams effectively humanizes this beautiful and awe-inspiring medieval church and its people that worshipped God in it for centuries. Thomas Cranmer, as archbishop of Canterbury, took part in the implementation of the Protestant Reformation that began in 1531. Despite the tragedy of dispossession, Cranmer was sympathetic to Catholic believers and endeavored to implement liturgical changes that were sensitive to Christian tradition in England, but also reflected Protestant theology. In 1553, Cranmer was arrested for treason under the reign of Queen Mary. During imprisonment, he recanted many of his Protestant beliefs. But when taken to be burned at the stake in 1556, he recanted from his recantations by placing his right hand, which had signed his erstwhile recantations, into the flames. In the end, Adams argues that the tragedies that played out with Cranmer on the national stage and on the local level with Roger Martyn and Long Melford offer a caution to Christians today. Sympathetic understanding amid church and wider cultural divisions in North America is the pathway to follow for post-Christendom Christians.

W. David Buschart's first chapter on tradition brings together two groups not usually in the same analysis: Calvinists and Anabaptists. Historically, both shared theological commonalities, but both also looked askance at one another for real and perceived faults. More specifically, while they shared a deep and abiding devotion to scripture, there were important nuances and differences when it came to views of the church, theology, church history, and tradition. For instance, Calvin emphasized historical continuity with the ancient church throughout church history, whereas Anabaptists assumed a discontinuity. Calvin sought to include the voices of the church fathers when interpreting the Bible, but the Anabaptists not so much. Likewise with the ancient creeds. Calvin's vision of the church was both local and universal, while the Anabaptist vision tended to focus on the local, or as Buschart states, theirs' was an "emphasis on particularity more than catholicity." Buschart's analysis concludes with a number of observations on the nature and role of tradition in the life of the church, observations that help Christians today sort out a number of related questions: what is the function and role of tradition, the nature and character of tradition, and the church and its history? Such issues, then and now, are central to Christian faithfulness and witness in a changing world.

Shepherd's chapter on anti-Semitism exposes the ugly and dark side of the Reformation. As he points out, virulent anti-Semitism has marked the history of the Christian treatment of Jews in Europe, and the reformers parroted much of it. Luther, Calvin, and other reformers, all shared in rhetoric that demeaned and dehumanized Jews, and some—most infamously Luther in his *On the Jews and Their Lies*—advocated violence against Jewish people and property. Shepherd also points out how even the humanists—often portrayed as the tolerant ones in the period—were equally as anti-Semitic as their Reformation protagonists. Sadly, Shepherd argues, the trajectory continued by the reformers "contributed prodigiously to the Holocaust" of the twentieth century. Shepherd roots the anti-Semitism partly in the sixteenth-century Jewish rejection of Jesus, but, most significantly, in what he coins "replacement theology." Convinced that anti-Semitism in the church has the same underpinnings, he offers an eight-point critique of "replacement theology" as a way to avoid the horrors of the past.

In his second chapter, Buschart shifts his discussion of tradition among Calvinists and Anabaptists to address directly the role of tradition in the church today. Should we, he asks, "put the past behind," as some seem to suggest? Not surprisingly, his answer is no, and he marshals a number of arguments in support. In the first part of his chapter he notes how one cannot separate the church from the past, even if one wanted to. The "radically historical" nature of the church, the embodiment of the faith among living beings, along with degrees of continuity with the past, mean that tradition is critical and unavoidable. The second part deals with retrieving (not replicating) tradition from the past, in particular, the tradition of the reformers. Buschart argues that this impulse to look back is flourishing, noting how having "looked around at the contemporary scene and found it wanting and in need, Christians are turning to the past for resources for a richly historical and a theologically more catholic Protestant faith and life." He is encouraged by modern initiatives to retrieve early church, Catholic, and Orthodox traditions, but he cautions against "leapfrogging over the traditions of Protestantism," for to do so risks losing out on the richness of a five hundred year tradition that could inform the church facing twenty-first century post-Christendom realities. Finally, a robust process of retrieval is marked by correction (to correct beliefs currently held), reaffirmation (see what has been shared with previous generations), reimagining (to see not merely Luther, but Christ at work then and now), enrichment (a deepening or new awareness), and reconciliation (a greater sense of catholicity).

Introduction

David Fitch deals with the unintended consequences of the Protestant Reformation movements and turns to the Radical Reformation, the Anabaptists, to resolve them. Fitch focuses on three ways the Reformations' legacy has malformed Protestant churches for mission in Canada and the United States. The first is the distinction between the visible/invisible church that makes the church optional for being a Christian. The solution is the Anabaptist ecclesiology of community-based life and practice that provides places for embodied and visible witness to the world. The second problem is the hallmark Reformation doctrine of justification by faith. Fitch argues that justification by faith separated faith and works and made salvation a matter of individual spirituality, which effectively emptied salvation of socio-political consequence. The Anabaptist wholistic vision of discipleship that is directly engaged in socio-political aspects of life offers a pathway to bear public witness in the increasingly post-Christian culture of North America. The third issue is the Bible alone (*sola scriptura*). This doctrine effectively dethroned the power of the Roman Catholic Church and the Pope. In contemporary pluralistic North America, however, it leaves the Bible adrift in cross currents of individual interpretation. In a society of Christendom, that was less of a problem, because common meanings were, well, common! But in post-Christendom that is no longer the case. Disconnected from ecclesial practices and meanings, the Bible is largely co-opted by cultural interpretation. The Anabaptist tradition of reading scripture within community and being shaped by that reading in community provides a model for recovering authentic Christian life and practices for post-Christendom.

Many Protestants associate the Reformation with Martin Luther and his iconic hymn entitled "A Mighty Fortress is Our God," and they also imagine gospel-oriented worship services belting out hymns that planted Protestant doctrines deep in the minds and hearts of congregants. As Wendy Porter's chapter demonstrates, however, the worship landscape was remarkably rich, diverse, and innovative among both Protestants and Catholics. It was also dangerous for those on the margins, such as the English Catholic composer William Byrd. Porter details the work, art, and craft of composing music and leading worship in a country wracked by religious tensions and divided loyalties. She also describes the underground activities of a Catholic worship leader in a Protestant nation, and the subversive nature of his ministry. She asks important questions about lessons learned for those living a post-Christendom world—an experience that Byrd may have felt when he looked at the foreign landscape of a Protestant England. Perhaps the most intriguing application of Byrd identified by Porter is the covert inclusion of words into a song, but without including the actual word. Such craftiness, she suggests, may be a way forward in an post-Christendom age of hostility and suspicion towards Christians and their socially offensive views.

The Reformation Conference also took part in Philpott Memorial Church's joint celebration of its 125th anniversary and Reformation Sunday service (2017). Plenary conference speaker, Jennifer Powell McNutt, preached the sermon for the service. Combining the conference with a church-based event and including the sermon from that celebratory service in this volume dovetails with the heart of the Protestant Reformations. As McNutt highlights, the Protestant Reformations sought to recover the gospel of Jesus Christ for the renewal of the church and its people. Moreover, she argues that task is the perennial one for the church. The growing context of post-Christendom presents new challenges for the church, but the fundamental mission remains the same: proclaim the gospel for the people of our world. McNutt's message covers key features of Luther's life and the Reformation movements and illustrates the Protestant priority on scripture with the parable of the sower in Mark 4:3–33.

The quincentennial celebrations have once again drawn attention to the events surrounding Luther and the *Ninety-Five Theses*. These chapters provide a sense of the religious ferment of the Reformation(s), giving evidence of the courage, insight, diversity, and failures of the Protestant reformers. They also provide a clear sense of the contemporary relevancy of the issues Luther and his followers addressed. Feelings of alienation from God, a longing for a deeper and more vibrant Christian faith, a need to bring structure to faith, and responding to harsh restrictions are just as much a post-Christendom reality as a late-medieval one. Of course, the task of appropriating the reformer's message today without the timebound elements of the sixteenth-century takes work and discernment, but the effort, as seen in these pages, is well worth it.

In conclusion, a few words of appreciation are in order. Financial support from a donor (who wishes to remain anonymous) made the conference possible, and, without her generosity, the event—including this follow up book—would not have been possible. Thank you! Nina Thomas (Vice President Enrollment Management and Marketing and Registrar) supported the vision for the conference and provided important leadership

Introduction

for planning and taking care of the logistical aspects of the conference. Vital in this respect was the support of Melissa West (Advancement and Marketing Assistant) and Virginia Wolfe (Finance Assistant). Stanley E. Porter (President) and Phil Zylla (Academic Dean) of McMaster Divinity College deserve our gratitude for making McMaster Divinity College and its resources available to host these conferences. Bonghyun Yoo, Don Springer, Adam Rudy, and Taylor Murray were our graduate assistants and helped with the myriad of logistical details and chores before and during the conference. Thanks as well to the roster of plenary and parallel paper presenters. Their time, expertise, and active participation were deeply appreciated. Thanks to Taylor Murray (the Centre's Graduate Assistant) for his excellent organizing and editing of this book. Finally, we would like to thank McMaster Divinity College Press and Wipf & Stock for recognizing the value of publishing the essays presented in this volume. In this respect, David Fuller (Managing Editor, MDC Press) provided necessary editorial assistance in the final stages of the preparation of the manuscript.

BIBLIOGRAPHY

Balserak, Jon. *Calvinism: A Very Short Introduction*. New York: Oxford University Press, 2017.
Crisp, Oliver. *Saving Calvinism: Expanding the Reformed Tradition*. Downers Grove, IL: IVP, 2016.
DeRusha, Michelle. *Katharina and Martin Luther: The Radical Marriage of a Runaway Nun and a Renegade Monk*. Grand Rapids: Baker, 2017.
Elwood, Christopher. *A Brief Introduction to John Calvin*. Louisville: Westminster John Knox, 2017.
García, Alberto, and John Nunes. *Wittenberg Meets the World: Reimagining the Reformation at the Margins*. Grand Rapids: Eerdmans, 2017.
Greengrass, Mark. *Christendom Destroyed: Europe 1517–1648*. London: Penguin, 2014.
Gregory, Brad S. *A Rebel in the Ranks: Why Martin Luther and the Reformation Still Matter*. New York: HarperOne, 2017.
———. *The Unintended Reformation: How a Religious Revolution Secularized Society*. Cambridge: Belknap, 2012.
Harris, Steven Edward. "The Power of the Word of God: Luther and Pentecostalism in Dialogue." *Post-Christendom Studies* 2 (2017–2018) 5–19.
Heath, Joshua L. W. "Two Kingdoms for Today: Luther for Post-Christendom Political Engagement." *Post-Christendom Studies* 2 (2017–2018) 87–108.
Jenkins, Philip. *The Next Christendom: The Coming of Global Christianity*. New York: Oxford University Press, 2002.
Kaufmann, Thomas. *A Short Life of Martin Luther*. Grand Rapids: Eerdmans, 2016.
Kittelson, James M., and Hans H. Wiersma. *Luther the Reformer: The Story of the Man and His Career*. 2nd ed. Minneapolis: Fortress, 2016.

Knowles, Michael P. "Preaching Before Posting: Lessons for the Postmodern Church from the Early Sermons of Martin Luther." *Post-Christendom Studies* 2 (2017–2018) 42–66.

Kolb, Robert. *Martin Luther and the Enduring Word of God: The Wittenberg School and Its Scripture-Centered Proclamation*. Grand Rapids: Baker Academic, 2016.

Leithart, Peter J. *The End of Protestantism: Pursuing Unity in a Fragmented Church*. Grand Rapids: Brazos, 2016.

Lutzer, Erwin W. *Rescuing the Gospel: The Story and Significance of the Reformation*. Grand Rapids: Baker, 2017.

Marty, Martin E. *October 31, 1517: Martin Luther and the Day that Changed the World*. Brewster, MA: Paraclete, 2016.

Paulson, Steven. *A Brief Introduction to Martin Luther*. Louisville: Westminster John Knox, 2017.

Payton, James R. Jr. "Reformation Ecumenism Reframed." *Post-Christendom Studies* 2 (2017–2018) 20–41.

Roper, Lyndal. *Martin Luther: Renegade and Prophet*. New York: Random House, 2017.

Schilling, Heinz. *Martin Luther: Rebel in an Age of Upheaval*. New York: Oxford University Press, 2017.

Sunshine, Glenn S. *A Brief Introduction to the Reformation*. Louisville: Westminster John Knox, 2017.

Van Neste, Ray, and J. Michael Garrett, eds. *Reformation 500: How the Greatest Revival Since Pentecost Continues to Shape the World Today*. Nashville: B&H Academic, 2017.

Vanhoozer, Kevin J. *Biblical Authority after Babel: Retrieving the Solas in the Spirit of Mere Protestant Christianity*. Grand Rapids: Brazos, 2016.

Walker, Noel. "Ninety-Five Tweets: A Twenty-First Century Reformation." *Post-Christendom Studies* (2017–2018) 67–86.

Walls, Jerry, and Kenneth Collins. *Why I Am Not Roman Catholic: What Remains at Stake 500 Years After the Reformation*. Grand Rapids: Baker Academic, 2017.

2

Martin Luther and the Origins of the Reformation

Victor A. Shepherd

It is March 1545. Luther has eleven months to live. He is not terminally ill. He has, however, been convicted of high treason, a capital offence. Anyone assisting him will also be deemed treasonous and, if caught, executed. Condemned by the Pope as a heretic since 1520, he has been an outlaw of the Holy Roman Empire since 1521. Anyone who assassinates him will be rewarded. He can never forget that life is short and death is sure. Now he is reviewing his vast written output, fine-tuning theological expositions that have convulsed Europe, infuriated church authorities, provoked academic debate, and above all comforted millions as they found themselves newly assured that the arms of the crucified Savior held them securely in a grip on them that would always be stronger than their grip on him.

At this time—March 1545—Luther is revisiting the complete edition of his Latin writings. While his Latin writings span decades, the preface to them is new, and one of the last items he will pen. Listen to him as he takes us back to an earlier moment in his life and theological career:

> I had indeed been captivated with an extraordinary ardor for understanding Paul in the Epistle to the Romans . . . a single word in chapter 1[:17], 'In it the righteousness of God is revealed' . . . had stood in my way. For I hated that word 'righteousness of God,' which, according to the use and custom of all the teachers, I had

been taught to understand philosophically regarding the formal or active righteousness, as they called it, with which God is righteous and punishes sinners.... I hated the righteous God who punishes sinners, and secretly... I was angry with God... the gospel threatening us with his righteousness and wrath.... Thus I raged with a fierce and troubled conscience.

At last, by the mercy of God, meditating day and night, I gave heed to the context of the words... 'He who through faith is righteous shall live.' There I began to understand that the righteousness of God... by which the righteous lives, is a gift of God, namely faith. ... Here I felt that I was altogether born again and had entered paradise itself through open gates. There a totally other face of the entire Scripture showed itself to me.... Thereupon... I also found in other terms an analogy, as, the work of God, that is, what God does in us, the power of God, with which he makes us strong, the wisdom of God, with which he makes us wise.[1]

What had been Luther's experience prior to this moment when the righteousness of God, so far from being that gift of God, owned in faith, which renders sinners rightly related to him, had instead been understood to be unrelieved condemnation that God, righteous in himself, visited upon hopelessly guilty sinners forever unrighteous in themselves?

HIS EARLY YEARS

Luther's experience, circumstantially his alone, inwardly appeared no different from the experience of humankind. For instance, death looms for everyone. One hundred-and-fifty years before Luther's era, the Black Death (bubonic plague) had carried off 40 percent to 45 percent of Europe. Three of Luther's friends had recently succumbed to a fresh outbreak. Only days ago one of his best friends died suddenly. Hunting one day with a companion, Luther accidentally fell on his dagger, severing an artery. He pressed his hand in his groin to stem the haemorrhage while his companion procured help, aware that he had come within a hair's breadth of death. Later, when Luther was walking near the town of Stotternheim, a thunderstorm overtook him. A lightning-bolt's near miss found him exclaiming, "St. Anne (she was the patron saint of miners, and Luther's father was a mine-owner), help me. I will become a monk."

---

1. *LW* 34:337.

In July 1505 Luther entered the Augustinian monastery in Erfurt. Monastic life appeared to agree with him, at least initially. Twenty years later, looking back on this period of his life, Luther smiled at the spiritual self-confidence he and others enjoyed at that time: "The greatest holiness one could imagine drew us into the cloister . . . we considered ourselves holy from head to toe."[2] Soon he found himself immersed in the study of scripture and church doctrine. Assigned to probe the academic question, "How does one find a gracious God?," the exercise quickly became a personal preoccupation whose anxiety no medieval discussion could relieve.

Ordained to the priesthood in 1507, Luther continued his work in scripture. An able Hebraist, Luther quarried in the book of Psalms, initially; unlike many contemporary Christians, he found the gospel on every page. Listen to him as he exulted as early as 1515 in Ps 119, whose 147th verse exclaims, "I came before the dawn and I cried, because I very much hoped in your words." Now lit up by this passage Luther enthused, "Indeed I come before the dawn . . . because you, God, promised to forgive me. . . . I come early and cry because I have hoped in your words. Your mercy, the mercy of a God who promises, has made me bold to pray out of season, as it were, *before I have any merits.*"[3]

At the same time, Luther's schooling in Renaissance Humanism at Erfurt University (the pre-eminent locus of humanist scholarship in Germany) contributed to his nascent theological formation and remained a major ingredient in his theological understanding (although less widely recognized than the humanist contribution of other Reformers such as Zwingli and Melanchthon and Calvin). "I am convinced," wrote Luther as early 1523, "that without humanist studies untainted theology cannot exist, and that has proved true. . . . There has never been a great revolution of God's word unless God has first prepared the way by the rise and flourishing of languages and learning."[4] In addition, his exposure to humanism heightened his distaste for theological speculation and rendered him averse to any theological articulation that assumed an Aristotelian underlay. For Luther was convinced that Aristotle, the dominant philosopher the medieval church had co-opted, had obscured and denatured the gospel for centuries.

---

2. Luther, *Weimarer Ausgabe*, 17.1:309. Hereinafter *WA* 17.1:309.

3. *LW* 11:51 (emphasis added).

4. *LW* 4:34.

The Reformation

In 1510 the Augustinian Order sent Luther to Rome. He walked (1500 kilometres), every step heightening his anticipation of the glories that awaited him in the city. Arriving in Rome, he was disillusioned by the ingloriousness that met him everywhere: the shabbiness of the environs, the poverty of the people, and not least, the throngs of prostitutes. Still, he managed to ascend the *Scala Sancta*, the sacred staircase, repeating the Lord's Prayer on each step. Told that such an undertaking would earn heavenly bliss for anyone the religious devotee named, he whiffed superstition. He walked home, having completed the only trip outside Germany he was to make.

Notwithstanding the theological misgivings his trip to Rome had aroused, Luther remained fixed in a theological meritocracy; namely, God accepts those whose goodness merits their acceptance; or at least God accepts those whose confession of sin is equal to the nature, depth and scope of their sin. Luther, profounder than most, knew he could confess only the sin he was aware of, and even then, would never grasp sin's enormity to God. He was inconsolable not because he was psychologically bizarre but because he was spiritually perceptive. Then how did Luther escape the cyclical trap of sin, misery, and condemnation before God?

INKLINGS OF REFORM

The way out, as mentioned earlier, was delivered to him through his study of the Psalms. He began lecturing on the Psalter in 1513. He would steep himself in it for the rest of his life. In it he found the gospel everywhere. Seeds were sown in his Psalms-studies that would bear fruit abundantly ever after. In no time Luther heard and rejoiced in the throb of that bass note which reverberates throughout the Bible and establishes the rhythm of the Christian life; namely, the truth and reality (not the mere idea) that what God declares, God effects. God's utterance brings forth the reality it announces, the all-determining truth and reality of the believer's life, as undeniable to the kingdom-sighted as it is incomprehensible to the kingdom-blind. To say the same thing in more biblical vocabulary, when God declares humans to be rightly-related to him not on the basis of what they do but on the basis of what he has done on their behalf in his Son—namely he has borne their sin and borne it away—then they *are* rightly-related to him. There is nothing they should do or can do to ingratiate themselves with him. Humans are as much a child of God right now (*rightly* now) as they can ever be. By faith they are bound so closely to that Son with whom the Father is pleased that when the Father looks upon the Son he sees them included in the Son and therefore pleased with them as well. At once Luther's tormented questions—What must I do? Have I done enough? Is my doing good enough? And how would I ever know?—each evaporated.

Years later Luther was to write a tract, *Two Kinds of Righteousness*.[5] The two kinds are "alien righteousness" and "proper righteousness." Alien righteousness is alien only (but crucially) in the sense that it comes from outside of oneself, comes from Christ—specifically from the Son's 'right' standing with the Father—and is always his gift, never one's own achievement. Proper righteousness, on the other hand, is the Christian, already rendered such by having "clothed" herself or himself in Christ's alien righteousness; proper righteousness is the Christian now repudiating the arrears of sin that still cling to her, zealously repudiating the old man or woman of sin who has already been slain at the cross, to be sure yet who refuses to die quietly. Paradoxically Luther exclaims that Christ's alien righteousness "swallows up all sins in a moment," even as by one's proper righteousness they aspire to distance themselves from Adam.

Put simply, because Christ's righteousness is one's own, they are forgiven by God and know it; because their old man/woman has already been slain at the cross, they may and must now put him to death. At all times, one must remember, the foundation and stable basis of the Christian life is what Christ has accomplished *for* humanity and forever vouchsafes *to* humanity: a new standing before God wherein one comes before him as the son or daughter accepted by him and at home on his knee.

This lattermost point requires amplification. Justification by faith had not been taught by any theologian Luther had read, especially by Gabriel Biel, or by anyone Luther had read about in Biel. Biel, the representative spokesperson for late medieval nominalist theology, had maintained that moral aspiration is in truth a seeking after God that God recognizes and rewards. At life's end, sinners can hope that his or her aspiration, "topped up," as it were, by God's grace, will suffice for their acquittal before God, their justification.

Reading scripture attentively, Luther saw that sinners, whose moral achievement is indisputable, wield their achievement as a bargaining point before God wherein they insist that their right-conduct in terms of a code is tantamount to that right-relatedness to God-in-person of which scripture

---

5. *LW* 31:293–306. All references to righteousness in this paragraph come from Luther's tract.

speaks. Sinners, Luther insisted, were dead *coram Deo*; not ill, not deficient, not defective, not lame, but dead. As such they achieve nothing and can claim nothing with respect to their predicament *coram Deo*. They need a new standing before God that a corpse cannot acquire. Therefore, justification *has* to be utterly gratuitous, sheer gift of God. In addition, such justification is the sure foundation and stable basis of the Christian life now, not an unsure, wished-for, wait-and-see outcome at life's end.

It was Luther's experience first. "Justification by faith" (shorthand for 'justification by grace through faith on account of Christ') became and remained the foundation of the Reformation. In his commentary on the Psalms, Luther extolled, "If this article stands, the church stands; if it falls, the church falls."[6] Reinforcing his point, Luther later added, "Without this article the world is nothing but death and darkness."[7] It was upheld thereafter as the bedrock and stable basis of the Christian life. Luther's position as a Reformer was established. From this position, he would think and write and preach for the next four years, all of it coming to a head when the Pope summoned him to a hearing in the city of Worms. As he came upon the city (he had travelled from eastern to western Germany) he wrote a friend, "All the way from Eisenach to here I have been sick. I am still sick. . . . But Christ lives, and we shall enter Worms in spite of all the gates of hell and the powers in the air." Days later he would find himself saying, with unparalleled courage in the face of the mightiest institution in Europe, "Here I stand. I can't do anything else. God help me."

Courage? We ought never underestimate the courage Luther's stand would require. Erasmus, possessing Luther's horror at abuses in the church yet lacking Luther's apprehension of the gospel; Erasmus, always ready to ridicule but forever reluctant to reform; Erasmus knew what courage was required, and knew just as surely that he did not have it. In his feeble self-extenuation he wrote, "mine was never the spirit to risk my life for the truth. . . . Popes and emperors when they make right decisions I follow, which is godly; if they decide wrongly, I tolerate them, which is safe."[8] Erasmus, Luther knew by 1530, "was not concerned for the cross but for peace."[9]

---

6. *WA* 40:III, 352–53.

7. *WA* 39:I, 205. *Sine hoc articulo mundus est plane mors et tenebrae.*

8. Erasmus, *The Correspondence of Erasmus*, 218, as quoted in Pettegree, *Brand Luther*, 231.

9. Luther, *Weimarer Ausgabe Briefwechsel*, II:387–89. Quoted in Pettegree, *Brand Luther*, 231.

Years later, saddened and annoyed at Erasmus' cowardice and shallowness, Luther would conclude, "Everything is a laughing matter for him."[10]

THE REFORMATION BEGINS

Constrained by the living Word of God, sharper than any two-edged sword, Luther was aware that much needed reforming, not least the matter of indulgences. Upset initially by the traffic surrounding indulgences, and soon offended by the logic of them, Luther penned his *Ninety-Five Theses* and hung them from the door of the church in Wittenberg. Hallowe'en—All Hallows' Eve—would never be the same after 1517. What was the indulgence traffic in Luther's day? Whom did it profit? Why was Luther vehement?

At this time the Pope needed to finance the remodeling of St. Peter's Basilica in Rome. He issued an indulgence, a certificate authorizing the remission of the temporal punishment of sin in return for payment. In Wittenberg the master-hawker was Johann Tetzel, a Dominican friar famed for his salesmanship. A slogan was said to accompany his sales pitch: "When a coin in the coffer rings, a soul from purgatory to heaven springs." In case poetry was ineffective in having hearers part with their coin, Tetzel supplemented his rhetoric with grisly pictures of deceased persons alive and writhing in purgatory, crying out to relatives to purchase their release. And if neither poetry nor terror moved them, Tetzel was aware that fervent devotion might. In this regard Tetzel announced that when indulgences are offered *and* cross-plus-papal-coat-of-arms are displayed, the cumulative effect is equal to the cross of Christ. Such a steroidal indulgence, Tetzel insisted, would pardon even someone who had violated the Virgin Mary.[11]

Luther was appalled. He assumed that the new archbishop of his territory, Albrecht of Mainz, would surely want to be informed of religious abuses occurring within his territory. Luther was aware of the immense power Albrecht wielded. Albrecht was, after all, not only archbishop and cardinal, he was also archchancellor of Germany and the most powerful political figure after Emperor Charles V.[12] Not least, Albrecht was one of

---

10. *LW* 54:81. The debate continues as to the place of Erasmus in the Reformation. Should he be regarded as a Reformer, albeit as one with more pointedly Humanist presuppositions and expectations, or does he fail to grasp the logic of the Reformers' gospel? For an approach to Erasmus markedly different from Luther's, see Küng, *Theology for the New Millennium*.

11. Hendrix, *Martin Luther*, 58.

12. Hendrix, *Martin Luther*, 136.

only seven men charged with electing the emperor of the Holy Roman Empire. Luther sent a copy of his protest to Albrecht of Mainz, together with a covering letter. The covering letter was unambiguous. "Once they acquire indulgence letters, the poor souls believe they can be sure of their salvation," Luther pressed; "Good God! Souls that are being instructed under your care are being sent to their death, and it will be harder and harder for you to account for all this. Therefore I could keep quiet no longer."[13] Four years later, when he was sequestered at the Wartburg, Luther would write to Philip Melanchthon, "I curse the hardness of heart that prevents me from drowning in the tears I should weep for the slain of my poor people."[14] Again, Luther's courage here is noteworthy. Years earlier Dr. Dietrich Morung, a priest in Würzburg, had preached from the city-church pulpit a sermon that questioned the entire indulgence mentality. Cardinal Raimudi Peraudi, papal commissioner for indulgences and papal legate to Germany, had had Morung excommunicated and then incarcerated for ten years. Luther knew what he was risking.[15]

And then Luther attached a second copy of his *Theses* to the door of the church in Wittenberg.[16] (He did not nail it, we might note in passing, since in the sixteenth century papers were affixed to doors with wax.)[17] It was customary in university towns to post topics inviting debate on public bulletin boards, since academic debate in those days was a civic event. All Luther had in mind was a public discussion of the theology underlying the indulgence practice and the finances floating it.

In Luther's era, when a major church position opened up, it was sold to the highest bidder. This practice was called "simony." Few clergy, however, were wealthy enough to bid on the position. Therefore, the church, seeking to maximize pecuniary gain, opened up the bidding to wealthy laypersons whose wealth ensured the topmost bid. Once the layperson had gained a church office meant only for clergy, he recovered his bidding-war costs through ecclesiastical taxation and monies otherwise pertaining to the office. Then and only then was the officeholder consecrated.

13. *LW* 48:46.
14. *LW* 48:215.
15. Pettegree, *Brand Luther*, 61.
16. In addition to sending a copy of the *Ninety-Five Theses* and an accompanying letter, *Letter of Martin Luther to Albrecht, Archbishop of Mainz* (*LW* 48:43–49) Luther also subsequently preached and published in German his sermon, *A Sermon on Indulgences and Grace* (*WA* 1:239–46).
17. See Wengert, *Martin Luther's 95 Theses*, ix.

Archbishop Albrecht of Mainz had done exactly this. When Albrecht had indicated his interest in the position, officials in Rome set him up with the Fuggers, a major banking enterprise in Europe. Now there was a three-party constellation: Albrecht, the papacy, and the Fuggers. Each party anticipated benefiting hugely. Tetzel was recruited to raise the money.

What theological understanding attended indulgences? Indulgences never purported to alter eternal punishment for sin. (Only God could.) They merely affected temporal punishment, which temporal punishment the church *could* rescind, since the church had imposed it in the first place. Here is how indulgences worked. One sins, repents before God, and is forgiven. Still, one needs to make reparation and receive temporal punishment for their sins, whereupon the church, through its clergy, assigns penance. It is possible, in this economy, for one to arrive at life's end and have temporal punishment still owing, insufficient penance having been assigned. The punishment owing is a debt that is "paid" (paid off) by means of "doing time" painfully in purgatory following one's death. A papally-authored indulgence, acquired through a cash payment, remits the debt and releases someone from purgatory.

In the popular understanding, however, some of the aforementioned subtleties were unknown. While according to Canon Law indulgences remitted sin's temporal punishment but did not forgive sin's guilt, Archbishop Albrecht's book *Instructio Summaria* left the matter ambiguous, with the result that the public understandably read "indulgence" as "forgiveness of all sins." Luther knew that when people purchased indulgences, they did so believing that they thereby ensured their salvation.[18]

Luther objected to the practice on several grounds. First, there was the crass materialism of it all, the "thingification" of the Christian life. Whereas the Christian life, Luther insisted, was the most intimate, personal relation between believers and their Lord, now it was a business or banking or institutional transaction. In his tract *Two Kinds of Righteousness* Luther was to insist that when one is rightly related to God through faith in Jesus Christ, such faith, so far from an abstract, cold, one-sidedly forensic transaction; such faith, rather, is an encounter in which Christ (the bridegroom) is heard saying, "I am yours," and the believer (the bride) is constrained to say at the same moment, "And I am yours." Justification is not a *hollow* declaration; it is an *effective* word from the Lord who is present, in person, in his utterance; justification, then, is a mutual embrace and mutual pledge of utmost

---

18. Lohse, *Martin Luther's Theology*, 101.

warmth and intimacy as Christ and his disciple encounter each other and embrace each other and are fused to each other. Indulgences, on the other hand, were utterly sub-personal and could only depersonalise participants.

In the second place, Luther opposed the church's usurping God's prerogative. The church of his era understood the "power of the keys" (Matt 16:19) to reside in institutional authority vested in it by Christ, enabling the church (i.e., the clergy) to remit temporal punishment or retain it. Luther, and all the Reformers following him, upheld the "power of the keys" as the efficacy of the gospel preached. The church proclaims the gospel, which gospel is nothing less than Jesus Christ in his presence and power. As the church attests the gospel, the Lord whose gospel it is, the Lord who ever remains Lord and judge of his body, the church, so as not to inhere it; this Lord acts in the power of the Spirit and forgives penitent believers. Plainly there is the most intimate relation between Christ and his people, head and body. Luther liked to speak of the *totus Christus*, the whole Christ. To have Christ at all is to have Christ entire, head and body. Nonetheless, the head is never buried in the body. Never does the Lord of the church collapse himself into the church or transfer his authority to it.

In the third place, Luther objected to the confusion between the penalty for sin and the consequences of sin. The penalty for sin is alienation from God arising from God's judgement. The consequences of sin are the "after-shocks" reverberating through perpetrators' lives and the lives of those they touch. The penalty for sin is cancelled, as penitent sinners own God's mercy. The consequences of sin—dismemberment or death, for instance, following the impaired driver's collision—remain as long as life lasts, spreading relentlessly like ripples from a stone dropped once into water.

In the fourth place, Luther deplored the flagrant commercialization of it all. Make no mistake: the indulgence traffic was hugely rich. Between 1486 and 1503 Cardinal Peraudi, a masterful indulgence-pusher, had raised over 500,000 guilders through the popular vehicle.[19] In the village of Vorau, an Austrian municipality so very small that by 2009 its population numbered only 1496, Peraudi was reputed to have sold 50,000 letters of indulgence.[20] Not only was the invention of the printing press to enter into its glory in the dissemination of Reformation tracts, treatises, tomes, and translations of the Bible; the invention of the printing press, double-edged

---

19. Hendrix, *Martin Luther*, 57.
20. Pettegree, *Brand Luther*, 61.

like every human invention in a fallen world, had already inked hundreds of thousands indulgence certificates. While Luther opposed indulgences for theological reasons (one of which was affording financial protection to exploited people), the indulgence traffic made millionaires out of printers as surely as it did church bureaucrats. Different persons from diverse spheres now fused their fury concerning Luther, as surely as Pilate and Herod became friends the day Jesus Christ was condemned.

In the letter to Albrecht that accompanied the *Ninety-Five Theses*, Luther underlined his conviction that "indulgences confer upon souls nothing of benefit for salvation or holiness." And then in the same letter he tersely reminded Albrecht, "it is the first and sole office of bishops that the people learn the gospel and the love of Christ."[21]

Luther followed up both the *Theses* (Latin) and the *Letter* (Latin) with his vastly more popular sermon in German, *A Sermon on Indulgences and Grace*.[22] It was the sermon in German, reprinted at least twenty-four times between 1518 and 1520, rather than the *Theses* in Latin, that made Luther a household name overnight. Tetzel, apoplectic at Luther's renown, riposted six months later (April 1518) with one hundred and six theses denouncing Luther's "errors."[23] Tetzel's retort was never reprinted.

Pope Leo X (the last non-priest to be made Pope) supported Tetzel and Albrecht. Leo labelled Luther "a wild boar in the Lord's vineyard" (i.e., purely destructive). Leo had become a cardinal at age 13 and Pope at 37. He allegedly remarked, "God has given us the papacy; now let us enjoy it." He spent colossal sums of money, and relished parading around Rome on Hanno, his albino elephant. (The elephant, admittedly, cost him little, since it was a gift of King Manuel I of Portugal.)[24] Leo pronounced Luther a heretic and excommunicated him.[25]

---

21. *LW* 48:44.

22. *WA* 1:239–46.

23. For an English version, see *Johann Tetzel's Rebuttal against Luther's Sermon Indulgences and Grace*, translated by Dewey Weiss Kramer.

24. Hendrix, *Martin Luther*, 67.

25. The matter of indulgences remains current. As the year 2000 approached and a new millennium loomed, Pope John Paul II issued a Jubilee Indulgence. See his Apostolic Letter *Tertio Millennio Adveniente (As the Third Millennium Approaches)* on 10 November 1994.

The Reformation

THE CLASH WITH THE CHURCH

The *Ninety-Five Theses* were posted in 1517. Much thereafter poured from Luther's pen. In 1520 there appeared three more unforgettable tracts: *Address to the Nobility of the German Nation*,[26] *The Babylonian Captivity of the Church*,[27] and *The Freedom of the Christian*.[28] The lattermost remains the most widely read item in all of Luther's writings. Not only is this tract moving on account of its understanding and expression; it is also comprehensive in its discussion as few other tracts are. Luther himself wrote of it, "Unless I am mistaken . . . it contains the whole of the Christian life in a brief form."

Before we probe Luther's tract we must be sure we understand "freedom" in conformity to scripture. In popular parlance, freedom is the capacity to choose among alternatives. Yet when Paul reminds the Christians in Galatia, "For freedom Christ has set us free" (Gal 5:1), he cannot mean that Christ has set humans free so that they may choose to obey Christ or disobey him. (Such freedom, so-called, is nothing less than the bondage of sin.) The apostle can only mean that Christ has set humans free to obey him—and this only. In other words, freedom is having Jesus Christ remove all impediments to obeying him; to say the same thing differently, freedom is the absence of any impediment to acting in accord—and *only* in accord—with one's true nature. Christ has freed his people to act in accordance with their true nature; namely, a child of God. In other words, Christ simultaneously frees humans *from* all claims upon one's faith and obedience that contradict one's nature as child of God and frees humans *for* everything that reflects one's nature as child of God. It is human nature as a child of God to love God and neighbor in utter self-abandonment. Luther succinctly sets out the theme of the tract:

> A Christian is a perfectly free lord of all, subject to none.
> A Christian is a perfectly dutiful servant of all, subject to all.[29]

Expanding on this statement Luther writes,

> We conclude, therefore, that a Christian lives not in himself, but in Christ and in his neighbour. Otherwise he is not a Christian.

26. *LW* 44:123–217.
27. *LW* 36:11–57.
28. *LW* 31:327–78.
29. All references to Luther's tract for the remainder of this section are from *LW* 31:327–78.

> He lives in Christ through faith, in his neighbour through love. By faith he is caught up beyond himself into God. By love he descends beneath himself into his neighbour.

Christians, *freed* by Christ for their true nature—*bound* to Christ by faith and *bound* to the neighbor by love—live henceforth in radical self-forgetfulness. Taken out of themselves, their self-absorption shrivels and their anxiety evaporates. The gospel effects this, and can effect it just because the gospel, as all the Reformers after Luther insisted, is not chiefly idea but rather power. The Reformers everywhere reflected Paul's conviction that the gospel is the *power* of God unto salvation (Rom 1:16).

Luther goes on to say that there is only one way of living in Christ by faith. There are, however, three ways of living in the neighbor by love. Firstly, one lives in the neighbor by love as they share our neighbor's material scarcity, and do so out of our material abundance, even material superfluity. Luther admits this costs little. If one has five shirts, giving one to a shirtless neighbor exacts little. Luther notes too that when one does this they also gain social recognition (today, we would say an income tax receipt for "gift in kind"). Secondly, one lives in the neighbor by love as they share the neighbor's suffering. Luther maintains this is costlier in that proximity to suffering in others engenders suffering in oneself. Painful though it is, however, we feel good about it; and if we do it well, we are rewarded for it (as the Order of Canada or the Lions' Club Humanitarian Award accorded Mother Teresa). Finally, says Luther not in his *Christian Freedom* tract but in a later one, one lives in the neighbor as they share the neighbor's disgrace, the neighbor's shame. This is by far the costliest way of living in the neighbor. Here there is no reward; here there is no social recognition. Here, on the other hand, there is nothing but social contempt and ostracism. Here one profoundly knows what it is to be "numbered among the transgressors," for was not our Lord before us publicly labelled with a disgrace he did not deserve? In concluding his discussion of this matter Luther insists that our service "takes no account of gratitude or ingratitude, of praise or blame, of gain or loss. . . . [the Christian] must freely and most willingly spends himself and all that he has"—including his reputation.

IMPLICATIONS OF HIS REFORMS

One more medieval tradition Luther overturned was clergy celibacy. His rejection of clergy celibacy was one instance of his rejection of sacerdotalism. Sacerdotalism is the notion that the clergy have spiritual powers invested in them by virtue of their ordination. The notion that the sacraments can be administered effectively only by clergy, for instance, is one aspect of sacerdotalism. Another notion is that the pronouncement of absolution following confession will leave the penitent forgiven by God only if absolution is pronounced by a clergyperson.

Luther insisted that Jesus Christ, our "great high priest," has fulfilled the priestly line of the Older Testament. For this reason, there is not, and there cannot be, a priestly class in the church. All Christians are priests before God. To be sure, Luther maintained, for the sake of order at Sunday worship, only someone whom the congregation has recognized and authorized is to preach and administer the sacraments, lest chaos overtake the congregation. Nevertheless, the distinction between clergy and laity *with respect to spiritual powers* has been eliminated.

Luther reinforced his understanding here by having congregants receive Holy Communion in both kinds, bread and wine, whereas lay people, to this point, had been given bread only (wine, along with bread, being consumed by the clergy only). While giving wine to lay people may seem a small point to us, in Luther's day it was huge: from now on the church was to be defined not in terms of a clergy hierarchy (priest, bishop, Pope) who had unique powers; the church was to be defined as the people of God, a "kingdom of priests," a "holy nation," in the words of the apostle Peter (2 Pet 2:9). Luther eliminated the clergy/laity distinction.

Marriage among the Reformation clergy was another sign of its disappearance. The medieval church had forbidden the clergy to marry (beginning in the tenth century) inasmuch as marriage was inferior to celibacy. Luther's contemporaries believed marriage was vitiated by the depravity of women. Women, it was said, had been the downfall of Adam, Samson, David, and Solomon. In the Aristotelian mindset that underlay much of the medieval church, women were said to be botched males: if copulation were error-free, a male would result every time.[30]

In addition, Luther faulted the church fathers, in particular Jerome, Cyprian, Gregory, and Augustine. Had not Cyprian, a giant in the Patristic era, written, "If you hear a woman speak, flee from her as if she were a hissing snake?"[31] The medieval church had expatiated on the various ways

---

30. For an amplification of this matter see Shepherd, *Interpreting Martin Luther*, 301 and Ozment, *Protestants*, 152–53.

31. *LW* 54:357.

in which marriage was fraught with sin, the last way being marital sex undertaken for the sheer pleasure of it.

Luther and his followers inverted the late medieval understanding by transferring the praise of monastic life to marriage. In no sense was marriage second-best. In the fourth century, Jerome had assigned numerical values to marriage and celibacy. On a scale of 0 to 100, Jerome assigned 100 to virginity, 60 to widowhood, and 30 to marriage. Marriage was last in this scheme because it was a concession to inferior persons who would derail spiritually and psychologically without the institution. Inverting all such calculations, Johann Bugenhagen, Luther's friend and pastor of the city church in Wittenberg, exclaimed, "It is faith, and not virginity, that fills paradise." (In this regard it is worth noting that while Pope John Paul II had canonized or beatified almost 300 people as of 1997, he had elevated no woman who was not a virgin.)[32]

Luther was not naïve in this matter. Always looking to scripture, he knew Jesus to have said that some men are born eunuchs, some become eunuchs for the kingdom of God, and some become eunuchs thanks to the violence of other men (Matt 19). Roughly, then, there are people who, for many different reasons (not least psychological difficulties) are incapable of sustaining a lifelong union; in addition, there are those who forgo marriage because of a vocation to celibacy; and there are those who, through sheer misfortune, are denied the opportunity to marry. None of this, however, undoes God's *mandate* to marry following God's pronouncement that it is not good to be alone. And needless to say, Luther, as Hebraist, was aware that marriage is the commonest metaphor everywhere in scripture for God's covenant relationship with his people. This fact alone guarantees that marriage ought never be slighted.

Luther exemplified his high view of marriage in his love for his wife, Katharina von Bora. She had been assigned to a convent at age six. Having appropriated Luther's understanding of the gospel as she matured, she had somehow conveyed word to Leonhard Koppe, a fish merchant, that she and others wanted to embrace the Reformation understanding of faith and life. In 1523, Koppe extricated twelve nuns from the convent in herring barrels. (This feat too required enormous courage. In Catholic Saxony, one year later, a man was beheaded for helping a nun escape.)[33] In 1525 Luther married Katharina. Together they had six children, and until he died he loved

---

32. Kent, *Wesley and the Wesleyans*, 106–7.
33. Hendrix, *Martin Luther*, 136.

her in exemplary fashion. Listen to Luther extol his beloved Katie in his 1531 sermon *On the Estate of Marriage*:

> God's word is actually inscribed on one's spouse. When a man looks at his wife as if she were the only woman on earth, and when a woman looks at her husband as if he were the only man on earth; yes, if . . . not even the sun itself sparkles any more brightly and lights up your eyes more than your own husband or wife, then right there you are face to face with God speaking.[34]

Luther delighted in his Katie as he delighted in nothing and no one else. He regarded husband and wife as God's gift to each other. And because the clergy and laity alike were God's people without spiritual distinction, the clergy should cherish the same gift—marriage—and thank God for it.

CONCLUSION

Brother Martin had no idea, in 1517, that his *Ninety-Five Theses* would precipitate an earthquake. His reading of scripture, however, reminded him that when God spoke at Sinai, God's voice shook the earth (Heb 12:28). And his reading of scripture confirmed every day his conviction that when the gospel is announced, Jesus Christ acts and speaks, once more shaking the earth—and all of this for the sake of that kingdom, Luther grasped with iron fast certainty, which cannot be shaken (Heb 12:28).

Luther's favorite Psalm was 118. "Although the entire psalter and all of holy scripture are dear to me as my only comfort and source of life," revelled Luther, "I fell in love especially with this psalm. Therefore I call it my own. . . . Here you see how the right hand of God mightily lifts the heart and comforts it in the midst of death. . . . Is not this astounding? The dying live; the suffering rejoice; the fallen rise; the disgraced are honored."[35] It was crucial that the disgraced be honored, for whereas Luther the brash monk had earlier boasted "We considered ourselves holy from head to toe," the older Luther, only eighteen months from death, wrote his friend, Georg Spalatin, "Now join with us prodigious and hardened sinners lest you diminish Christ for us. . . . You can be a bogus sinner and have Christ for a fictitious savior. Instead, get used to the fact that Christ is a genuine savior and that you are a real sinner."[36]

---

34. *LW* 51:17–42.
35. *LW* 14:45; also 14 and 86.
36. *WA* 10:639.

While Luther maintained Ps 118 to be his favorite, his most frequently cited was Ps 50:15: "Call upon me in the day of trouble" (says the Lord); "I will deliver you, and you shall glorify me." Luther, in trouble from the moment he was pronounced an outlaw (1521) until he died 25 years later, had called upon God relentlessly. Was he delivered? Certainly he believed he was. Did he glorify God? His theological legacy—450 treatises, 3,000 printed sermons, 2,600 extant letters—is largely a paean of praise to God.

Two weeks before his death (18 February 1546) Luther, now in Eisleben, learned that his wife Katharina, minding children in Wittenberg, was anxious concerning his illness. He wrote her telling her that her anxieties for him were groundless: "I have a caretaker who is better than you and all the angels; he lies in the cradle and rests on a virgin's bosom, and yet, nevertheless, he sits at the right hand of God, the Father almighty. Therefore, be at peace."[37] The clarion call for the church in a post-Christian context is to believe and proclaim that same message.

BIBLIOGRAPHY

Brecht, Martin. *Martin Luther: The Preservation of the Church*. Vol. 3. 1532–1546. Translated by James L. Schaaf. Minneapolis: Fortress, 1993.

Erasmus, Desiderius. *The Correspondence of Erasmus*, edited by R. A. Mynors. 12 vols. Toronto: University of Toronto Press, 1974–2003.

Hendrix, Scott H. *Martin Luther: Visionary Reformer*. New Haven: Yale University Press, 2015.

John Paul II. *Tertio Millennio Adveniente (As the Third Millennium Approaches)*. November 10, 1994. N.p. Online: https://w2.vatican.va/content/john-paul-ii/en/apost_letters/1994/documents/hf_jp-ii_apl_19941110_tertio-millennio-adveniente.html

Kent, John. *Wesley and the Wesleyans*. Cambridge: Cambridge University Press, 2002.

Küng, Hans. *Theology for the Third Millennium*. Translated by Peter Heinegg. New York: Doubleday, 1988.

Lohse, Bernhard. *Martin Luther's Theology*. Translated by Roy A. Harrisville. Minneapolis: Fortress, 1999.

Luther, Martin. *Luther's Works*. Vol. 31, edited by Harold J. Grimm. Saint Louis: Concordia, 1957.

———. *Luther's Works*. Vol. 34, edited by Lewis W. Spitz. Saint Louis: Concordia, 1959.

———. *Weimarer Ausgabe, D. Martin Luthers Werke*. Vol. 17, edited by Stephan Roths. Weimar: Herman Bohlau, 1907.

Ozment, Steven. *Protestants*. New York: Doubleday, 1991.

Pettegree, Andrew. *Brand Luther: 1517, Printing, and the Making of the Reformation*. New York: Penguin, 2015.

Shepherd, Victor. *Interpreting Martin Luther: An Introduction to his Life and Thought*. Toronto: BPS, 2016.

---

37. Brecht, *Martin Luther*, 373.

Tetzel, Johann. *Johann Tetzel's Rebuttal Against Luther's Sermon Indulgences and Grace.* Translated by Dewey Weiss Kramer. Atlanta: Pitts Theology Library, 2012.

Wengert, Timothy J. *Martin Luther's 95 Theses.* Minneapolis: Fortress, 2015.

3

Luther, the Ninety-Five Theses, and Ecumenism

That They May be One in 2017

JAMES KELLER

THE YEAR 2017 WAS one of commemoration and celebration for all of Christendom, not merely for those churches bearing the Reformation's genetic material. Essential elements of the Reformation have landing zones across the traditions. The *Ninety-Five Theses* of Martin Luther (1483–1546) were expressions of ecumenical concern for the unity of Christ's Mystical Body. In and through Holy Baptism all Christians mutually recognize each other as brothers and sisters in Christ. The churches of the Unaltered *Augsburg Confession* realize, or at least acknowledge, that they and the communities in which they live out their Christian faith belong unambiguously to the one true Body of Jesus Christ. Nevertheless, in this the quincentenary anniversary of the publication of the *Ninety-Five Theses*, hope is growing that the mutual condemnations issued in the sixteenth century have lost their teeth and become no more than historical footnotes.

Many church historians have released Luther from the charge that the *Ninety-Five Theses* were to be a theological gauntlet.[1] Luther's hope for eternal life rested on Jesus Christ and his invisible Body, not on the visible, institutional church with its centuries of accumulated baggage.

---

1. McGrath, *Christianity's Dangerous Idea*, 47–48; Evans, *The Roots of the Reformation*, 289–90.

Nevertheless, Luther did express regret that the external unity within the empirical church, already suffering from a multitude of schismatic cuts from various Christian fellowships, was now further subjected to a painful rendering through his hand. Luther may have expressed compunction for the breach but assigned ultimate responsibility for the rupture to those in the ecclesiastical power structure unwilling or unable to stop the hemorrhaging indulgences had caused. As this chapter demonstrates, Luther believed strenuously that a seismic event was on the horizon, and only a direct act of God could stave off the appearance of a dangerous fissure in the Body of Christ.

In this chapter, I examine the ecumenical content and value of Luther's *Ninety-Five Theses* from three perspectives. First, I place the *Theses* in their historical context so they interpret pre-Tridentine Roman Catholicism. Luther endeavored to restore a Catholicism that had not been in existence for centuries, the primeval church of Christ whose sole task was to call sinners to repentance and faith through Word and Sacrament. Luther's vision at the time of the *Theses* did not stray beyond the theological parameters of what at the time would be considered standard procedure. Second, it must be remembered that the *Ninety-Five Theses* were not *of the Reformation*, but were rather a document of reform, conceived and executed for a theological disputation that would never materialize. Third, I argue that the *Theses* were intended as an ecumenical mechanism for reform, not reformation. Reform, for Luther, was an exercise in renewal of the institutional Catholic Church consisting of bishops, priests, deacons, and the people of God, as well as the renewal of Christianity *in toto*. His approach did not and could not have signaled a desire that a rebranded church should become a reality. In this way, the Luther of the *Ninety-Five Theses* should be understood properly as a man with the desire for reform, rather than a Reformer.[2] In short, the Luther of the *Ninety-Five Theses*, and prior to his excommunication, was a proto-ecumenist, but not a conscious one. More to the point, he was a Christian originalist, an evangelical Catholic who reflected on his ecclesial age with genuine gospel concern for all of Christendom.

INDULGENCES IN LUTHER'S CONTEXT

It would be incorrect to assign responsibility for the Reformation and its aftermath to *Luther sola Luther*. The church of Luther's day had been

---

2. Kasper, *Martin Luther*, 13–14.

declining *theologically* for some centuries prior, even if the Papacy and leadership failed to recognize it at every moment. The freefall began in the chancel, when public worship ceased to be the nexus of authentic Christian spirituality and the major source of temporal comfort and peace. Medieval liturgies were often more mystical and allegorical than literal, and salvation was rarely presented as the unique possession of God's chosen people as they gathered before the altar to receive His gifts of Word and Sacrament. Scripture was neglected wholesale, though many clerics agreed that it should be positioned prominently in Christian life.[3] Church leadership refused to provide vernacular versions of the sacred books that would, if used routinely, edify clergy and laity alike. Most unfortunately, the medieval church found herself in possession of secular power and responsibility that drew spiritual energy and resources from her dominical responsibilities. The church of Luther's day was fairly saturated with contemporary culture, and Christians went along.[4] Luther arrived at a spiritual nadir.

The society Luther observed both within and without the church had drifted from traditional church teachings, often bent on indulging passions and inclinations over gospel truth. Worse still, many Roman cardinals and officials seemed oblivious to the decline, unfortunately unconcerned over crumbling ecclesiastical and spiritual foundations that some medieval movements had already sought to reform. Honesty should have compelled the Curia that they had botched the "Luther affair," as short-reigned Pope Adrian VI (1459–1523) pointedly admitted in an oddly unguarded moment.[5] Every Christian born within a century of the posting of the *Theses* in 1517 knew the Roman Church required significant reform from stem to stern. The *Devotio moderna*, often credited as a source of all significant sixteenth-century reforms, was an earnest effort to re-energize personal morality, religiosity, and piety.[6] The church herself made a stab at reform in the lead-up to 1517. Several councils given the task of reforming the medieval church were convened,[7] and hopes ran high that some positive change

---

3. McNally, "The Ninety-Five Theses of Martin Luther," 439–40.

4. The *Devotio moderna* were exemplars here. See below.

5. Adrian believed that the same Curia that had stumbled with the Augustinian was none other than the font for all of the evils present in the church of the day. He has planned to issue the rather strident critique at the Diet of Nuremberg (January 1523), but at the last moment sent an emissary.

6. Ozment, *The Age of Reform*, 97.

7. Constance (1414–1418), Basle (1431–1449), Florence (1438–1445), and Lateran V (1512–1517).

would come. However, ecclesial inertia and a lack of comprehensiveness resulted in half-hearted and patchy efforts that failed to meet the needs of the church catholic.

Long-standing abuses of churchly authority had caused deep harm to the Christian layperson in particular, and the Christian faith in general. Religion *qua* religion, insofar as it was practiced, was focused not so much on piety, but on human expediency. By the dawn of the sixteenth century indulgences were offered enthusiastically and with dramatic flair, usually associated with good works for some worthy cause such as funding defence against the invading Turks or rebuilding some church or holy site. In the fifteen years prior to 1517, seven major indulgence campaigns fanned out across Germany, raising funds for everything from a crusade against schismatic Ruthenians to the repair of dykes in the Netherlands.[8] The needs of St. Peter's in Rome were but one project promoted by the indulgence preachers, yet it would raise Luther's ire and drive him to ask for a referendum on the subject of indulgences. Luther's protest was so effective that the St. Peter's fundraising campaign may have been the last major effort to transact indulgences before the practice was discontinued.

As the preaching of indulgences, appositely labelled *sacrum negotium* ("holy business") increased apace, Luther became increasingly distressed and disgusted at the distortions to true Christianity that were being passed off as spirituality. There was much to address. The *Ninety-Five Theses* that flowed from Luther's pen were concerned with several abuses, but aimed especial frustration at the doctrine pertaining to indulgences, which were an ancient church practice with continued and widespread support.[9] An indulgence offered the Christian a reduction or even complete commuting of any penitential acts and temporal punishments that the church might choose to impose.[10] Most Christians and clergy had no issue with the exchange or even the sale of indulgences, since it was widely accepted that the church had been commanded to recognize sin and, when she was confident the sinner had achieved acceptable contrition, had the sovereign right and,

---

8. McNally, "Ninety-Five Theses of Martin Luther," 447–49.

9. Luther's own elector, Frederick the Wise, in 1509, "had expanded the collection [of indulgenced relics] that he had inherited to a total of 5,005 items, with the possibility of 1,443 years of indulgence. Nine years later, the size of the collection had grown to 17,443 items, carrying with them the possibility of the equivalent of 127,709 years and 116 days of public penance in the primitive Church's fashion." Piepkorn, "Lutheran Theologian," 524.

10. Brecht, *Martin Luther*, 176.

presumably, the competence to remit it. Before such remittance could be declared and the sinner reconciled, the church imposed any satisfaction for penance she deemed necessary. The penitent could not expect full remission until the specifics of this satisfaction were completed.[11] Regrettably, no firm theology of penance separated into its component parts—confession, reconciliation, satisfaction, intercession, and substitution—existed in the medieval church, or even to the present day. The transformation of the sacrament of penance required the practice of penance be worked in systematically as the doctrine of penance, the precursor to the Confession and Absolution practiced in the churches of the *Augustana*.

At this juncture, Luther seemed to have had no quarrel with the Roman rite of penance,[12] since the *Theses* addressing it spoke of the vicarious satisfaction won for all persons in and through the Lord Jesus Christ.[13] As a dutiful preacher in pre-Trent Wittenberg, Luther would have instructed his flock on the proper place indulgences should occupy in the life of the Christian. Moreover, if the church had stopped at the promulgation of vicarious satisfaction, it is very likely the Lutheran Reformation would not have gained traction. But Roman theology declared that individual Christians, acting within their Christian vocations, can and should "help" each other *en route* to salvation, and that their good works, done under God's grace, earn merit that may be "shared." When the church exercised the Keys by absolving the sinner in the name of Christ, she believed herself to have made intercession on his behalf, and remitted his personal, declared guilt before God. Even so, satisfaction to mollify the penalties that had adhered to the sinner over time was still required. The church, then, intercedes with

---

11. Moorman, *Indulgences*, 198–99.

12. "The sacrament of Penance consisted of three parts: contrition (sorrow for sin out of love of God), confession (privately to a priest who granted absolution), and satisfaction (of the remaining temporal punishment through works prescribed by a priest depending on the severity of the sins." Wengert, *Martin Luther's Ninety-Five Theses*, location 124.

13. Wengert states, "Luther's experience with indulgences was broader than most people imagine. While still a student at Erfurt, Luther probably heard the indulgence preaching of Raimund Peraudi (1435–1505) . . . [F]rom 1502–1504, Peraudi preached a plenary indulgence throughout Germany, with the money being set aside to support a crusade against the Turks. Among other places, Peraudi was in Erfurt on 29 October 1502, at which time Luther was a student there. This means that in all likelihood Luther personally experienced the preaching of one of the most popular indulgence preachers in Germany." Wengert, *Martin Luther's Ninety-Five Theses*, location 196–97.

God on the sinner's behalf to set aside the temporal compulsion to satisfy what had been contracted in a lifetime of sinful behavior.[14]

That merit could be "shared" was a popular notion in Luther's day. Even more so was the view that indulgences had efficacy in themselves that was subject to the jurisdiction of the church—they could be framed to offer satisfactions unique to time or circumstance. The fundamental problem for Luther lay in the assumption that every forgiven sin—venial sins forgiven by their very identification, and mortal sins forgiven in response to true contrition—must have a residual element of temporal punishment to be satisfied in this life or expiated in purgatory. In fairness, it could be argued that the potential for portable merit is not unique to Catholic theology since it is a Third Article issue, wherein such merit, purified by the Holy Spirit, is the final cause of the communion of saints as well as the Christian's necessary location within the Body of Christ. Orthodox churches believe that sinners are absolved "in the stead and by the command of Christ," without any merit or worthiness in us. The church directs the penitent away from self and to Christ, who alone can intercede to remit original sin, while substituting Himself for the personal sins one has committed. The medieval theology of penance, however, added a requirement of satisfaction to the admixture, insisting that since penalties for various sins accrue over time, the penitent must work to compensate for the judgment that must be imposed to sate God's righteous anger. The church then claimed that God had not only given the keys to her, but also the duty to impose appropriate satisfactions to fulfill the temporal obligations sinful behavior engenders. In the eleventh century, a theology of indulgences was nascent, but growing.[15] By the beginning of the fourteenth century, the doctrine of indulgences had taken flesh and was firmly rooted dogma, with the following elements entrenched: absolution of sin and the commuting of any temporal punishments that might be justly imposed, the intercession of the church on the penitent's behalf, and substitution of good works for penalties contracted in the daily act of sinning.

In the broad sense, the doctrine of indulgences as originally formulated had various defensible features. The commitment to the solidarity

---

14. Aquinas believed that any one that had taken a monastic vow of poverty, chastity, and obedience enjoyed a form of "second baptism" or "indulgence" that eliminated all guilt from earlier in life, as well as the punishment for any actual misdeeds. Wengert, *Martin Luther's Ninety-Five Theses*, 153–54.

15. The first plenary (complete) indulgence may have been granted to men who participated in the First Crusade. Brecht, *Martin Luther*, 177.

of all Christians as the true Body of Christ is one of them. Clement VI (1291–1352) declared in the papal Bull *Unigenitus Dei* that the doctrine is

> [the] very treasure [of the merits of Christ and the saints]. . . . He entrusted to be dispensed for the salutary profit of the faithful through blessed Peter, the bearer of heaven's keys, and his successors, His vicars on earth, and to be applied mercifully, for fitting and reasonable causes, to those who are truly penitent and have confessed; at times for the total, at times for the partial remission of the temporal punishment due to sins, whether by a general or a particular grant, as they deem it expedient with God.[16]

Clement had established the applicability of indulgences to living souls. In 1476, more than a century later, Pope Sixtus IV (1414–1484) extended the same privileges to the dead. The timing could not have been better. Indulgences for the dead ran parallel with the spiritual presuppositions of the people of the times—deep concern for one's own salvation, consciousness of personal sinfulness and its necessary consequences, and dread over the promised return of Christ for universal judgment.[17] Purgatory and the torments of hell were already prominent themes in medieval piety. With Sixtus' Bull *Salvator noster* (1476), the Roman Church could now preach that indulgences could be attained by the living for themselves and for the deceased—they were considered favors granted by God only to those who could perform good works in a state of grace or friendship with God. *Salvator* declared:

> With the longings of such great paternal affection as with God's help we can achieve, in reliance on the divine mercy and the plenitude of our power, we grant by concession and indulgence as follows: If any parents, friends or other Christians are moved by obligations of piety towards these very souls who are exposed to the fire of purgatory for the expiation of punishments which by

---

16. Clement VI, *Unigenitus Dei*, in McNally, "Ninety-Five Theses of Martin Luther," 443. Interestingly, it was this Bull that buoyed Cardinal Cajetan's argument against Martin Luther at the Colloquy at Augsburg in October 1518. Cajetan knew that the Bull was a trump card since it appealed to papal authority traced back to St. Peter himself. Luther was aware of this as well, and declared that his authority was much higher and more compelling—scripture itself.

17. "One should not say that an indulgence effects the release of a *particular person* from purgatory, since we do not know if this person has made himself ready to be freed from purgatory. Still, Luther's theological elaboration of the problem has shown that the church's help for the souls in purgatory through indulgences is greater than what she does for the living." Wicks, "Martin Luther's Treatise on Indulgences," 515, emphasis added.

> divine justice are their due: let them during the stated period of ten years give a fixed amount or value of money, as laid down by its dean and chapter or by our own collector, for the repair of the church of saints, paying either in person at the Church or by duly accredited messengers: *it is then our will that plenary remission should avail by intercession for the said souls in purgatory, to win them relief from their punishments*—the souls, that is, for whose sakes the stated quantity or value of money has been paid in the manner declared.[18]

Until Sixtus ascended the papal throne, the average man in search of solace had little option but to turn to good works as visible expressions of his good will before a vengeful God. Now he could gain sure and certain hope against the agonizing punishment of purgatory, and for a swift entrance into the divine embrace of Heaven.[19]

This monetization of indulgences reflected Luther's own perception that indulgences must lead to fraudulent security and even leniency with respect to sin. It is not easy for the thoroughly modern person to grasp the significance of indulgences for medieval Christians. Yet the laity viewed indulgences as spiritual privileges that could help sustain them, body and soul to life eternal. The downside of indulgences was their tendency to make religion a largely external experience, a mechanistic practice of virtuous acts that distracted the ordinary Christian into performing esoteric good works in order to earn remittance of temporal punishment due to sin the church could not possibly enumerate in the confessional anyway. In his largely overlooked Treatise on Indulgences, Luther lashed out that

> [i]ndulgences . . . do not, at least per se, grant the grace which makes a person just or more just. They grant instead only the remission of penance and of imposed satisfaction, which though does not mean that one who then dies goes immediately to heaven. But most of the people are simple and have been deceived into thinking that a plenary indulgence drives out all sin, and one is thus ready for heaven. So they sin with abandon, and thereby burden themselves with the bonds of concupiscence.[20]

18. *Salvator noster* (emphasis added).

19. The *Catechism of the Catholic Church* declares: "An indulgence is a remission before God of the temporal punishment due to sin whose guilt has already been forgiven which the faithful Christian who is duly disposed gains under prescribed conditions through the action of the Church which, as the minister of redemption, dispenses and applies with authority the treasury of the satisfaction of Christ and the saints."

20. As cited in Wicks, "Martin Luther's Treatise on Indulgences," 494.

In any case, the medieval theology of indulgences held no comfort for the sinner gripped by fear of God Himself. If Christ were scripted to be Lord of Judgment, then uncertainty of salvation is the only possible outcome for the already tortured soul. Luther was therefore justified in his insistence that the precise value of an indulgence could not be ascertained with the specificity claimed by Tetzel and the indulgence preachers.

Virtually from their inception, indulgences could be either earned through pious acts of charity, or purchased with money contributed to an approved churchly cause. It was the externalization of religion that exercised Luther most acutely, perhaps because indulgences often led to religious cynicism and disappointment. So great was his disdain for those preaching indulgences that Luther encouraged pious church leaders to immediately expel them from their dioceses and prevent others from entering. Unfortunately, not all churchmen agreed with him. "Because the pope and the bishops refused reform, [in 1517] Luther had to be satisfied with an emergency arrangement on the basis of his understanding of the common priesthood of believers. However, he was confident that the truth of the gospel would be implemented, and therefore, he basically left open the door to a possible rapprochement in the future."[21]

In August 1514, Albrecht of Brandenburg (1490–1545), then only twenty three years old, was elected Archbishop of Mainz, his third archbishopric along with Magdeburg and Halberstadt. To hold the position of archbishop in three separate dioceses, to say nothing of Albrecht's tender years, was essentially unheard of. Yet even to the most disinterested observer it was clear that Albrecht had not ascended to the honor on the basis of his personal merit. Moreover, the addition of Mainz to his diocesan inventory was manifestly contrary to canon law and rationality. In order to expedite the crown transfer, Albrecht agreed to pay into papal coffers the enormous sum of 24,000 ducats. Not even a man of privilege such as Albrecht could muster such a sum without help. Fortunately, the firm of Fugger, acting financial agents for the Vatican, fronted Albrecht the necessary funds, along with the requirement to allow indulgence preaching within his bishoprics.

The way was now clear for the carpet-bombing of indulgence preaching in Germany, which Pope Leo X (1475–1521) allowed unreservedly, for the "good work" of contributing to the construction of St. Peter's basilica in Rome.[22] Leo's first plenary indulgence of 31 March 1515—*Sacrosancti sal-*

---

21. Kasper, *Martin Luther*, 32.

22. To pave the way, Albrecht had a pamphlet prepared, called the *Instructio*

vatoris et redemptoris nostri—had already raised Luther's hackles, and now the indulgence preaching gloves were off. *Sacrosancti* called for Albrecht to receive half of the indulgence proceeds that accrued to him as profit, while the other half would be transferred to the Fuggers as both payment and interest. The Fuggers left nothing to chance, requiring that one of their representatives be present at each indulgence preaching session to audit the returns. The whole affair was scandalous from beginning to end. In his Treatise on Indulgences, which Archbishop Albrecht received coincident with the *Ninety-Five Theses* themselves, Luther vented,

> [a]lthough indulgences are the very merits of Christ and of His saints and so should be treated with all reverence, they have in fact nonetheless become a shocking exercise of greed. For who actually seeks the salvation of souls through indulgences, and not instead money for his coffers? This is evident from the way indulgences are preached. For the commissioners and preachers do nothing but extol indulgences and incite the people to contribute. You hear no one instructing the people about what indulgences are, or about how much they grant, or about the purpose they serve. Instead, all you hear is how much one must contribute. The people are always left in ignorance, so that they come to think that by gaining indulgences they are at once saved.[23]

Johann Tetzel (ca. 1465–1519), the Dominican inquisitor of heretics and the sub-commissioner for the promotion of the St. Peter's indulgence, was deployed to Albrecht's dioceses to preach indulgences, and by early 1517 he was doing so with great energy. It was largely for this reason, however, that Tetzel has become a pariah in Reformation history and the case of indulgences, owing to his ruthless pulpit manner and apparent disregard for the laity and their weaknesses. Tetzel was a master showman, his sermons lively, compelling, and often theologically sound. In the early days of his deployment Tetzel met with considerable success. Interestingly, his preaching was orthodox in large measure prior to October 1517—he would

---

summaria, which described in some detail the "graces" that Pope Leo had granted to the Indulgence. The graces enumerated were: 1. Complete remission of all sins, and instantaneous release from purgatory. 2. A letter of indulgence which extended beyond the eight-year endpoint of the papal Bull. 3. Participation in all that the church universal possesses until the Consummation. 4. Indulgences for the souls in purgatory, which does not require the penitent to be truly contrite, but rather to have placed a sufficient contribution in the chest.

23. As cited in Wicks, "Martin Luther's Treatise on Indulgences," 493.

even concede that indulgences hold no unique merit without repentance and heartfelt confession as their preface.[24] But time and personal pride moved Tetzel away from any semblance of gospel truth to the presentation of indulgences that distorted their Catholic intent. Where gospel truth was lacking, Tetzel topped up the mix with generous portions of sentiment and emotion, these becoming the backbone of his appeal to the masses that had thronged to hear him.

Luther chanced upon Tetzel probably in late autumn 1517, when Tetzel was preaching at Jüterbog and Zerbst, near Wittenberg. By his own admission, Luther knew little of indulgences at that time, his exposure to their preaching having little lasting effect it seems, stating that "I did not yet know—as surely as my Lord Christ has redeemed me—what indulgences were, but no one else knew, either. I carefully began to preach that one could do something better and more certain than to purchase indulgences."[25] Luther also examined canon law concerning indulgences in some detail to avoid distorting their Catholic sense.[26] At first blush Luther was not particularly concerned about indulgences. His mind changed, however, as he became more familiar with Tetzel and the potential damage indulgences could inflict on the humble Christian.

It was clear to most that after the posting of the *Ninety-Five Theses*, Tetzel and his homiletical confreres began to lose ground. Sales of indulgences dropped precipitously, and the lay persons that had thronged to Tetzel's sermons drifted back to their usual daily pursuits with their money still in their pockets. In hopes of stopping the bleeding, Tetzel composed a sharp *Rebuttal* in 106 Theses to Luther's *Theses*, which was published early in 1518. *Rebuttal's* publication coincided with that of Luther's *Sermon on Indulgence and Grace*, although Luther's paper outsold Tetzel's by a wide margin. Tetzel attacked Luther with ferocity, a thinly-veiled act of slander to which Luther was becoming accustomed. In responding to Luther's Ninth Thesis,[27] for example, Tetzel wrote:

> Even if the Christian church right now would decide and declare that indulgence removes more than the works of satisfaction, it would still be a thousand times better, if no Christian would buy

24. McNally, "Ninety-Five Theses of Martin Luther," 464.
25. McNally, "Ninety-Five Theses of Martin Luther," 443.
26. Wengert, *Martin Luther's Ninety-Five Theses*, 279.
27. "Therefore the Holy Spirit through the pope is kind to us insofar as the pope in his decrees always makes exception of the article of death and of necessity."

> or desire an indulgence but would rather do the works and bear the suffering. For indulgence is nothing else, and cannot become anything else, than a release from good works and wholesome suffering. Men should rightly welcome these rather than avoid them, in spite of the fact that some modern preachers have invented two kinds of suffering: remedial and satisfactory, that is, some suffering is for satisfaction, some for amending one's ways. But we have more freedom to disdain this and all such prattle (Thanks be to God!) than they do to invent it. For all suffering indeed everything that God inflicts, is beneficial and useful for Christians.[28]

As time wore on, Tetzel's preaching became what might be referred to charitably as un-catholic. His tenor placed teeth on edge, and the venality of his assaults on critics of indulgences moved Luther to complain publicly that all Tetzel and his entourage were interested in was filthy lucre.

> With its offer of indulgences the church obliged the fears of its members. It presented itself at the great transcendent institution of salvation whose arm reached as far as heaven, purgatory, and hell, and which could have a share in the eternal fate of each individual. That was one of the foundations of its influence; yet at the same time it was enormously vulnerable at this point, especially because the basis of this extensive indulgence theory stood on shaky ground.[29]

So armed, Luther decided to exercise one of the rights possessed by doctors of the church, to hold disputations (public debates) on any subject the Faculty at the University of Wittenberg deemed worthy. Luther was already a relative veteran of disputations such as these, having defended his own work and that of others at various times. The *Ninety-Five Theses* may or may not have been posted physically in Wittenberg, but the stage was now set: Pope Leo must respond to Tetzel's overreach as quickly as possible. This was the culmination of the religious indignity that confronted Luther on All Hallows Eve, 1517.

AN EXPOSITION OF LUTHER'S NINETY-FIVE THESES

As we have seen, Luther was no fan of indulgences, nor of the preachers who foisted them on a populace in constant search of spiritual reassurance. He seems not to have been greatly dismayed with church leadership at the

---

28. Tetzel, *Rebuttal against Luther's Sermon on Indulgences and Grace*, 20.
29. Brecht, *Martin Luther*, 177.

time, whom he viewed as regrettably uninformed on the abuses attached to their sale and utilization. He writes,

> Hence, when in the year 1517 indulgences were sold (I wanted to say promoted) in these regions for most shameful gain—I was then a preacher, a young doctor of theology, so to speak—and I began to dissuade the people and to urge them not to listen to the clamors of the indulgence hawkers; they had better things to do. I certainly thought that in this case I should have a protector in the pope, on whose trustworthiness I then leaned strongly, for in his decrees he most clearly damned the immoderation of the quaestors, as he called the indulgence preachers. Soon afterward I wrote two letters, one to Albrecht, the archbishop of Mainz, who got half of the money from the indulgences, the pope the other half—something I did not know at the time—the other to the ordinary (as they call them) Jerome, the bishop of Brandenburg. I begged them to stop the shameless blasphemy of the quaestors. But the poor little brother was despised. Despised, I published the *Theses* and at the same time a German *Sermon on Indulgences*, shortly thereafter also the *Explanations*, in which, to the pope's honor, I developed the idea that indulgences should indeed not be condemned, *but that good works of love should be preferred to them.*[30]

Luther was doubtless aware that he was fighting an uphill battle when it came to indulgences. *Unigenitus* with no little irony had deemed indulgences "the treasure of the Church."[31] The Catholic faithful had become accustomed to the promised merits of indulgences, as well as the means of their distribution. It was the distribution that Luther had sought to rectify, more so than the indulgences themselves. In 1517 Luther probed for clarification on the nature of indulgences and their subsequent function in the life of the Christian—he did not call for their abolition outright. The *Theses*, then, as well as the Treatise on Indulgences,[32] serve as object lessons in Luther's not-yet crystallized thought on the subject—for the moment he kept his legendary polemical edge well under check. From Luther's perspective, the pitiable religious situation in the churches was the result of institutional rot, and had obscured any benefit indulgences may have offered Christians.

---

30. *LW* 34:329–30. Emphasis added.

31. Clement VI, jubilee bull *Unigenitus Dei Filius* 27 January 1343. (DS 1025, 1026 and 1027).

32. Wicks, "Martin Luther's Treatise on Indulgences," 491.

The *Theses* made clear that for Luther, a discussion on the nature and value of indulgences offered an unanticipated ecumenical opportunity, refocusing the whole church on the universal gospel.

Turning to the *Theses* themselves: In the first four Theses, Luther insisted that interior religion everywhere and always supersede outward performance. To that end, the Christian practice of penance must remain the primary interior focus of the gospel, which is unserviceable without disciplines of the flesh (Thesis 3). Penance is evangelical, particularly when it reflects the entire temporal existence of the Christian. Luther's understanding of penance required a tangible change of heart for the sinner who hates his or her sin and attempts on a daily basis to amend his life and do better. Penance is not an event, but a process, and a never-ending one at that. It transcends the actual sacrament of penance, which is in constant state of flux, and requires satisfactions such as fasting, prayers, and alms.[33]

Luther's first impression of indulgences was that of a bifurcated and unwieldy existential system operating within the individual Christian. The first step is justification, whereby grace is "infused" as a singular event, followed by daily repentance, ideally the operative element in growth of grace in the Christian. In the same instant, the church through her under-shepherds imposes the sacrament of penance, and can summarily dismiss the same through indulgences. However, the wall of separation between these processes is permeable. In 1517, Luther would not divorce the two, leaving at least the possibility that indulgences may have an effect on the progression of justification.

> Infused grace is an interior illumination of the mind and a kindling of the will. This is an eternal emanation into the soul like rays of the sun, and it does not become inactive after a plenary indulgence. This grace is necessary for the extirpation of concupiscence, until it is completely rooted out. This process is complete when a person is so filled with disgust for this life that he sighs longingly for God and finally breaks free of the body out of desire for God. Clearly, only a few who gain a plenary indulgence as so disposed. Further, a plenary indulgence is only granted to those who have proper sorrow and have confessed.[34]

---

33. Unfortunately, "imposed sacramental penance had consequences of a tragic nature. This was the Achilles' heel upon which Luther's adversaries fastened, and his reaction to their attack led directly to the Reformation as a movement that divided the Church." Wicks, "Luther's Treatise on Indulgences," 511.

34. As cited in Wicks, "Martin Luther's Treatise on Indulgences," 497.

In Thesis 5, Luther began an extended discussion of the church as institution, and her given and perceived role in the salvation of souls. The Pope, in Luther's view at that time, is the supreme authority in all things spiritual, as well as the instigator and foundation of any indulgence preaching. The Pope is a territorial power at best, if an indelible one, who can remit sins in the canonical realm alone; forgiveness is offered when the faithful declare to one another God's sovereign power to forgive sins and cleanse from all unrighteousness. Despite protestations to the contrary, the Pope cannot forgive sins—he can only reassure sinners of Gods' forgiveness. Furthermore, the only penalties that the church can remit unilaterally are those that she herself has imposed. Thesis 6 declares that "the pope cannot remit any guilt, except by declaring that it has been remitted by God and by assenting to God's remission; though, to be sure, he may grant remission in cases reserved to his judgment. If his right to grant remission in such cases were despised, the guilt would remain entirely unforgiven."[35] The sinner cannot be reconciled to God until he is first reconciled to the church and her members. The reality, however, is that one can be reconciled with the church and remain disconnected to God. This is the ecumenical reality of a Pope with limited powers—all things are ultimately in the hands of the true God.

Luther did not stand opposed to punishment meted out according to the church's fourth commandment authority; he was, after all, a good Augustinian cleric that had taken lifetime vows of fealty to the Pope insofar as the Pope remains orthodox with respect to penance. What Luther could not accept was the unsupportable claim that the Pope could apply temporal penalties to the dead, or grant posthumous grace to those whose loved ones had the means to purchase it. Indulgences could do no more than remit sins that had been imposed on the church militant by canon law.

> Thesis 7: God remits guilt to no one whom He does not, at the same time, humble in all things and bring into subjection to His vicar, the priest.[36]

> Thesis 8: The penitential canons are imposed only on the living, and, according to them, nothing should be imposed on the dying.[37]

---

35. Luther, *Disputation*, 35.
36. Luther, *Disputation*, 36.
37. Luther, *Disputation*, 36.

Thesis 10: Ignorant and wicked are the doings of those priests who, in the case of the dying, reserve canonical penances for purgatory.[38]

The whole system of penalties imposed by the church in the present moment is, for Luther, nothing more than a phantom to establish blind, and often profitable, obedience to the church and her clergy. Furthermore, if the keys could reach beyond the temporal and into the immortal, then it stands to reason that the one who wields the keys must necessarily possess the power to empty purgatory of all who await God's gracious release.[39] Luther's ecumenical spirit is on display here.

Theses 13 through 17 focused on death as the soul's preparation for eternal life, and the role indulgences may play in such preparation. Contrary to indulgence doctrine, the dying person cannot be held responsible for unpaid soteriological debts since they are freed by death from all penalties; they are already dead to canonical rules, and have a right to be released from them.[40] Luther's own road experience helped him sympathize with the dying man on the edge of despair due to his own lack of charity and dissolute life. For Luther, the consuming fire of the event of dying renders any additional punishments the church may assess posthumously, including purgatory and its horrors, as largely redundant.

Thesis 28—Luther's trenchant and colloquial critique of Tetzel and Albrecht—may be the most widely recognized of the Ninety-Five. "It is certain that when money clinks in the money chest, greed and avarice can be increased; but when the church intercedes, the result is in the hands of God alone."[41] Anyone familiar with indulgence preaching in early sixteenth-century Germany could not mistake Luther's target and purpose. No external act, *qua* external act, earns merit for those souls in purgatory. The Pope, the Archbishop, Tetzel *et al* could declare that contributions intended for St. Peter's offered a special indulgence that did not require

---

38. Luther, *Disputation*, 36.

39. Luther: "Souls in purgatory have no joy or peace, in fact they share nothing from heaven, since the punishment of purgatory is considered the same as that of hell, differing only in duration. But in speaking of despair I have added, 'hear despair,' for that type of despair finally comes to an end. Moreover, the soul, as long as it is in purgatory, feels nothing but despair, not because it despairs, but because it is so disturbed and perplexed with anxiety that it does not feel capable of hope. The Spirit alone helps them in their weakness [Rom. 8:26]." Luther, *Explanation to the 95 Theses*, 99.

40. Luther, *Explanation*, 99.

41. Luther, *Disputation*, 38.

contrition formed by faith and charity.[42] If the quality of contrition for any penitent is uncertain at best, the remission of sin promised by indulgence preachers would be uncertain as well. The person who is truly repentant already enjoys full remission of sin and guilt according to divine promise. He has no need for indulgences, except perhaps as a spiritual placebo. "For God places no demands upon one who is perfectly contrite, neither for actual sins nor for habitual, i.e. for the tinder and 'original' sin. What good then are indulgences?"[43] Luther's task, then, was to show how erroneous and empty the indulgence preachers were when they gave the masses the impression that the indulgences they hawked granted infused grace needed to make them ready to enter heaven. Indulgences have nothing to do with the urgency of rooting out concupiscence, growing in charity, and leaving unhealthy attachment to the world behind.

The contrast between contrition and indulgence is categorical and problematical. Contrition is by nature evangelical and ecumenical, while indulgence is narrowly ecclesial and divisive. Contrition asks for true repentance and offers unconditional remission in return; indulgence simply eases the penalty for sin, and causes the Christian to despise what is promised through it. Luther believed with the historical church that a Christian who has offended God should be thankful for the sorrow his sin has engendered, and humbled by the grace shown to him by the Almighty. The church does have an influence on the cleansing of extreme sin. "God justifies the sinner in the midst of anguish of conscience; the Church's absolution is a word of assurance and solace that makes one certain of God's hidden work. The one thing the penitent must do is believe that he is most certainly justified and forgiven."[44]

One of the best means Luther found to challenge the sale of indulgences ecumenically was by devaluing them. Theses 41—68 contrast the

---

42. Luther to Albrecht: "There is sold in the country under the protection of your illustrious name the papal indulgence for the building of St. Peter's in Rome. . . . How is it possible that the indulgence preachers convey security and fearlessness to the people through false fables and futile promises about indulgences? Indulgences do not contribute to the salvation and sanctification of souls, but only remit temporal punishment which is imposed according to canon law. . . . It should be the foremost and only care of all bishops to teach the gospel and the love of Christ to the people. . . . What great danger and shame wait for a bishop who allows the gospel to be silenced, but suffers the pompous proclamation of indulgences and is more concerned about indulgences than the gospel?" Wengert, *Martin Luther's Ninety-Five Theses*, 279.

43. Wicks, "Martin Luther's Treatise on Indulgences," 503.

44. Wicks, "Martin Luther's Treatise on Indulgences," 513.

power of indulgences against the superior capacity of acts of charity[45] and the proclamation of the gospel.[46] Indulgences can never take the place of the pure practice of true Christian religion, a right attitude toward the needs of others, and a proper understanding of the gospel. It was the gospel that Luther contended was being displaced in favor of the preaching of indulgences. The indulgence preachers claimed that theirs were the supreme graces, in that they produced the greatest monetary returns. Luther knew better: even if the grace of indulgences should exist, they could never compare to the grace of God and the power of the Cross.[47]

Luther made many remarks critical of the indulgence preachers, but he never recommended active disobedience against them. In Thesis 69 Luther avers, "[b]ishops and curates are bound to admit the commissaries of papal indulgences with all reverence," since their directive came from what Luther believed was legitimate authority that must be respected even if their intransigence is at maximum. At the same time, the bishops should be required to dissuade indulgence preachers from exceeding their directives, particularly those that are a detriment to the church. Thesis 75 declares, "To imagine that papal indulgences are so great that they could absolve a person even for doing the impossible by violating the mother of God is insanity."[48] Thesis 80: "The bishops, parish priests, and theologians who allow such sermons free course among the people will have to answer for this."[49]

The *Theses* continue with a series of sarcastic entries that are virtual commentaries on the state of the papacy that indulgence preaching had regretfully created. The wholesale disregard for the sanctity of the Christian faith indulgence preaching elicited infuriated Luther, particularly when the

---

45. Thesis 41: "Papal indulgences must be preached with caution, lest people erroneously think that they are preferable to other good works of love." Luther, *Disputation*, 39.

46. Thesis 62: "The true treasure of the church is the most holy gospel of the glory and grace of God." Luther, *Disputation*, 42.

47. Luther: "We must, therefore, recall that grace is of two kinds, namely, the grace of remission and infused grace, with the former being extrinsic and the latter intrinsic. The grace of remission is a release from the temporal punishment imposed by a confessor, which one must undergo on earth or in purgatory, if it still remains [at death] . . . But this release in no way diminishes concupiscence and the infection of our nature. Neither does it increase charity or grant grace and internal virtue. All these, however, must take place before one enters the kingdom of God, for 'flesh and blood will not inherit the kingdom of God.'" Wicks, "Martin Luther's Treatise on Indulgences," 496.

48. Luther, *Disputation*, 43.

49. Luther, *Disputation*, 44.

Holy See gleefully accepted the funds raised while decrying any reported abuses. A few cases in point:

> (Thesis) 82: . . . Why does not the pope empty purgatory for the sake of the holiest love and the direst need of souls as a matter of the highest justice, given that he redeems countless souls for filthy lucre to build the Basilica [of St. Peter] as a completely trial matter.

> (Thesis) 83: Again, 'Why continue funeral and anniversary Masses for the dead instead of returning or permitting the withdrawal of the endowments founded for them, since it is against the law to pray for those already redeemed?'

> (Thesis) 84: Again, 'What is this new piety of God and the pope that, for the sake of money, they permit someone who is impious and an enemy to redeem [from purgatory] a pious, God-fearing soul and yet do not, for the sake of the need of that very pious and beloved soul, redeem it purely out of love?'[50]

Despite the anti-papal tone of much of the *Theses*, Luther ends on a positive note: If, therefore, indulgences were preached according to the spirit and intention of the Pope, all these doubts would be readily resolved. Indeed, they would not exist. Away, then, with all those prophets who say to the people of Christ, '"Peace, peace," when there is no peace!"[51] It should be noted that Luther was only posing questions that the laity had been offering up for years. By October 1517, the time to initiate a conversation on indulgences had come.[52]

THE NINETY-FIVE THESES AS ECUMENICAL DOCUMENT

It has been my position in this paper to characterize confessional Lutheranism in general and Lutherans in particular as both evangelical and ecumenical in the best possible senses of each. While we grieve over the perceived lack of unity between Christian traditions, we continue to anticipate and pray for the winds of healthy ecumenism to blow that they may be one promptly and completely. The Australian Lutheran Kurt Marquart,

---

50. Luther, *Disputation*, 44.

51. Jer 6:14 (ESV).

52. The *Theses* appear dense and overly academic, but they still managed to generate great interest among academics, clergy, and literate laypersons. They were translated into German soon after their appearance, increasing their accessibility, and were reprinted as many as four times before the end of 1517.

commenting on the current state of ecumenism in Christendom, reminded Lutherans specifically that ecumenism occurs as a matter of course when Christians respect one another and strive to place the centrality and animating principle of the gospel over an amorphous ecumenical "experience" which sacrifices theological rigor in the interests of Christians "getting along." In fact, the best ecumenical discussions occur without the display of our unique ecclesial stamps. As Marquart writes,

> [I]t should be noted that the "one Lord, one faith, one baptism" of the "one body" in Ephesians 4:4–5 is meant as a present reality, not as an ideal still to be achieved, much less one to be achieved by human church politics! Scripture speaks not of any "Ecumenical Movement" but of the ecumenical status of the Church! *The Church is already one.* This oneness is given in the one Lord and the one. This oneness is given in the one Lord and the one faith, and is not an imaginary abstraction, of a piece with "some Platonic republic."[53]

That vision of an "ecumenical movement" needs to be noted in an age of innovative attempts at unity.

The Luther of the *Ninety-Five Theses* remained a loyal Catholic despite attempts to paint him as a conscious dissident as early as 1513. He sought reform, not Reformation. In the years prior to October 1517 Luther's theological interests were shifting away from the medieval theology in which he was schooled. His expositions on the books of Romans and Galatians had been completed to positive reviews. His pen flowed liberally with personal correspondence, and his preaching began to be noticed beyond the confines of little Wittenberg, though a relative dearth of it is extant. In all likelihood, Luther's famed "Reformation breakthrough" to recover the true gospel occurred somewhere in this three-year period, although one would be hard-pressed to declare there to have been a discrete moment in time when the scales of medieval theology fell from Luther's eyes, revealing for him the path to reform that would reshape the church and the centuries to come. In short, Luther of the *Ninety-Five Theses* was a primeval ecumenist, albeit an anonymous one.

Until 1520, when circumstances temporal and ecclesial forced his hand, Luther preached, lectured, and wrote as an intentionally Catholic theologian with no particular animus to vent. He could and did maintain

---

53. Marquart, "The Church of the Augsburg Confession as the True Ecumenical Movement," 62. Emphasis added.

contrary to his opponents that ecclesial authority had not ruled sufficiently on many issues, indulgences among them, leaving those as grist for the disputation mill. This allowed Luther to stand apart from the theological consensus of the time on indulgences while remaining what he maintained was a loyal Catholic cleric and academic. Luther believed that his sharp but not mean-spirited critiques of Leo X should have been taken in the spirit of collegiality, and should not have placed him on the Holy See's list of *persona non grata*, the weigh station before excommunication. He also believed that as a good Catholic he should have been able to bring to Archbishop Albrecht's attention the scandalous over-reach of the indulgence preachers, and be given assurances that some effort was being expended to correct the problem.

By 1517, the focus of Luther's scholarship was the divine mandate for and benefit of pure inward penitence and genuine humility, not the possibility of an exodus from Holy Mother Church for reasons of spiritual abuse or malfeasance. Any Christian may lay claim to righteousness due to pious effort, but even if those righteous acts were heavily aided by grace they would still be woefully inadequate to change one's fate before divine judgment. The Christian is overmatched by sin, and therefore must find a different means of reconciliation with God—for Luther, the only option open was true penitence, condemning one's own sins in light of the righteousness of God. This view is summed up in the famous Thesis 1: "When our Lord and Master Jesus Christ said, 'Repent,' he willed the entire life of believers to be one of repentance."[54] The Christian, then, should never view penitence as a burden to escape, but a blessed participation in the cross of Christ. It is perfectly understandable that Luther would find the preaching of indulgences which advised a financial contribution could substitute for sorrow over sin reprehensible, and more than a simple abuse. With the *Ninety-Five Theses* Luther showed no desire to challenge Papal authority—his was a protest of a theological nature, because the gospel was at stake.

In a letter to Archbishop Albrecht dated 31 October 1517, Luther reflected on many of the issues brought forward by the *Theses*. His greatest disquiet was not over the questionable theology behind and implications of indulgences, but rather his deep and abiding pastoral concern for the ordinary Christian. Luther's appeal is heartfelt and uncomplicated: the people require assurance of salvation founded on faith, not indulgences. They need the church, warts and all, to be for them what the Lord promised.

---

54. Luther, *Disputation*, 34.

> Under your most distinguished title, papal indulgences are being disseminated among the people for the construction of St. Peter's [in Rome]. In these matters, I do not so much find fault with the cries of the preachers, which I have not heard, but I do bewail the people's completely false understanding, gleaned from these fellows, which they spread everywhere among the common folk. For example, these poor souls believe: that if they were to purchase these letters of indulgence they would then be assured of their salvation; likewise, that souls immediately leap from purgatory when they have thrown a contribution into the chest; and then that the graces [of indulgences] are so great that no sin is of such magnitude that it cannot be forgiven—even if (as they say) someone should rape the Mother of God, were this possible; likewise, that through these indulgences a person is freed from every penalty and guilt. O great God! In this way, excellent Father, souls committed to your care are being directed to death.[55]

Luther was for the most part certain that the disgraceful peddling of indulgences was occurring without Albrecht's knowledge or *imprimatur*. Regardless of preachers' voices to the contrary, no indulgence could reconcile humanity to God, or destroy the punishments of purgatory. For Luther, true repentance was in short supply when indulgences were readily available. In a letter sent to Albrecht early in 1518, he respectfully advised the archbishop to take the matter of indulgences in hand as soon as possible, since to delay would allow an unknown foe to refute the archbishop's will concerning indulgence retailing and the preaching that supported it. Luther's tone was not aggressive, but it is hard not to detect a veiled threat, even if he did not intend the letter to serve as a kind of ultimatum. The *Ninety-Five Theses* were never intended to be threatening—they were simply to be discussion points concerning an accepted church practice that had become stained with error. The *Theses* themselves were unambiguous and lucid, offering a clear alternative to the errors Luther believed were being peddled by the indulgence preachers. Luther was genuinely concerned about the critical reactions he might expect and had already encountered. The letter was not so much an apology for his exploits, but a winsome presentation of the contents of one man's humble heart in the service of God's chosen people.

---

55. Luther, "Letter from Martin Luther to Albrecht, Archbishop of Mainz 31 October 1517," 52.

Archbishop Albrecht would do the Augustinian a great honor should he accept Luther's advice in an ecumenical, royal, and charitable manner.[56]

Another key indicator of Luther's commitment to ecumenism and reconciliation is his use of the phrase "assurance of salvation" (Thesis 16).[57] This seemingly innocuous locution was debated extensively by Luther and some of the Roman interlocutors sent in 1518 at Leo X's behest to demand of him immediate and unqualified recantation. Luther had no desire to square off with Papal pit bulls like Cardinal Cajetan (1469–1534), particularly when he had already averred that the *Ninety-Five Theses* were for debate purposes only. Cajetan challenged Luther strenuously on several points, but in particular on whether or not faith was necessary to "assure" one of efficacious sacramental absolution. Did Luther really claim that a penitent Christian must move beyond common conviction to the greatest possible certitude before she is fully absolved by God? Cajetan reminded Luther that unfaltering assurance of salvation is available through Christ alone, therefore one could never know if he had achieved proper contrition, much less be certain of forgiveness.[58] It seemed that Luther's view was "foreign to the Christian faith," and intended to "build a new church."[59] Luther blanched.

Luther's response was sharp, but largely respectful for the often-volatile young monk. For Luther, faith is simple: it is nothing else than believing that for the sake of Christ I have in the present moment what God promises and reveals. The penitent *must* believe that the words of absolution apply to him, since they are tied directly to Christ who gives to His church the keys to earth and heaven (Matt 16:19). For Luther, the obstruction indulgences presents was their tendency to reduce objective, saving faith to an interesting but unessential element of the Christian life. In effect, the Pope had supplanted his uncertain, human words for the certain, divine words of Christ Himself. To be unsure of forgiveness makes Christ to be a liar, a sin of staggering proportion. The way one "feels" in the confessional is

---

56. Brecht, *Martin Luther*, 191.

57. Luther, *Disputation*, 36.

58. "This is more evident today when we consider Cardinal Cajetan's conclusion, after studying Luther's writings, that Luther's understanding of faith certainly implied the founding of a new church. However, this judgment is conclusive only within Cajetan's own theological system. If one leaves this system behind and turns to Luther's way of thinking, concerns and intentions change to a significant extent." Thönissen, "Reform and Reformation," 41.

59. Thönissen, "Reform and Reformation," 41.

irrelevant—prepare for the sacraments by faith, not mortification. Reception of grace is not predicated on worthiness, which would lead inevitably to presumption or despair. In this exchange at least, Luther proved to be the true ecumenical churchman, encouraging the church to which he was loyal to reform through recovery of the pure creedal teachings common to all Christendom.[60]

It is self-evident that the medieval church was not theologically homogeneous. Luther was occupied with an internal struggle within the church, which was not alone in Christendom.[61] Several competing understandings of justification already existed within the church catholic,[62] and had done so virtually from the genesis of the Christian faith 1,500 years previous. Luther's objection to the "certainty sale" of indulgences did not materialize from the ether. The medieval nominalists Gabriel Biel (ca. 1425–1495) and William of Ockham (1285–1347) were known to be at least respectful Catholics—Luther charged them with espousing a radically Pelagian view of salvation. Thomas Aquinas (1225–1274)—whom the church had canonized in 1323, most likely in deference to his seminal work the *Summa Theologiæ*—systematized the Christian faith from an Aristotelian perspective, a labor on which Luther did not look with unqualified favor.[63] The *Ninety-Five Theses* cast light on the plurality of views of salvation with their thoroughgoing monergism and realism—they implied correctly that while the Church Militant has been and always will be unified under the Cross, she can never hope to achieve temporal unity until the internal contradictions have been resolved.

One must likewise remember that Luther's theological approach was not "scholastic" in the proper sense. The Schoolmen had different loci of emphasis, in particular the articulation of the dogma of the church and its philosophical moorings. Luther, on the other hand, displayed little interest

---

60. The Council of Trent upheld Cajetan's position, showing that it too had misunderstood Luther.

61. "Ecumenical dialogues have some similarities with medieval disputations. Partners who represent different traditions sit at the same table. This very dialogue includes the question of the truth of certain doctrines, since it does not allow the participants simply to say that their own convictions are true simply because they are the position of their own church. In the perception of many theologians, ecumenism is connected with compromise, whereas theology is proud to be committed to the search of truth and of truth alone." Dieter, "Luther Research and Ecumenism," 165.

62. E.g., Monergism, Pelagianism, and Semi-Pelagianism to name three.

63. Wilson, "Six Ways Ecumenical Progress is Possible," 314.

in such doctrinal disputes. Orthodoxy was of course indispensable, but it must lead inevitably to orthopraxis in the life of the Christian. Thesis 68: " they are in truth the least of all when compared to the grace of God and the goodness of the cross."[64] The manner of living espoused by Luther is normative for the individual Christian in the world, and the church as a whole. "Reformation" of the church did not mean adjustment and adaptation to resident circumstances, but genuine *re-formatio* to the original pristine Christianity, insofar as that is possible. Christ crucified is the ground of faith, the fount and source of transformation in the church that continues until the consummation of all things.

Christendom writ large suffers the disease of amorphous theology and internal distrust to the current day. Nevertheless, the great bulk of Luther scholarship is concerned not with the damage done by the Augustinian, but over categorizations that resulted in deeply rooted misunderstanding. From a confessional Lutheran perspective, the *Ninety-Five Theses* were profoundly ecumenical in nature. To declare them otherwise misses their historical context. By 1517 Luther had turned his quill to the implications of the return to the true and simple gospel the Holy Spirit had directed him to in recent years. The Sacrament of Penance was in his crosshairs, since it seemed to draw attention from the Cross and placed it on the quality of personal confession and pious effort. Yet as the *Ninety-Five Theses* make plain, Luther's opposition to indulgences did not include repeal. Luther wished, on the other hand, for the priests to offer the "assurance of salvation" he himself had sought desperately by speaking to the penitent of the forgiveness of sins that had already occurred through true repentance. Faith is the only appropriate response to God's grace, revealed as it is in the Word.

Luther's view of scripture was clearly on display in the *Ninety-Five Theses*.[65] His early Catholic antagonists like Cajetan and Johannes Eck (1486–1543) prosecuted Luther as a sectarian, claiming his view of God's Word was at best a contradiction to the authority of the Magisterium of the church, and at worst a clarion call to apostasy. Luther responded with typical clarity: nothing could take the place of scripture as the sole source of authority for the church. God will severely chastise all those who alter or displace the clear words of scripture, particularly those who offer remission of sin without repentance and faith.[66] Ecumenism in itself allows that

---

64. Luther, *Disputation*, 42.
65. Luther, *Explanation of the Ninety-Five Theses*, 80.
66. Wood, "Baptism and Christian Life," 199–200.

those within the church have lived in manifest sin of one kind or another. The result is a church that has reaped a harvest of division that is by no means accidental or circumstantial; Christ willed there to be unity among His disciples.[67] In other words, there can be no restoration of confessional concurrence without the difficult task of confession, absolution, and faith that undergird it.

Although Luther was not consciously ecumenical, his was an ecumenical approach to the church that showed great deference to the eighth commandment. On 31 October 1517, he believed himself to be neither a schismatic nor a heretic; he was a university professor of still little renown who self-identified as a monk, a loyal son of the Church of Rome. Luther saw the abuses of indulgence peddling with clarity, and spoke out unambiguously against them. From the posting of the *Theses* in 1517 until his final papal condemnation in 1521, Luther treated indulgences as a largely open question to be deliberated in a respectful, ecumenical fashion. This was the tenor of the *Ninety-Five Theses*. He would certainly alter his stance on the subject if his errors were pointed out by scripture, the Fathers, or human reason. He refused to take the route of expediency by falsely claiming the church to be unified in all things, even if such a claim were made in principle only. "The Reformation did not intend to found new churches but wanted reform, the renewal of the whole of Christendom in the spirit of truth of God. . . . [It] gives clear evidence of the fact that true reform of the church can only come out of a profound encounter with the word of God in which the Church finds [her] true identity."[68] Thus, ecumenism demands that confessional Lutherans remain on the side of scripture and sacrament, even when circumstances threaten and boundaries crumble. Luther knew that there could be no doctrinal *quid pro quo* with Rome—with the *Ninety-Five Theses* he showed a willingness to speak truth to the authority, and that even as he stood firm against abuse he remained a loyal Catholic, wishing the church to relent and return to the state of Spirit-given grace she had enjoyed for centuries.

CONCLUSION

On 9 November 1518, Pope Leo X published the bull *Cum postquam*, which Leo hoped would be definitive in correcting the theological excess

---

67. Wilson, "Six Ways Ecumenical Progress is Possible," 325.

68. Koch, "The Commemoration of the Reformation as an Ecumenical Opportunity," n.p.

and pastoral abuse that indulgence preaching had wrought. Leo believed that Luther and his objections could be used to some advantage, in this case to draw the church back from the wilderness to the pastureland of correct Catholic doctrine. The Bull declared that "(1) that the Church can grant indulgences to the living and the dead; (2) that indulgences are conceded by apostolic authority from 'the treasury of the merits of Jesus Christ and the saints;' (3) that indulgences are granted *per modum absolutionis* and *per modum suffragii*; [and] (4) that guilt is remitted by the sacrament of penance, temporal punishment 'by means of an ecclesiastical indulgence.'"[69] Leo wished for future generations of Catholics to have what he contended was the unvarnished truth concerning indulgences, both in the sixteenth century and for future generations. Luther's later excommunication was regrettable, and probably illegal, but Luther by his own admission had removed himself from the embrace of Holy Mother Church, and had come to comprehend the Christian faith and the gospel as something distinct from what was propagated by church leadership. Despite Luther's best ecumenical attempts, the rift was set in stone.

In the context of history, no means exist to identify, much less assess, moral turpitude—who knows what lurks in the heart of a person? And if that knowledge is unavailable, how can one accuse another of ethical laxity or nefarious intent? In 1517, the clarion call of Luther to bring the church into alignment with herself and her orthodox history fell on largely deaf ears. For his part, Luther must have ascertained that his Disputation on Indulgences, while ecumenical in aim, would have the opposite effect in many for whom indulgences were accepted and open-ended dogma. It turns out that history is more complicated than we might think—it does not offer up its answers readily. But from her inception the Christian church has maintained her animating energy to be the abiding presence of the Holy Spirit, Whose blessings move the church through time and space with purpose and meaning. The true meaning of history may take decades or even centuries to make itself known, oftentimes with contradiction and conflict. The Reformation is by no means distinct—it cannot be understood as a whole. The ecumenical concerns of 2017 have most certainly shaped some of this paper's assertions. God willing more ramifications and influences of the *Ninety-Five Theses* will emerge in the Holy Spirit's good time.

Soli Deo Gloria!

---

69. McNally, "Ninety-Five Theses of Martin Luther," 478.

The Reformation
BIBLIOGRAPHY

Brecht, Martin. *Martin Luther: His Road to Reformation 1483–1521*. Translated by James L. Schaaf. Minneapolis: Fortress, 1985.

Catechism of the Catholic Church. London: Geoffrey Chapman, 1999.

Dieter, Theodor. "Luther Research and Ecumenism." *Dialog* 47.2 (2008) 157–66.

Evans, G. R. *The Roots of the Reformation: Tradition, Emergence and Rupture*. Downers Grove, IL: IVP, 2012.

Kasper, Walter. *Martin Luther: An Ecumenical Perspective*. Translated by William Madges. New York: Paulist, 2016.

Koch, Kurt Cardinal. "The Commemoration of the Reformation as an Ecumenical Opportunity: Towards a Joint Declaration on Church, Ministry and Eucharist." Paper delivered to the Spring Assembly of the Finnish Ecumenical Council in Helsinki, 27 April 2015.

Luther, Martin. *Disputation of Doctor Martin Luther on the Power and Efficacy of Indulgences: October 31, 1517*. Bellingham, WA: Logos Bible Software.

———. *Explanation of the Ninety-Five Theses*. In *Luther's Works*, 31:17–33. Edited by Harold Grimm and Helmut T. Lehmann. Philadelphia: Fortress, 1957.

———. *Luther's Works*, Vol. 34, edited by Helmut T. Lehmann and Lewis W. Spitz. Philadelphia: Fortress, 1960.

Marquart, Kurt. "The Church of the Augsburg Confession as the True Ecumenical Movement: Was the Reformation Ecumenical," 62–110. Online: http://www.ctsfw.net/media/pdfs/marquartchurchoftheaugsburgconfession.pdf.

McNally, Robert. "Ninety-Five Theses of Martin Luther: 1517–1967." *Theological Studies* 28 (1967) 439–80.

Moorman, Mary C. *Indulgences: Luther, Catholicism, and the Imputation of Merit*. Steubenville, OH: Emmaus Academic, 2017.

Ozment, Steven. *The Age of Reform: 1250–1550*. New Haven: Yale University Press, 1980.

Piepkorn, Arthur Carl. "A Lutheran Theologian looks at the Ninety-Five Theses in 1967." *Theological Studies* 28 (1967) 519–30.

Sixtus IV. *Salvator noster*. Abbreviated. Online: rels365fa10.pbworks.com/w/page/30170987/Salvator%20noster%20and%20Unigenitus

Tetzel, Johann. *Rebuttal against Luther's Sermon on Indulgences and Grace*, edited by M. Patrick Graham. Translated by Dewey Weiss Kramer. Atlanta: Pitts Theology Library, 1987.

Thönissen, Wolfgang. "Reform and Reformation: Ecumenical Approaches in Light of the Document From Conflict to Communion." *Claritas-Journal of Dialogue & Culture* 5.2 (October 2016) 38–49.

Wengert, Timothy, ed. *The Roots of Reform*. Vol. 1 of *The Annotated Luther*. Minneapolis: Fortress, 2015.

———. *Martin Luther's Ninety-Five Theses with Introduction, Commentary, and Study Guide*. Minneapolis: Fortress Press, 2015.

Wicks, Jared. "Martin Luther's Treatise on Indulgences." *Theological Studies* 28 (1967) 481–518.

Wilson, Sarah. "Six Ways Ecumenical Progress is Possible." *Concordia Journal* 39 (2013) 310–32.

Wood, Susan B. "Baptism and Christian Life." In *Luther Refracted: The Reformer's Ecumenical Legacy*, edited by Piotr J. Malysz and Derek R. Nelson, 193–214. Minneapolis: Fortress, 2017.

4

Thomas Cranmer, Roger Martyn, and the Transformation of Worship in the English Reformation

Gwenfair Walters Adams

THERE IT WAS, RIGHT in front of me: The Church of the Holy Trinity, Long Melford, Suffolk—the parish church with the longest nave in England. I had asked my doctoral supervisor, Eamon Duffy, for his recommendation for a particularly interesting parish church to photograph and talk about for my candidating lecture at Gordon-Conwell Theological Seminary. He suggested Long Melford. So, here I was, standing at the bottom of the churchyard. After contemplating the building's beautiful façade for a few minutes, I pulled my rollerboard (filled with camera equipment) up the path to the south door. There I discovered an elderly gentleman looking out expectantly. At first he seemed to be waiting for *me*, but it turned out that he was waiting for a journalist who had scheduled an appointment with him for a tour of the church. She was late, so he offered to show me around until she came, which ended up being an hour or so later. I got the full tour, and it was fascinating.

In this building, in 1527 (or 1526), as in any year, the priests had baptized many babies. But that year, one of them would turn out to be quite important to the history of this particular church—and, as it turns out, to our understanding of the English Reformation, especially to our insight into the impact of the Reformation on the lives of people in the pews. The priest christened this baby boy Roger Martyn. Martyn would live for eighty-eight years, his life crossing over into the seventeenth century.

When Martyn was born, the church was still steeped in medieval religious culture, quite untouched by the Reformation that had begun ten years earlier in Germany. But soon, by the time he was about twelve years old, the Reformation would reach this wool town. Martyn would live through the dramatic religious changes that the reigns of Henry VIII, Edward VI, Mary, Elizabeth I, and James I would bring. By studying Long Melford through Martyn's experience, we can catch a glimpse of what life was like in the English Reformation at the "micro" level for those who resisted the cataclysmic changes. We will weave into his account that of a key figure at the "macro" level, Thomas Cranmer, who, through his decisions made at the national level, was responsible for much of the transformation in Long Melford's worship. By contrasting these two men, we discover a story of reformation and recusancy played out in the changing rituals, service books, vestments, and furnishings of a local medieval church.

THE CHURCH OF ROGER MARTYN'S CHILDHOOD

In his later years, Roger Martyn would write a detailed description of church life in the parish in the 1530s. The document reveals a poignant, wistful longing for the church of his childhood, the version of the church he would remain loyal to for his entire life, even though it would cost him dearly. My tour guide pointed out many traces of this childhood world.

First, there was the font where Roger Martyn had been baptized. My guide informed me that it was the one thing that had survived from the centuries-earlier phase of the church that had stood on the site. The building I was now standing in had been completed a mere two decades before the Reformation. It had originally been a small Saxon church that had been granted to the town by King Edward the Confessor (1042–1066). That building had been a place of worship for centuries. Then John Clopton, a wealthy wool merchant—his life spared in the Wars of the Roses—decided to build a larger church for Long Melford, out of gratitude to God. The new church was built around and above the old church, and the people worshipped in the little church until the big one was completed, and then the tiny church was torn down, and everyone worshipped in the larger space.

The Martyns and the Cloptons, both wealthy families in a wealthy wool merchant town, donated significant funds for this new building. Each family had major parts of the church named for them. Around the clerestory are inscriptions asking passersby to pray for them and their families as the benefactors of the church building.

The Cloptons had their own family chapel inside the parish church. Their private chapel had its own entrance so that the family worshipped separately from the rest of the church, but at the same time. A squint in the wall allowed their priest to see from their family chapel, across the corner of their chantry priest's chapel, to a view of the high altar of the main church, so that all the priests could coordinate their masses with the one taking place in the chancel, keeping one step behind so that they did not outpace the primary mass.

The Cloptons' chantry priest had his own chapel, right next to the Clopton family chapel. A chantry priest's job was to offer up masses for the dead on a daily basis for the ancestors of those who funded them. It seems that the Cloptons' chantry priest may have also been an anchorite, which meant that he stayed in the church building, in his two rooms at all times, never leaving. Centuries later, the bones of a goose were discovered in the chimney of his fireplace. It seems that he may have been cooking the fowl during Lent when he should have been abstaining from meat, and that he may have heard someone coming and stuffed the evidence up the chimney! Up on the wall in his chapel there are niches where statues of the twelve apostles stood guard. They were probably not too happy about his violation of the Lenten fast.

Gracing the walls of the Clopton chapels were two poems by John Lydgate. Lydgate was a famous poet of his time, and John Clopton—the Clopton whose wool merchant money financed much of the church—knew him personally. One of the two poems was called "Testament," and it included Christ speaking to the reader, reminding him or her of his sacrifice on the cross, made out of love for them. The latter part of the poem repeated variations on the refrain, "Grant, ere I die, shrift, housel, repentance,"[1] expressing the common desire to avoid sudden death so that one could have the last rites before it was too late. The final stanza lands above the Clopton chapel altar, exhorting the worshipper to be aware of how short the pilgrimage of life is.[2] The other poem, *Quis Dabit Meo Capiti Fontem Lacrimarum* expressed the sorrowing of Mary Magdalene at the cross, modeling for the reader the need to sorrow along with her, an expression of the highly affective devotion to the cross of the late medieval period.

1. Lydgate, *Early English Poetry*, 252.
2. Gibson, *The Theater of Devotion*, 89.

Roger Martyn was born about thirty years after this church—the building that his great, great, great grandfather had helped finance—was completed. He grew up attending a church in which there were at least seven altars running concurrently at Mass. The Holy Trinity altar was the high altar. The Cloptons had two altars, including one dedicated to St. Anne. The one in the Martyn family's aisle was the Jesus altar, and then there was the one dedicated to Mary in the Lady Chapel.

In his later reminiscences, Martyn would describe the church in detail. He remembered what was in his family's aisle, or chapel. He referred to it as the Jesus aisle, in reference to the Jesus altar at its head. Behind the altar was a table with a crucifix on it, with the two thieves hanging on each side. There were two tabernacles that reached from the ground all the way to the ceiling. Tabernacles held the hosts for viewing and veneration. The one at the north end of the altar had an image of Jesus holding a ball in his hand, which Martyn thought signified his containing the "whole round world." On the south end of the altar was "a fair image of our Blessed Lady having the afflicted body of her dear Son, as he was taken down off the Cross lying along on her lap, the tears as it were running down pitifully upon her beautiful cheeks, as it seemed bedewing the said sweet body of her Son, and therefore named the Image of our Lady of Pity."[3] Neither tabernacle survived the Reformation, but a stained glass image of our Lady of Pity did. The Virgin Mary held Christ's lifeless body, hundreds of wounds bleeding in trinitarian clusters.

Then there was the Rood Loft with the Rood and Mary and John on each side. "Rood" was the medieval English word for cross. The Rood loft was a tall, wooden screen that spanned the breadth of the church, and the side facing the congregation was painted with images of the twelve apostles. It may have looked something like the one that has been restored at St. George's Church in Dunster, built in 1499, around the same time as Holy Trinity Church's, with the apostles like the ones at St. Firmin Church, North Crawley, and the rood itself like the one at St. Birinius at Dorchester-on-Thames. The ceiling of the entire church was, in Martyn's words, "beautified with fair gilt stars."[4] You can see some of them still in the Clopton Chantry chapel. In the vestry there was a press that held many "rich copes and Suits of Vestments" in such a way that they did not "frumple."[5]

3. Parker, *History of Long Melford*, 71.
4. Parker, *History of Long Melford*, 71.
5. Parker, *History of Long Melford*, 72.

Along with his account of childhood church memories, a listing of church contents appears in Roger Martyn's handwriting. It is a 1529 listing, so it would not have been written originally by Martyn, who would, of course, have been only two years old at the time. Presumably he copied the inventory as an adult, perhaps when he became the churchwarden for Holy Trinity during Mary's reign. The listing is quite instructive, for it tells us what objects the church owned before the Reformation started chipping away at them. It is a very long list. There are thirteen chalices, a monstrance (a portable vessel in which the host was carried in processions), three paxes (small crucifixes to be passed around and kissed) and a pyx (for holding reserved sacrament, often hung above altar), two basins for hand washing, two crosses, two chrismatories (holding the holy oils for anointing at baptism, confirmation, and last rites), and two ships (boat-shaped silver vessels that held incense until it was placed in censors), two silver candlesticks, two silver censers, and two silver cruets. The list includes a relic that benefactor John Clopton had given to his son, the knight William who, in turn, gave it to the Church. It was believed to be part of the pillar "that our Saviour Christ was bound to."[6]

The Lady Chapel had a special sculpture of the Blessed Virgin Mary that attracted pilgrims, and the inventory showed her popularity, for she had many objects dedicated to her honor, including girdles, rings, beads, buckles—jewels and an apron together weighing 22 oz. She had a white-bordered coat for the major feast days, a crimson velvet coat, and a white damask coat, the latter with a matching altar cloth trimmed with green velvet.

Vestments for the main chapel included seventeen copes, chasubles, tunicles, and other garments in red velvet, scarlet velvet, blue velvet with stars, bawdkin (silk with gold thread) with birds, red sarsnet (soft silk), white damask, black damask, blue satin, and red silk. There were six altar cloths of crimson velvet, blue damask, and silk with blue birds and blue velvet.

There were ten mass books, four antiphonals, and a dozen grails (graduals), eleven processionaries (processionals), three manuals, two martolages (martyrologies of the lives and deaths of saints), two hymnals, and an ordinal. Three dozen altar cloths and fourteen towels, more than twenty corporasses (cloths for the consecration of the host), seven coverlets, seventeen golden candlesticks, dozens of cloths for the various images

6. Parker, *History of Long Melford*, 77.

of saints—there were at least a dozen saints, including St. James, Catherine, Margaret, Mary Magdalene, Edmund, Sythe (Sitha or Zita), George, Thomas, Christopher, Andrew, and Loy.

Holy Trinity had at least six guilds dedicated to the Holy Trinity, Jesus, Corpus Christ, Our Lady, St. Peter, and St. Thomas the Martyr. These were groups of people who came together around a common devotion to a saint who served as their patron, while they made sure to keep a taper (or candle) burning in front of his or her image.

This seems to have been an active, engaged, church with a significant number of devoted parishioners. It was the church that Roger Martyn was born into, and he would have had no idea how dramatically things would change during his lifetime.

CRANMER'S CONVERSION

In the same year that Roger Martyn was born, about 70 miles away, in London, a thirty-seven year old man was also oblivious to the fact that he was about to begin his own turbulent journey. It was Thomas Cranmer (1489–1556) who was meeting Henry VIII for the first time. Little did he know in 1527 that he was embarking on a relationship that would bring him to the very heart of the English Reformation, and that it would make him, arguably, its most significant religious figure. While Martyn would live the Reformation at the micro level, Cranmer would live it at the macro level. As far as we know, they never met. It is almost certain Cranmer never heard of Martyn. Martyn may or may not have heard of Cranmer. But Cranmer's actions, decisions, and words would have a profound shaping influence on the worship practices of Martyn and his beloved church.

There is something fascinating about looking at the Reformation through the eyes of both of these men. Both were devout. Both held their views passionately. But they were on two very different sides of each of the events that unfolded. We will consider the changes first through Cranmer's eyes, for he is the one who starts to experience them first.

In 1531, the first of a long series of Acts and Injunctions was passed that began to dismantle Roman Catholicism in England. At first the Acts were related to the King's divorce and involved the king being declared the Supreme Head of the Church of England and the country cutting itself off from papal authority. Cranmer was involved in helping with the King's divorce and the break from the papacy, basing it on a theology of the divine right of kings and princes. But these would not yet affect Long Melford's worship.

On 30 March 1533, when Roger Martyn was only six years old, Cranmer became the archbishop of Canterbury, and thus one of the most powerful religious figures in England, the other being the vice-gerent and Lord, Thomas Cromwell. Cranmer had been in holy orders as far back as 1520. He had also, quite ironically, been married (secretly!) for almost a year. Priests were not supposed to be married, let alone archbishops!

We do not know exactly when or how Cranmer became involved with the Reformation. He had been exposed to Lutheran theology in his student days at Jesus College, Cambridge University. Lutheran ideas had arrived in England in the early 1520s and students began discussing them in the White Horse Tavern in Cambridge. But Cranmer does not appear to have been a member of "Little Germany," as the Tavern had come to be called, and he seems to have sided with Erasmus rather than Luther at this time, as his annotations in his copy of Erasmus' *De Libero Arbitrio* (1524 edition) indicate.[7] Also, in the late 1520s, as he became one of the key champions of Henry VIII's bid to divorce Katherine of Aragon, his antipathy towards Lutheranism was fed by Luther's strong stance against Henry VIII's divorce.[8] So, it is possible that when he became archbishop in 1533, he was still a bit theologically conservative. Bishop Brooks, for example, who presided at Cranmer's trial in 1555, said, "Who was thought as then more devout? Who was more religious in the face of the world? Who was thought to have more conscience of vow-making, and observing the order of the church, more earnest in the defence of the real presence of Christ's body and blood in the sacrament of the altar, than ye were?"[9] At the same time, though, Cranmer's wife was the niece of a Reformer, Andreas Osiander, a German Lutheran theologian. Cranmer's marriage to her may point to an emerging openness towards the Reformation.

Throughout the Reformation, Cranmer would tend towards peacemaking and towards saving people's lives from the death penalty. He attempted to save the loyally Catholic Thomas More's life when he could not sign the Oath of Supremacy that declared Henry Supreme Head of the Church in England. He succeeded in keeping Catholic Princess Mary from

---

7. Null, *Thomas Cranmer's Doctrine of Repentance*, 93.
8. MacCulloch, *Thomas Cranmer*, 68.
9. Foxe, *Foxe's Book of Martyrs*, 3:657.

going to the Tower because of *her* inability to sign the Oath. This would, of course, later prove to be ironic, and very much to his detriment.

MARTYN'S MEDIEVAL CHILDHOOD

Meanwhile, Roger Martyn was a child growing up in a church that was still very medieval in spite of what was happening on the Continent and at the macro level of his own country. He would later describe the celebrations held on Holy Days in the church, and so we learn what parish church life was like just before the Reformation began to have an impact in Long Melford. He remembers that on Palm Sunday:

> The Blessed Sacrament was carried in procession about the Churchyard under a fair canopy born by 4 yeomen. The procession coming to the churchgate, went westward, and they with the Blessed Sacrament went eastward. And when the procession came against the door of Mr. Clopton's aisle, they, with the Blessed Sacrament, and with a little bell and singing, approached at the east end of our Ladie's Chapel, at which time a boy with a thing in his hand pointed to it, signifying a prophet as I think, sang standing on the tyrett that is on the said Mr Clopton's aisle door, "Ecce Rex tuus, venit, etc." and then all did kneel down, and then, rising up, went and met the Sacrament, and so then, went singing together into the Church, and coming near the Porch, a boy or one of the Clerks, did cast over among the boys, flowers, and singing cakes, etc.[10]

On Maundy Thursday, a painted timber frame was erected in the Choir, with holes for candles to be placed near the Easter Sepulchre. On Good Friday, a priest stood near the Rood and sang the Passion account. Then someone would be posted to keep vigil at the burning taper that had been placed on John Clopton's tomb. It was the most prominent tomb in the church at the time and sat between the Clopton Chapel and the main altar of the church. A host, representing Christ's dead body, was "buried" on it on Good Friday and kept there until Easter morning when it would be taken out and used in the Easter morning Mass. A painting of Christ's resurrection decorated the underside of the canopy above the tomb, where if John Clopton had emerged from his repose, it would have been his first sight. The painting was highly appropriate for the most important purpose

---

10. Parker, *History of Long Melford*, 72.

the tomb served each year, as an Easter Sepulchre, the focal point of the Paschal liturgy.

As a child, Martyn would have had little or no idea, presumably, of what was happening at the macro level. He would not have known about the significance of Henry VIII's desire to divorce his wife, the machinations towards which began around the same year that Martyn was born, as that was the year that Henry became infatuated with Anne Boleyn. He would probably not have known about Henry's breaking things off with the papacy. Or of his having his close friend Thomas More beheaded for treason in 1535. He may have heard of the beheading of the Queen (the former Anne Boleyn) in 1536. He would not have known that Cranmer attempted to defend her. But all this would not have directly affected Long Melford. The first effects of the Reformation seem to have come three years later, in 1539.

THE DISSOLUTION OF THE MONASTERIES

In that year, the monks stopped chanting the daily office in the Lady Chapel of Holy Trinity. Henry had dissolved the larger monasteries—and Long Melford felt the impact. The monastery at Bury St. Edmunds was dissolved. Lydgate, whose poems graced the Clopton chapel, had been a monk in that monastery. Based in the nearby town of Bury St. Edmunds, it had a country estate right down the hill from the Long Melford's church. The Bury St. Edmunds monastery was one of the largest in England. By 1535, its net annual income was about eight times the average for a monastery.[11] Moreover, where the national average number of monks per monastic house was a dozen, Bury St. Edmunds had about sixty monks. When the monks stayed in Long Melford, they walked across the churchyard many times each day to worship in the Lady Chapel that was attached to the parish church. The Lady Chapel where they worshipped had been financed by John Clopton, and the parish church itself had been built with the assistance of the monks.

Now the monks were gone. They no longer chanted during the services. They no longer trekked up the hill eight times a day to the Lady Chapel. Their property was taken over by the Crown. Later, under Queen Mary, it would be granted to Sir William Cordell. He would incorporate parts of the past monastery into his new home. The new buildings would be large enough that when Elizabeth I came to visit, Cordell was able to entertain

---

11. Haigh, *English Reformations*, 4.

her and her sizable retinue. He would eventually be buried in the chapel in the chancel, his tomb quite prominent. By then, the monks were long gone.

Incidentally, in 2017, a new theory emerged about the body of St. Edmund, who had been a ninth century king of East Angles and whose body had been buried at the monastery of Bury St. Edmunds—hence the name Bury St. Edmunds. Barry Wall, a local historian suggests that the Abbot of Bury St. Edmunds, as soon as he saw that his monastery was going to be taken over by the crown, had his monks, in the dark of night, smuggle the body from the monastery into the Lady Chapel at Long Melford, and bury it in the floor.[12] As far as I know, no one has dug up the floor of the Lady Chapel to see if the body is actually there.

Cranmer likely had little to do with the dissolution of the monasteries.[13] It was Henry who was interested in the vast land holdings and the jewels and precious metals of the riches held by the monasteries. He wanted the wealth for the significant expenses he was incurring through war. The annual net income of the monasteries, from the rents, was quite large. So, he, with Parliament, passed laws dissolving the smaller monasteries in 1536 and the larger monasteries in 1539. It was the latter that had disbanded Bury St. Edmunds. What was Cranmer's role in all of this? It was the Crown to which all the wealth went, not to the church, so he did not have anything to gain from the transfer of land and treasures—except, apparently, that many of the manuscripts went to his library.[14] Cranmer tried to help the monks. In fact, early on in the process he had written to Cromwell that he was willing to go to the Carthusian monks to try to persuade them to cooperate so that they would not be punished with being burned at the stake for treason for refusing to sign agreement with the Act of Supremacy.[15] Politics rather than Protestantism were primarily driving the monastery closures.

Strangely, though, that same year (June 1539), we have the Six Articles. There had been some earlier Injunctions that seemed to be moving the Reformation forward, but now Henry was reverting back to a more conservative stance in areas other than monasticism and pushed Parliament to declare the necessity of holding to transubstantiation. The articles also required that the laity should receive communion in one kind only, that is in the form of the Host but not the wine; that priests should not marry, that

12. *Suffolk Free Press*, "Could Saint Edmund be Buried in Long Melford?"
13. MacCulloch, *Thomas Cranmer*, 135.
14. Selwyn, "Cranmer's Library," 59.
15. *Three Chapters of Letters Relating to the Suppression of the Monasteries*, 173–74.

vows of chastity must be upheld (particularly ironic since Henry was in the process of dissolving all the monasteries), and that private masses and auricular confession continue.

These Six Articles came to be known by Reformers as "the bloody whip with six strings." Cranmer signed them out of fear. We know of this fear from a description by his friend, the Scottish Reformer Alexander Alesius, who Cranmer helped to escape from England before he would be forced to sign agreement to the articles:

> "Happy man that you are," said he, "you can escape! Would that I were at liberty to do the same; truly my see would not hold me back. You must make haste to escape before the island may be cut off, unless you are willing to sign the decree, as I have done, compelled by fear—for I repent of what I have done, and if I had known that my only punishment would have been deposition from the Archbishopric (as I hear that my Lord Latimer is deposed), of a truth I would not have subscribed."[16]

Cranmer wished that he could be assured that only his high church position rather than his very life would be taken from him if he refused to sign the Articles. He sent his wife back to Germany for her safety. By this time it was quite clear that Cranmer was starting to align with Reformation ideas and ideals. But fear and danger were keeping him from moving things forward as quickly as he would like.

THE ENGLISH BIBLE ENTERED LONG MELFORD

Ironically, given the conservatism of the Six Articles, 1539 was also the year that the Great Bible—the English Bible—entered the churches. Henry had allowed, in 1536, for an Injunction (by Cromwell) to be passed that required an English Bible to be placed in each parish church, but it seems that, due to translation and publishing issues, it was not until 1539 that the first Bibles actually made it into the churches. The timing was particularly poignant—even frustrating—since William Tyndale had been burned at the stake for heresy after translating the scriptures from Greek and Hebrew into English. He died saying, "Lord! Open the eyes of the King of England." That was in 1536. The same year as the first injunction requiring a Bible in each church! On top of that, the Bibles that would eventually end up in the churches were based on his translation!

---

16. Quoted in MacCulloch, *Thomas Cranmer*, 251.

The first injunction of 1536, and the ones in 1538 and 1539, all required Bibles to be in every church, but they did not attach any sanctions. So, many churches resisted the injunctions. But in 1541, sanctions were added so that a church had to pay forty shillings per month in penalties if they did not purchase a Bible. The Bible itself would have cost them only twelve shillings, so forty shillings per month was a major incentive. Therefore, churches started purchasing English Bibles.[17]

When did Long Melford acquire its first officially sanctioned English Bible? The churchwardens' accounts at Long Melford for that year seem to be missing. But other churches in Suffolk seem not to have purchased Bibles within the five years of the first injunction requiring it. Cratfield (50 miles away), Boxford (9 miles away), and Mildenhall (28 miles away) purchased Bibles in 1541.[18] It is likely that Long Melford finally succumbed and purchased its first official English Bible around the same time, when Roger Martyn was a young teenager.

While Long Melford was resisting the vernacular Bible, Cranmer was advocating it. Cromwell was the one who first pushed for the vernacular Bible, but when the Great Bible was published, its frontispiece included a depiction of Cranmer receiving the Bible from King Henry VIII and then handing the Bible to his priests who in turn gave copies of it to the people and preached to them from a pulpit. Seven editions of the Great Bible were produced within a two and a half year period. The second through seventh all included a preface from Cranmer. This preface gives us a glimpse of Cranmer's heart in reference to the scriptures, which he referred to as "the most precious jewel, and the most holy relic that remaineth upon earth."[19] Here, we can already see the attempts that Cranmer made to find a middle way, a way of balance, for he directed his preface to two types of readers, those that "be too slow, and need the spur" and those that "seem too quick, and need more of the bridle."[20] Long Melford, it would appear, fell into that first category. That category included those who "refuse to read, or to hear read the Scripture in the vulgar tongues."[21] He addressed them first.

---

17. Thompson, "Local Reception of Religious Change under Henry VIII and Edward VII," 75.

18. Thompson, "Local Reception of Religious Change under Henry VIII and Edward VII," 76.

19. Bray, ed., *Documents of the English Reformation*, 239–40.

20. Bray, ed., *Documents of the English Reformation*, 234.

21. Bray, ed., *Documents of the English Reformation*, 234.

How could they "be so mad as to refuse in darkness light; in hunger, food; in cold, fire."[22] The Bible is light, food, and fire. He understood that people have a hard time adapting to change, that when first exposed to something, they might reject it. Perhaps they are like those in the North Pole who have never seen the sun and may at first be offended at its bright glow.[23] Cranmer turned to John Chrysostom's *De Lazaro* for help. He stated that in the scriptures:

> Here may all manner of persons, men, women, young, old, learned, unlearned, rich, poor, priests, laymen, lords, ladies, officers, tenants, and mean men, virgins, wives, widows, lawyers, merchants, artificers, husbandmen, and all manner of persons of what estate or condition soever they be, may in this book learn all things what they ought to believe, what they ought to do, and what they should not do, as well concerning Almighty God, as also concerning themselves and all other. Briefly, to the reading of the Scripture none can be enemy, but that either be so sick, that they love not to hear of any medicine, or else that be so ignorant that they know not Scripture to be the most healthful medicine.[24]

Thus Cranmer drew on Chrysostom for aid in inviting resistant readers to come to the scriptures.

DESTRUCTION OF CHURCH FABRIC AND ITEMS

Eight years later, dramatic changes came to Long Melford. In 1547, the churchwarden of Holy Trinity wrote a list of the items that were sold. Roger Martyn later interpolated in his own hand, "The begynyng of the spoyle of Melford churche."[25] It began with 340 pounds of brass and 300 pounds of wax being sold. The brass would have been from the brasses over people's burial spots within the church. The wax would have been for burning in front of the images. The rood loft was dismantled. The great images were sold off. Walls were whitewashed and Bible texts written on them. Many items went missing, either given up to the king's commissioners who had come to claim the items for the crown, or taken by church members, presumably in order to protect them from pillage.

---

22. Bray, ed., *Documents of the English Reformation*, 234.
23. Bray, ed., *Documents of the English Reformation*, 234.
24. Cranmer, "Preface to the Bible," 111.
25. Dymond and Paine, *Spoil of Long Melford*.

Roger Martyn, the great, great, great grandson of Laurence Martyn the early benefactor of the church, tried to rescue items. So did William Clopton, son of the other key benefactor, John Clopton. Referred to as Master Clopton, he was the one who bought back the alabaster panels of St. Anne's altar that his ancestors had given to Holy Trinity: "a lytell tabyll in Sent Anny's Chappell and all the gere therein."[26] In the eighteenth century, some workmen were pulling up the floor in the church, and they discovered the alabaster of the Epiphany that used to be part of the altar. It is quite possible that John Clopton's great-grandson was the one who had hidden it there.[27] He also bought up many other liturgical objects to keep them safe.

One can only imagine what was going on in his and Roger Martyn's minds and hearts as they watched their childhood church, the one their recent ancestors had built at great expense, start to be stripped of so many of their worship treasures. It is not clear that they would have been aware of the developments at the macro level that drove all these changes.

LITURGICAL CHANGES UNDER HENRY VIII'S REIGN

So, what *was* going on at the macro level? Well, some of it was politically driven, as with the monastic closures. In 1536, for example, Henry had upgraded his favorite ship the *Mary Rose* with new cannons, and he needed brass to melt down for war. Some of it was theologically driven. The Reformation shift away from the cult of the saints, for example, was making it illegal to venerate the saints by keeping tapers alight before their images, so the wax was no longer needed.

What was Cranmer's involvement, in particular, in these changes? Cranmer did have concerns about the cult of the saints. In an early draft for the Ten Articles (1536), he had expressed concern—ridicule, even— about the laity praying to St. Apollonia when they had toothaches and to St. Barbara when in a thunderstorm.[28] But now Cranmer was even more involved in another project that would impact the worship in parish churches throughout England. That was the liturgy itself. The changes came in increments. Early on, they involved eliminating references to the Pope from all the service books. Then Cranmer started translating various parts of the

---

26. Parker, *History of Long Melford*, 140.
27. Parker, *History of Long Melford*, 140.
28. MacCulloch, ed., *The Reign of Henry VIII*, 176.

liturgy into English: in 1544 it was the processional; in 1545, the litany and the primer; and he added biblical saints to the *sanctorale*.[29]

Then, in 1547, after 20 years of walking a wildly shaking tightrope as confidante to King Henry VIII, Cranmer had become the King's closest friend. In many ways, it was like having a porcupine as one's best friend. Cranmer never knew when a deadly quill was headed his way. Remember, the king had beheaded two wives and his close friend, Thomas More. He was constantly changing his mind on religious matters. But Cranmer had survived his reign and had managed to move the Reformation forward even in the midst of fear and danger. Finally, Henry, after twenty years of veering from Catholicism, to rejecting the papacy, to hanging on to Catholic practices, seems to have landed in a rather surprising place in his faith in his final days. As he lay dying, he kept Cranmer at his side rather than calling for a Catholic priest. He did not request last rites, something quite unexpected for someone who had remained so theologically and sacramentally conservative in spite of his rejection of the papacy. Instead, as Foxe's *Book of Martyrs* explains about the king's deathbed: "Then the archbishop, exhorting him to put his trust in Christ, and to call upon his mercy, desired him, though he could not speak, yet to give some token with his eyes or with his hand, that he trusted in the Lord. Then the King, holding him with his hand, did wring his hand in his as hard as he could."[30] Diarmaid MacCulloch notes that "Thus ended the most long-lasting relationship of love which either man had known." Cranmer stopped shaving and grew a beard—some said it was out of grief for the loss of the King.[31]

LITURGICAL CHANGES UNDER EDWARD VI'S REIGN

In 1547, Edward VI succeeded his father. We will not get into the complicated details of the succession of a nine-year old. But what we can say of the Reformation is that it moved forward dramatically under this young man who had been raised as a Protestant.

When we examine the churchwardens' accounts back at Long Melford, we discover the impact of changes being made at the macro level. In the 1549–1550 entries, there is a purchase of "the service booke, set forth by parliament" and the start of a sell off of mass books, processionals, ordinals,

---

29. MacCulloch, *Thomas Cranmer*, 327–34.
30. Quoted by MacCulloch, *Thomas Cranmer*, 360.
31. MacCulloch, *Thomas Cranmer*, 360–61.

graduals, among other items.³² Early in 1552, the Crown appointed new commissioners to survey, again, all church goods in all parishes, and to decide what should go to the crown and what could be retained by each church. Roger Martyn records that just before Edward VI's death, all the plate and vestments of the church were handed over to the commissioners except for two chalices.³³ A rather dramatic change from the long list back in 1529. That was all gone, except for two vessels for wine, which the laity would now be receiving. It was not just the objects that were vanishing, it was also the ceremonies and processions. A new liturgy was dramatically reshaping the church. One can only imagine Roger Martyn's bewilderment as the remaining vessels, vestments, and traditions of his childhood were stripped away.

CRANMER'S ROLE IN THE LITURGICAL CHANGES

What was Cranmer's role in all these changes? Well, he was the one writing the new liturgies. After Henry VIII's death, Cranmer was able to move forward with more freedom. Although he had to be careful not to move too quickly in case the people thought he and the other Reformers were manipulating the young prince Edward VI. In his "Homily of Good Works," Cranmer gives us clues as to why he is so concerned to eliminate so many of the popular religious practices. First, it relates to epistemology. He calls people back to the Bible and what it teaches, as their authority. He sees the medieval practices as fabricated in men's minds out of "blind zeal and devotion" rather than being in obedience to the Holy Scriptures.³⁴ He believes that they are based on "false doctrine, superstition, idolatry."³⁵ When it comes to images, he is concerned about the pilgrimages to them, the kneeling before them, censing of them, kissing of them. He wants to bring back the "sweet and savoury bread of God's own word" rather than the "pharisaical and papistical leaven of man's feigned religion."³⁶

Second, was a concern for soteriology. He is worried that people have used all sorts of things to "attain to the eternal life, or remission of sin."³⁷ He lists many examples of these practices: "as of beads, of lady psalters,

32. Dymond and Paine, *Spoil of Long Melford*.
33. Dymond and Paine, *Spoil of Long Melford*, 54n126.
34. Cranmer, "Homily of Good Works," 146.
35. Cranmer, "Homily of Good Works," 147.
36. Cranmer, "Homily of Good Works," 148.
37. Cranmer, "Homily of Good Works," 148.

and rosaries, of fifteen Oos, of St Barnard's verses, of St Agathe's letters, of purgatory, of masses satisfactory, of stations and jubilees, of feigned relics, of hallowed beads, bells, bread, water, palms, candles, fire, and such other."[38] What has suffered is God's commandments, and therefore, God's glory. What should be done is this:

> Wherefore, as you have any zeal to the right and pure honouring of God; as you have any regard to your own souls, and to the life that is to come, which is both without pain and without end, apply yourselves chiefly above all thing[s] to read and to hear God's word; mark diligently therein what his will is you shall do, and with all your endeavor apply yourselves to follow the same. First, you must have an assured faith in God, and give yourselves wholly unto him, love him in prosperity and adversity, and dread to offend him evermore. Then, for his sake, love all men, friends and foes, because they be his creation and image, and redeemed by Christ as ye are.[39]

Cranmer goes on to give details about how to do this. Now, most of what he prescribes relates to morality. This shift from medieval worship practices to Reformation *moral* practices reveals how Cranmer has perceived so many of the church practices as having been done as 'works.' Worship needs to be done for the glory of God rather than to earn one's salvation, and works belong in sanctification, not justification, and in morality, not in doxology.

This sermon was part of the Homilies that were called for by the Injunctions of Religious Reform of 31 July 1547. Whereas earlier injunctions had dealt more with the *fabric* of the church, these injunctions were related to the *rituals* of the church.[40] This is the point where many of the ceremonies that Roger Martyn had described from his childhood ceased.

When the *Book of Common Prayer* was published in 1549, it included a Preface that explained why Cranmer was completely reworking the liturgy for the churches. First, he explained that the early church fathers intended that the whole of the scriptures be read through every year in the liturgy. This was so that people would be "stirred up to godliness," that they would be able to teach each other "wholesome doctrine," and to correct those who were "adversaries to the truth." That they would come to know God better and better and would be "inflamed with the love of his true

---

38. Cranmer, "Homily of Good Works," 148.
39. Cranmer, "Homily of Good Works," 148–49.
40. Duffy, "Cranmer and Popular Religion," 199–216.

religion." But over time, this had been supplanted by "uncertain stories, legends, responds, verses, vain repetitions, commemorations, and synodals" to the point where very little scripture was read at all.[41] Secondly, Paul spoke the language of the people, but by now, in England, the service was in Latin and most people could not understand it. The Psalms all used to be read on a regular basis, but now only a few portions were used regularly and the rest omitted. Finally, the liturgy had become so complicated with so many different books to juggle that more time was spent figuring out what to read than was taken to actually read it!

So, Cranmer greatly simplified the liturgy. The priests would need only the *Book of Common Prayer* and the Bible, which would save congregations money. Instead of there being different uses in Salisbury, Hereford, Bangor, York, and Lincoln, now all would share the same liturgy. He then sought to explain why some ceremonies had been kept while others were discarded. Some were in accord with the scriptures. Some were edifying to the people, which was also a biblical principle. He recognized that some people would want to hang onto all the old ceremonies, while others would want to throw all of them out and start with brand new ones. He was not going to try to please either group, but rather, he was going to try to please God, and thus profit both groups. On the one hand, without any ceremonies, it was difficult to maintain order and discipline in the service. On the other hand, certain ceremonies that might be fine in and of themselves, had become so associated with abuses that they needed to be eliminated. Therefore, he had chosen to keep those ceremonies that laid out clearly what they meant and what purpose they served. Also, he was doing this only for *his* people. Other nations should do what they thought was best for the "setting forth of God's honour and glory."[42]

After the 1549 version, Cranmer received feedback from John Calvin, Martin Bucer (writing just two months before his death),[43] Peter Martyr Vermigli, and others. When you look at the Eucharistic liturgies of the *Book of Common Prayer* of 1549 and of 1552, you discover many Reformation principles at their heart. The shift from Latin to English meant that everyone could understand every word. No more private masses were said for the dead. Where the laity had been denied receipt of communion except

---

41. Cranmer, *Miscellaneous Writings and Letters of Thomas Cranmer* (hereafter PSII), 517.

42. PSII, 519.

43. Thompson, *Liturgies of the Western Church*, 238.

at Easter, now they were invited to participate every time. Where they had been allowed only the Host, now they would receive both the bread and the wine. No more transubstantiation or veneration of the Host. The laity had gotten in the habit of gazing almost magically at the Mass, especially at the elevation of the Host, but now they were not meant merely to gaze but rather to receive. No more prayers for the dead or intercessions to the saints; the saints were now exemplars rather than intercessors. Auricular confession was allowed but no longer required. There was a shift from altar to table. The canon was preserved but it was divested of sacrifice language. Instead of Christ being offered as a sacrifice in the Mass—for his sacrifice was once and for all—now the people were exhorted to offer *themselves*, in response, as living sacrifices, and to offer a sacrifice of praise and of thanksgiving. The Eucharist was now more of a holy supper than a reenactment of the crucifixion, and Christ was our Mediator, "Not weighing oure merits, but pardoning oure offenses."[44]

The 1552 version of the *Book of Common Prayer* never had a real chance, though, for Edward VI died in 1553, and with him, so did Cranmer's dream for a Protestant England—at least, for a while. Cranmer would not live to see it resurrected.

RESTORATION OF CATHOLIC WORSHIP AT LONG MELFORD

Things changed dramatically again at Long Melford. Just after they had handed almost everything over to King Edwards' commissioners, Catholic Mary ascended the throne. (And by "just after," we mean the very same year!) It was too late to bring back the monks, but not too late to reestablish the Mass. Martyn records the purchases of many goods to restore the old worship. It is a long list again. There is some poignancy to the list, however. Many of the objects are damaged. The rood comes back in parts. The organs need mending. The wooden crosses require painting and gilding, as does the rood. The cross on the green is repaired. Fabrics for the chancel cross, the Trinity, and St. Peter demand dye and fringe.

Restoration runs through Martyn's inventory. Candles flicker again at the death of a loved one. Church ales revive. Priests don vestments and use elaborate vessels for the liturgy once again. Roger Martyn and Richard Clopton, as churchwardens and as members of wealthy families, pay for

---

44. Thompson, *Liturgies of the Western Church*, 281.

much of this themselves. They purchase wax for candles and pay for images to be washed. The Easter Sepulchre is restored, and the church pays someone to keep vigil there at Easter. One can imagine the delight that Roger Martyn was feeling as he set about restoring the fabric and rituals, the worship practices of his childhood.

An interesting "what if?" can be posited at this point, raising questions about what might have happened had the macro and micro stories intersected directly. When Queen Mary ascended the throne, Martyn was twenty five or so years old. The *English Baronetage of 1741* indicates that his grandfather was invited to be a member of Mary's Privy Council—the Secretary of State, to be exact—but that he turned it down.[45] If he had accepted it, Martyn's family would have entered that macro level where Cranmer had resided ever since the year of Martyn's birth, and his grandfather would have been directly involved in determining Cranmer's fate, for it was the Privy Council that sent Cranmer to prison in Oxford.

CRANMER'S FINAL YEARS

That brings us back to Cranmer. As Roger Martyn was rejoicing over the reign of Queen Mary, Cranmer's life, on the other hand, came into danger. In 1553, he was arrested for treason. He was kept in prison for many months, without books, and he began to doubt his Protestant principles. He ended up recanting of many of his beliefs. According to canon law, this could have allowed him to be spared death. However, Queen Mary wrote to the Pope, "His iniquity and obstinacy was so great against God and your Grace that your clemency and mercy could have no place with him."[46] Years before, Cranmer had protected Mary from going to the Tower and possible death; but she did not return the favor. His death sentence still stood in spite of his recantation.

Then Cranmer did something surprising: he recanted of his recantation. When he came to be burned at the stake, he committed himself to putting his right hand into the flames first, because it was the hand that had betrayed his beliefs by signing repeated recantations against his Protestant beliefs. John Foxe recounted Cranmer's final words:

> And now I come to the great thing which so much troubleth my conscience, more than any thing that ever I did or said in my

---

45. *Proceedings of the Bury & West Suffolk Archaeological Institute*, 84.
46. MacCulloch, *Thomas Cranmer*, 597.

whole life, and that is the setting abroad of a writing contrary to the truth; which now here I renounce and refuse, as things written with my hand contrary to the truth which I thought in my heart, and written for fear of death, and to save my life, if it might be; and that is, all such bills and papers which I have written or signed with my hand since my degradation, wherein I have written many things untrue. And forasmuch as my hand hath offended, writing contrary to my heart, therefore my hand shall first be punished; for when I come to the fire it shall first be burned.[47]

He followed through, placing his right hand into the flames first, and he died for his Protestant beliefs in 1556.

In 1558—only two years later—Mary died and her half-sister, Elizabeth I, ascended the throne. She was Anne Boleyn's daughter and a Protestant. Quite remarkably, she was able to bring peace and stability to a nation that had been through such turmoil and change. She charted a *via media* course through the religious terrain. Her ministers took Cranmer's 1552 *Book of Common Prayer* and his *Forty Two Articles* and produced the 1559 *Book of Common Prayer* and the *Thirty Nine Articles*, versions of which became authoritative documents for centuries. Although Cranmer was gone, his influence continued strongly.

MARTYN'S FINAL YEARS

Even after Elizabeth's accession, though, Roger Martyn continued to bring back more and more items for Catholic worship in Long Melford. But at some point that came to an end. Later, his recusancy—the term for the Catholic resistance to Protestant worship—got him into trouble; one story, which may be apocryphal, had him hiding out in a haystack. In 1590, the Privy Council minutes record that a letter was sent to the Sheriffs of Suffolk and Norfolk that required a group of recusants to report to the custody of Thomas Grey, the keeper at Wisbech Castle, an ecclesiastical prison at the time. Roger Martyn's name is included.[48] It is believed that he had been hiding catholic priests in his home and that he ended up in prison for several years as a result. At some point he wrote the wistful reminiscences of Long Melford's communal catholic piety that we summarized at the beginning. When he died in his eighties, in the reign of James I, having lived through the reigns of six monarchs—if you include the nine days of Lady

---

47. Foxe, *Fox's Book of Martyrs*, 392.
48. Acts of the Privy Council of England, 10.

Jane Grey—he would finally be buried in his beloved church, in his family's chapel, and if you visit Long Melford, you can see the brass of him and his two (consecutive) wives.

CONCLUSION

Thomas Cranmer and Roger Martyn: two devout men, both with high ideals. Both living in dangerous times when one's life was literally at stake when one worshipped. One was attempting to restore the purity and God-glorifying nature of Word-shaped worship. The other was trying to hang on to the beauty of community, symbolism, ritual, and celebration and probably could not understand why those in authority seemed to be trying to take these things away. I find myself wondering what might have happened had Cranmer and Martyn been able to talk deeply with one another—in a safe context, where neither one of them would have had to risk imprisonment or death. Could they have avoided some of the unintended consequences that came with the Reformation? Could the best of both their worlds have found a way to co-exist?

We no longer burn one another at the stake in the West. But we too live in times of turbulent change, where politics sometimes impinge on the life of the church. Perhaps it would be wise for us to listen carefully to one another, and to study the side effects of our decisions—to pay attention to the interplay of macro and micro levels in our church contexts.

I conclude with two prayer books and an invitation.

In 2014, historian Frances Young convinced Cambridge University library to purchase a Book of Hours that had been in the Rookwood family for many years. And then, in 2016, when he had the opportunity to study the manuscript more carefully, Young discovered that one of Roger Martyn's ancestors—perhaps the original co-benefactor of Holy Trinity—had very likely commissioned its production back in the 1460s. It has the names "Roogers" and "Martin" written in it.[49] It is quite likely that Roger Martyn, the subject of this chapter, inherited it at least as early as Mary's reign, and that he held on to it until his death. In 1538, Henry VIII had ordered that all images of St. Thomas of Canterbury (i.e., Thomas à Becket) be destroyed, including ones in prayer books. He had been afraid of the example Thomas à Becket had set in standing against the King Henry of his day. This prayer book has the St. Thomas image still intact, indicating

---

49. Young, "Roger Martin's Prayer Book?"

that it had been protected, probably, therefore, by Martyn's grandfather, father, and himself, all refusing to deface the image of the saint. Someone, probably Martyn himself, copied prayers from Erasmus' *Precationes aliquot* (probably the 1542 edition) into the prayer book during Mary's reign, including Catholic prayers to the Virgin Mary.[50] If this book was indeed the Martyns' prayer book, it means that in the end, Roger Martyn had been able to hold onto *something* that encapsulated so much of what he had been trying to preserve at the Church of the Holy Trinity in Long Melford: The beauty of the visual arts, the sanctity of holy objects, the continuity of the Latin language, the use of the traditional liturgy of Sarum, the key place of the cult of the saints. He had been able to hold all of these in his hands in the pages of this precious book.

Cranmer also left behind a prayer book, or, actually, prayer *books*. There are eighty-five million Anglican believers around the world today, most of whom use versions of Cranmer's 1549 and 1552 *Books of Common Prayer* in worship every week, and in many cases, every *day*. That means that perhaps more than one in a 100 humans alive today uses a version of Cranmer's prayer book.

And the invitation: I hope that if you travel to England someday, you will include a visit to Roger Martyn's church in Long Melford. Ponder a font in which babies have been baptized for a thousand years. Read poetry on a wall. Look through the squint from the Clopton chapel to the high altar. Kneel down and look up at the resurrection above the Easter Sepulchre. Imagine monks chanting in the Lady Chapel and wonder if a twelve hundred year-old king-saint is buried under the floor.

And then, sit in a pew and take two books out of the rack in front of you. Hold the English Bible and the *Book of Common Prayer* in your lap and appreciate the fact that you can read them in your own language. Then perhaps offer up "a sacrifice of praise and thanksgiving, most humbly beseeching [God] to grant that by the merits and death of [his] Son Jesus Christ, and through faith in his blood, we and all [God's] whole church, may obtain remission of our sins, and all other benefits of Christ's passion."[51]

And then do as I did. Go to the nearby café for tea. They have the most delicious sticky toffee pudding!

---

50. Young, "Resistance and Devotion in Tudor Suffolk: Roger Martin's Prayer Book."
51. *The First Prayer-Book*, 80.

BIBLIOGRAPHY

Acts of the Privy Council of England, April 5, 1590 in *Acts of the Privy Council of England*, Vol. 19 (1590), edited by John Roche Dasent. London: Mackie & Co., 1899.

Bray, Gerald, ed. *Documents of the English Reformation*. Minneapolis: Fortress, 1940.

Cranmer, Thomas. *Miscellaneous Writings and Letters of Thomas Cranmer*, edited by John Edmund Cox. Cambridge: Parker Society, 1846.

———. "Preface to the Bible." In *The Remains of Thomas Cranmer*, edited by Henry Jenkyns, 2:104–17. Oxford: Oxford University Press, 1833.

Duffy, Eamon. "Cranmer and Popular Religion." In *Thomas Cranmer: Churchman and Scholar*, 199–216. Woodbridge, Suffolk: Boydell and Brewer, 1993.

Dymond, David, and Clive Paine. *Spoil of Long Melford*. Ipswich, England: Suffolk, 1992.

Foxe, John. *Foxe's Book of Martyrs*. Philadelphia: James B. Smith, 1860.

———. *Foxe's Book of Martyrs*. Vol. 3, edited by John Cumming. London: George Virtue, 1844.

Gibson, Gail McMurray. *The Theater of Devotion*. Chicago: University of Chicago Press, 1995.

Haigh, Christopher. *English Reformations: Religion, Politics, and Society under the Tudors*. Oxford: Clarendon, 1993.

Lydgate, Dan John. *Early English Poetry, Ballads, Popular Literature of the Middle Ages*, edited by James Orchard Halliwell. London: Percy Society, 1840.

MacCulloch, Diarmaid. *Thomas Cranmer*. New Haven: Yale University Press, 1996.

MacCulloch, Diarmaid, ed. *The Reign of Henry VIII: Politics, Policy, and Piety*. New York: St. Martin's, 1995.

Null, Ashley. *Thomas Cranmer's Doctrine of Repentance: Renewing the Power to Love*. Oxford: Oxford University Press, 2007.

Parker, William. *History of Long Melford*. London: Wyman and Sons, 1873.

Proceedings of the Bury & West Suffolk Archaeological Institute. Vol. 2. 1859.

The First Prayer-Book as Issued by the Authority of the Parliament of the Second Year of King Edward VI. London: Parker and Co., 1883.

Thompson, Bard. *Liturgies of the Western Church*. Philadelphia: Fortress, 1980.

Thompson, William Keene. "Local Reception of Religious Change under Henry VIII and Edward VI: Evidence from Four Suffolk Parishes." MA thesis, Portland State University, 2012.

Three Chapters of Letters Relating to the Suppression of the Monasteries. Camden Old Series 26. Cambridge: Royal Historical Society, 1843.

Selwyn, D. G. "Cranmer's Library." In *Thomas Cranmer: Churchman and Scholar*, edited by Paul Ayris and David Selwyn, 39–72. Woodbridge, Suffolk: Boydell, 1993.

Suffolk Free Press, "Could Saint Edmund be Buried in Long Melford?" 26 May 2017. N.p. Online: https://www.suffolkfreepress.co.uk/news/could-saint-edmund-be-buried-in-long-melford-1-7980883.

Young, Francis. "Resistance and Devotion in Tudor Suffolk: Roger Martin's Prayer Book." Paper presented at Catholic East Anglia Conference, Cathedral of St. John the Baptist, Norwich, 11 June 2016.

———. "Roger Martin's Prayer Book?" 18 February 2015. N.p. Online: https://drfrancisyoung.com/2016/02/18/roger-martins-prayer-book/.

5

Calvin, the Anabaptists, and Tradition

W. David Buschart

ANYONE WHO IS EVEN casually acquainted with the Christian Reformations of the sixteenth century may find it a bit puzzling to encounter a single chapter that covers both Calvin and sixteenth-century Anabaptists. In 1544, Calvin wrote two tracts, one of them against the Anabaptists and one of them against "libertines," in which he set forth his critique of the Anabaptist *Schleitheim Confession*, criticized Anabaptist interpretation of scripture, and called-out what he regarded as their synergistic view of free will.[1] For their part, Anabaptists thought that in both their teachings and practices the magisterial Reformers such as Calvin were seriously inconsistent with regard to the stated commitment to the principle of *sola scriptura*. Many Anabaptists believed that these other would-be reformers "[put] their own interests above faithful obedience to Scripture."[2] Calvin accused both Anabaptists and Roman Catholics of "bury[ing] the Word of God . . . mak[ing] room for their own falsehoods" by making extravagant claims for the current revelatory work of the Holy Spirit,[3] and Anabaptists believed that Calvin and other magisterial reformers continued

---

1. Balke, *Calvin and the Anabaptist Radicals*, 150–54.
2. Murray, *Biblical Interpretation*, 49.
3. Calvin, "Reply to Sadolet," 230. While the English-language edition of Calvin's letter that will be cited here renders Sadoleto's name without the final "o" (thus, Sadolet), it is far more common in both English-language and other sources to include this letter, so that is the form that is employed here.

to be under the interpretive and behavioral spell of traditions of the Roman Catholic Church.[4]

Calvin believed that Anabaptists *wanted to* honor scripture. "It is a sect," he writes, "which accepts the Holy Scripture as do we."[5] And, in a similar fashion, many Anabaptists believed that magisterial reformers such as Calvin *sincerely proclaimed the principle of sola scriptura* but became sidetracked with competing commitments—such as inherited traditions—and so did not follow through with a consistent and complete application of *sola scriptura*. This chapter seeks to approach this conjunction of the fountainheads of two Reformation traditions, Calvinist and Anabaptist, in the spirit of Richard Mouw's characterization of the relationship between the two as "an intra-family argument."[6] We will consider each as representing one of the major streams of the Protestant Reformation.

With this in view, here are some of the parameters for the path forward. The focus will be predominantly theological, while seeking also to be responsible with respect to discretely historical matters. We will consider each subject on its own—that is, first Calvin, and then the Anabaptists—rather than a parallel or side-by-side juxtaposition throughout. This brief study simply seeks to see Calvin in his own right and the Anabaptists in their own right, rather than constantly looking at each through the lens of the other. There will be, nonetheless, a few comparative observations along the way and at the conclusion.

As we listen to Calvin and the Anabaptists, the thematic focus will be on the nature and function of Christian tradition. Speaking of sixteenth-century Christianity, the contemporary Anabaptist scholar Stuart Murray has observed that "everyone was struggling to define the Bible's role vis-à-vis scholarship and tradition on the one hand, and the illumination of the Holy Spirit on the other."[7] "The relationship between Scripture and church traditions was," he asserts, "exposed to critical scrutiny as rarely before."[8] In the few pages that follow, we seek to listen and learn from this struggle.

---

4. Murray, *Biblical Interpretation*, 26.

5. John Calvin, quoted in Balke, "Calvin and the Anabaptists," 150.

6. Mouw, "Reflections on My Encounter," 121. Mouw suggests, "These disputes reach a high intensity because the differences between the two groups are of a more intimate character than are the arguments of either group with, say, the Lutherans or the Catholics."

7. Murray, *Biblical Interpretation*, 19.

8. Murray, *Biblical Interpretation*, 26.

CALVIN

John Calvin's name is today intimately associated, and understandably so, with *sola scriptura*, *sola gratia*, *sola fide*, *solus Christus*, and *soli Deo Gloria*. Of these *solas* the one most frequently associated with the topic of our attention here is *sola scriptura*. This formal principle of the Protestant Reformation is clearly important to the nature and function of tradition in the Reformation, including the work of Calvin.

However, the window into Calvin's beliefs about and practices with respect to tradition would be too small if it was large enough to view only tradition and scripture side-by-side. Obviously, Calvin's basic beliefs about the nature and authority of scripture must, and will, be considered. However, we will here also consider two other matters which serve to more adequately frame Calvin's, and for that matter anyone else's, view of tradition. Those two additional matters are ecclesiology and history. Thus, in service of this modestly larger approach to the inquiry, we will make our way toward an understanding of Calvin's view of tradition under two headings: first, scripture and theology, and then, the church and history.

Scripture and Theology

SCRIPTURE

No inquiry into any aspect of John Calvin's thought can proceed without a healthy acknowledgment of how deep his respect for scripture was, and how important scripture was for all that he did. Early in *Institutes of the Christian Religion* Calvin wrote that "the church recognizes Scripture to be the truth of its own God, as a pious duty it unhesitatingly venerates Scripture."[9] More simply put, "the Sacred Scriptures . . . breathe something divine."[10] Thus, as Anthony Lane observes, for Calvin "[t]he Scriptures are the only infallible norm and the teaching of the fathers is to be judged in the light of Scripture."[11] "The rule of faith is" for Calvin, Lane observes, "to be sought in the Word of God, in Scripture, in the oracles of God, not in tradition."[12] The Bible, the canonical scriptures of Christianity, are the one and only *norma normans* (the rule that rules)—the supreme authority for

---

9. Calvin, *Institutes*, I.vii.2.
10. Calvin, *Institutes*, I.viii.1.
11. Lane, *John Calvin*, 35.
12. Lane, *John Calvin*, 171.

faith and life. All that the church believes and teaches, all that the church does, is ultimately accountable to the scriptures.

RELATIONSHIP BETWEEN SCRIPTURE AND THEOLOGY

Bruce Gordon has helpfully described the relationship between scripture and theology in Calvin's thought as a "symbiotic relationship." "[T]o be able to interpret scripture properly," Gordon observes, "one already had to be versed in doctrine and scripture. . . . [S]cripture could not stand without a framework of interpretation."[13] For Calvin, "[t]heology is necessary," writes T. F. Torrance, "because the Scriptures are not subject to private interpretation."[14] Thus, some appropriate complexity and nuance is to be seen in Calvin's view of *sola scriptura*.

For Calvin, and other Magisterial reformers, *sola scriptura* did not mean *nuda scriptura*. It did not mean, to adopt the image of Jesuit theologian Bernard Lonergan, that one ought to come to the interpretation of scripture with "an empty head." To the contrary, in order to rightly interpret the Word of God, believes Calvin, one should come to it with two-fold knowledge: knowledge of scripture beyond the particular book or passage that one is interpreting at the moment, and some knowledge of theology. This second component—knowledge of theology—constitutes an open door for theological tradition. But before we attempt to walk through that door, the *wider* angle of approach suggested above needs to be taken by considering Calvin's views of history and of the church, particular as these have a bearing on his understanding and use of tradition.

The Church and History

IMPORTANCE OF THE CHURCH

The church matters. It is important. Likewise, the church was important to Calvin's, and anyone else's, understanding of tradition. In 1539 Cardinal James Sadoleto wrote a letter to the senate and people of Geneva, imploring them to return to communion with the Roman Catholic Church. In a letter of reply, Calvin underscored his commitment to "unity of faith and brotherly concord" by saying of the church, "we revere her as our mother,

---

13. Gordon, *Calvin*, 108. T. F. Torrance writes, "The fundamental purpose of theology is to serve the interpretation of Holy Scripture" (*Hermeneutics of John Calvin*, 70).

14. Torrance, *Hermeneutics of John Calvin*, 70.

so we desire to remain in her bosom."[15] He employed this imagery twenty years later, in the final (1559) edition of the *Institutes*, where he asserted the ongoing importance of the church in the lives of Christians: "God is pleased to gather his sons [into the bosom of the church] not only that they may be nourished by her help and ministry as long as they are infants and children, but also that they may be guided by her motherly care until they mature and at last reach the goal of faith."[16] The church was important to Calvin not only as a subject of theological reflection; his theological reflection about the church included the strong affirmation, on which he acted, of the fundamental importance the church itself to Christians, importance for both entering into and carrying on life in Christ.

Historical Path of the Church

It is also important for present purposes, with a focus on the role of tradition, to briefly observe what Calvin believed about the historical path of the church—both the path the church's historical journey *should* follow and what path it *has in fact taken* up to Calvin's day. Like other reformers, such as Martin Luther and Ulrich Zwingli, Calvin regarded the early church as representing something of "a golden classical period."[17] In the first Book of the *Institutes*, Calvin described the early church as one in which "religion was still flourishing, and a purer doctrine [was] thriving."[18] In his letter to Cardinal Sadoleto, cited above, Calvin challenged the bishop by contrasting the present state of the church of Rome with the "pristine splendor" of the early church.[19] Indeed, in response to the cardinal's summons to Geneva to return to Rome, Calvin frequently made reference to Christian "antiquity" or "the ancient church." Further, he drew two kinds of comparisons between his own day and that of the ancient church.

The question of the relationship—that is, the actual historical path—between the ancient church and the then-contemporary church was a matter of repeated debate and disagreement among all contenders, whether Roman or Reformed. Each believed that the contemporary church *of which they were a member* had traveled that path and that *their church stood in*

---

15. Calvin, "Reply to Sadolet," 231. For the text of Sadoleto's letter, as well as Calvin's letter of reply, see Olin, ed., *A Reformation Debate*.

16. Calvin, *Institutes*, IV.i.1.

17. Lane, *John Calvin*, 40; Lane here refers to Calvin, *Institutes*, I.xi.13.

18. Calvin, *Institutes*, I.xi.13.

19. Calvin, "Reply to Sadolet," 232.

continuity with the early church.[20] Indeed, Sadoleto's historical argument about the relationship between the Christian past and its ecclesiastical present was not original to him. However, because it was a significant part of his appeal to the Genevans, this matter was correspondingly a significant component of Calvin's response.

Sadoleto charged that the Reformation was new, and thus was a departure from the historical path of the true church. In this line of argumentation we arrive at an extremely important component of any view of Christian tradition: the understanding, whatever understanding that might be, of *continuity and change* in the church, of the relationship between the *"old" and the "new"* in Christian thought and action. In his letter of response to Sadoleto, Calvin devoted considerable attention to this matter. When he did so, he drew two types of comparisons between the past and the present: comparisons between the ancient church and the present-day church of Rome, and comparisons between the ancient church and the church envisioned by himself and like-minded reformers. When Calvin *compared the present visible church of Rome with the early Christian church*, he found the contemporary to be woefully incompatible with the ancient. "[H]ow widely you differ," wrote Calvin, "from holy antiquity."[21] He turned Sadoleto's accusations of "novelties" and "newness," back on their source. It was the contemporary Roman church, particularly as it had passed through medieval waters, which had embraced novelties and thereby departed from the path of the true church. The papacy and other offices in the Roman church "criminally mangled and almost destroyed" completely, Calvin wrote, the form of true Christianity bequeathed by the early church.[22] It was the church of Rome, not the reformers, that had embraced novelties and departures from the path of the true church.

As previously indicated, Calvin undertook a second point of comparison, namely *between the ancient church and the church envisioned and pursued by the reformers*. When he turned to this he said to Sadoleto, "our

---

20. An early instance of debate over this matter can be seen in portions of the exchanges between the Roman Catholic theologian Johann Eck and reformer Martin Luther during the Leipzig disputation of 1519. For brief accounts, see for example Headley, *Luther's View of Church*, 44–45, 163–65, and 225–27; and Junghans, "Leipzig Disputation," 2:417–18. This disputation also highlights the fact that Christian views of history and of the church are intimately interrelated.

21. Calvin, "Reply to Sadolet," 240.

22. Calvin, "Reply to Sadolet," 231.

agreement with antiquity is far closer than yours."[23] "As to our doctrine," Calvin stated, "we do not hesitate to appeal to the ancient Church."[24] Thus, in contrast to Rome, which had undertaken a new way, Calvin and the reformers were appealing to and seeking to stand in the old way. They did not regard themselves as innovators; they were faithful stewards of an ancient trust. Reform of the church was conceived, in part, in terms of the restoration of the church to its pristine splendor.[25] Reform was nothing but the desire "that religion be revived."[26] Thus, Calvin said to Sadoleto, "all we have attempted has been to renew the ancient form of the Church."[27]

This form of argumentation—relating the present to the early Christian past, and casting this relationship in terms of newness and novelty versus sameness and continuity—was by no means limited to the episode with Sadoleto and Geneva. For but one other example, consider the letter to King Francis I of France, which accompanied the 1536 and most subsequent editions of the *Institutes*. At least one-quarter of the text of this appeal to the king was devoted specifically to historical matters, including accusations of "newness," with particular attention to teaching that is inconsistent (or not) with the early church fathers, as well as the related issue of appeal to "long-standing custom."[28] Calvin reported to King Francis that the reformers' teachings were "new to them"—that is, new to their Roman Catholic opponents—while there was "nothing new among us"—that is, those who with Calvin were preaching and teaching the Pauline message of justification in Christ.[29] As was the case in his letter to Sadoleto, Calvin's application of the descriptor "new" to the Roman church combined with his assertion that there was "nothing new" about the reformers shapes the character and trajectory of the reform that was pursued. Simply put, their

---

23. Calvin, "Reply to Sadolet," 231. Note that there is a second continuum of comparison being employed. In addition to the present and the past there is the comparison between Rome and Geneva.

24. Calvin, "Reply to Sadolet," 233.

25. Calvin, "Reply to Sadolet," 232.

26. Calvin, "Reply to Sadolet," 256.

27. Calvin, "Reply to Sadolet," 231.

28. In the McNeill-Battles edition of the *Institutes*, 5.5 out of 20 pages of Calvin's letter are devoted specifically to historical matters. See "Prefatory Address to King Francis I of France," in *Institutes*, I:14–23.

29. Calvin, "Prefatory Address to King Francis I," 16.

path of reform was one of "recovery" of "antiquity," rather than a schismatic invention.[30]

Conclusion: Calvin and Tradition

Against this backdrop of the relationship between scripture and theology and the relationship between the church and history, we can offer some summary observations about Calvin's view of and use of tradition.

Scripture

Calvin's unswervingly high view of scripture was accompanied by a deep concern that it be properly interpreted. He recognized that this interpretation could not be done alone. The interpreter needs the wisdom of others. Consequently, in his efforts to honor and set forth the teachings of scripture, Calvin was also a "student of the church fathers" and a respecter of the early church councils. Thus, "we are armed not only with the virtue of the Divine Word, but," Calvin wrote, "also with the aid of the holy Fathers."[31]

The Church

Despite opponents' charge that the teachings of Calvin and other reformers were, in Bruce Gordon's words, "a new weapon which had slashed the Church's artery, its traditions," Calvin was adamant that this reformation was neither schismatic nor disrespectful toward authentic tradition. As noted above, Calvin "revere[d]" the church as "the mother" of all true Christians and was eager to interpret scripture properly so as to "remain in her [the church's] bosom." Calvin was eager to receive any and all wisdom the early church had to offer, whether it come through the writings of an individual church father or the pronouncements of an early ecumenical council. Traditions, however, that were inconsistent with scripture were to be abandoned and, if necessary, explicitly opposed.

History

It is imperative also to rightly interpret history. A critical interpretive key for reading history correctly is the relationship between change and continuity. Whether exegeting scripture or pointing to the true church, Calvin believed that it was crucial to stand in continuity with the early church.

30. Calvin, "Prefatory Address to King Francis I," 16.
31. Calvin, "Reply to Sadolet," 240, 255.

This was not because it was "early" but because the teaching of the early church was, for the most part, in accord with the teaching of scripture. It was the Roman church of the sixteenth century—not the reformers—that had departed from the path of the true church. Calvin was not pursuing novelties or innovations. He sought to be a faithful steward of—to faithfully hand on—the teachings of the Word of God.

Tradition

R. Ward Holder's description of Calvin appears to be very much on the mark. He writes, "Calvin rarely did anything wholly new, nor did he self-consciously set out to do so."[32] He "was not the innovator that his opponents claimed he was, or the innovator that others of his opponents . . . wished he could become. Further, he was not even the innovator that some of his disciples suggested in their devotion to his memory. Instead, Calvin used traditional elements in order to renew theology so as to edify the church . . . [and] in order to renew biblical religion."[33]

ANABAPTISTS

Having heard from and about Calvin and tradition, the time has come to listen to other voices of reformation: the early Anabaptists. "While we could consider the Reformers as a group"—that is, the so-called Magisterial Reformers—"with a basically homogeneous hermeneutic, we cannot do so for the Anabaptists. One difference is the absence of any Anabaptist theologian of comparable status to Luther, Zwingli, or Calvin."[34] This is the observation of Mennonite scholar Stuart Murray, and it is a view that is shared by many, perhaps most, students of the Reformation era, be they Reformed or Anabaptist.

Furthermore, there is a wide and diverse array of figures and ideas that are associated with the descriptor "Anabaptist" when applied to the sixteenth century and beyond. Thus, describing his own path into advanced study of Anabaptist history and theology, Mennonite scholar Karl Koop reports, "what I encountered in my own heritage—the Anabaptist-Mennonite tradition—was a diversity that apparently lacked any unity and

---

32. Holder, "Tradition and Renewal," 385.
33. Holder, "Tradition and Renewal," 384–85.
34. Murray, *Biblical Interpretation*, 29.

coherence."[35] (Koop's inclusion of the word "apparently" is important, for his own studies eventually lead him to discover a certain theological unity in the unfolding development of the Anabaptist tradition. But his observations, along with those of many other scholars, about the degree of diversity within Anabaptism is nonetheless indicative of a truly wide-ranging diversity.) Consequently, the following description of and comment on the nature and role of tradition in early Anabaptism, even if accurate, will inevitably be incomplete. The same two major headings that structured our consideration of Calvin's thought will serve us well here also: early Anabaptist views of scripture and theology, followed by views of the church and history.

Scripture and Theology

Sixteenth-century Anabaptists had an intense commitment to knowing and, equally if not more importantly, living out the teachings of the Bible. In 1524, Conrad Grebel and some colleagues wrote to Thomas Müntzer, "There is more than enough of wisdom and counsel in the Scripture, how all classes and all men may be taught, governed, instructed, and turned to piety."[36] What weight should that wisdom and counsel of scripture carry? "Whatever we are not taught by clear passages or examples," said Grebel and friends, "must be regarded as forbidden."[37] This same commitment to scripture is seen, for example, in the unfolding Anabaptist confessional tradition. Anabaptist confessions such as the *Kempen Confession* of 1545 and the Swiss Brethren *Confession of Hesse* of 1578 are permeated with phrases such as "Witness of the Holy Scriptures" and "according to the Holy Scripture" and "according to God's holy word," combined with the frequent citation or quotation of specific passages of scripture.[38] The firmness and pervasiveness of Anabaptist commitment to scripture was unmistakable.

Relationship between Scripture and Theology

In contrast with the Magisterial Reformation, which had considerable numbers of leaders with advanced university education, there was a marked

---

35. Koop, *Confessions of Faith*, 7; also 9.

36. Grebel et al., "Letters to Thomas Müntzer," 79.

37. Grebel et al., "Letters to Thomas Müntzer," 75.

38. See "Swiss Brethren Confession of Hess," 45–92 and "Kempen Confession," 95–108.

absence of formally educated leadership in early Anabaptism. This was largely the result of a tragically clear reason: virtually all of the leaders of the first generation of Anabaptists died rather young, and often in martyrdom.

The point being addressed at the moment is the relationship between scripture and theology. What does this—persecution, martyrdom—have to do with the relationship between scripture and theology? A life on the margins, a life of persecution, does not typically provide the resources of time and opportunity necessary for formal education or for extended theological reflection and writing. This *Sitz im Leben*—groups of people who were "mainly poor, uneducated, and persecuted"—contributed to a certain inclination or posture with respect to how rightly to read and interpret the Bible.[39] This inclination or posture can be described in terms of both rejection and affirmation. Walter Klaassen provides a description of rejection, suggesting that from its beginnings in the sixteenth century the Anabaptist tradition has been marked by "hostile distrust of traditional and contemporary theologians, theology, and theologizing."[40] With rather pervasively and deeply pragmatic interests, combined with sometimes being the objects of physical violence inflicted by people associated with the Magisterial Reformation, Anabaptists were not drawn toward more intellectually-informed, more complex or "sophisticated" biblical interpretation and theological formulation. This included the tasks associated with studying and incorporating tradition. "This was an approach," observes Murray, "that was suspicious of the distorting influence of power and status, that empowered ordinary Christians as interpreters, that relied actively on the anticipated guidance of the Holy Spirit, that encouraged congregational hermeneutics and that emphasized application over intellectual discussion."[41] They wanted to be, they sought to be, people of the Book—and note the definite article, *the* Book.

The Church and History

IMPORTANCE OF THE CHURCH

As was the case with Calvin, the church mattered, it mattered deeply, to Anabaptists. As was suggested to be the case with anyone's view of tradition,

---

39. Murray, *Biblical Interpretation*, 11.
40. Klaassen, *Anabaptism*, 37.
41. Murray, "Anabaptism as a Conversation Partner," 97.

we must have an adequate understanding of Anabaptist views of the church in order to have a right understanding of Anabaptist views of and practices with regard to tradition.

Anabaptist interpreters of sixteenth-century Anabaptism as different as Harold S. Bender and J. Denny Weaver share a recognition of the importance of ecclesiology to Anabaptist identity. Thus Weaver suggests, "the ecclesiology of Anabaptism is a comprehensive perspective with potential implications for every aspect of Christian life and thought."[42] Our particular interest here is in the ways that Anabaptist ecclesiology informs and is informed by Anabaptist views of tradition. Toward that end, we will first note some emphases in the Anabaptist understanding of the nature of the church, and second, in the understanding of the historical path of the church.

NATURE OF THE CHURCH

There are three sixteenth-century Anabaptist emphases with regard to ecclesiology to be noted here. It is worth noting that each of these is an "emphasis," not a binary "either/or," and that they are emphases of particular importance to the relationship between Anabaptist ecclesiology and the interpretation of the Bible and the role that tradition does or does not play in that regard.

First, relatively speaking, there is an emphasis on *particularity* more than catholicity—on the *local* church more than the universal church. In part because of the high priority they placed on the importance of lived-with-integrity Christian faith,[43] which was further intensified by persecution, Anabaptists were clearly, and understandably, almost singularly concerned with the local incarnation of the church. This emphasis was not always explicitly articulated, but is often clearly evident in the way that Anabaptists went about interpreting the Bible and formulating theological beliefs. Thus, as Murray observes with respect to biblical hermeneutics, "Anabaptist approaches were developing in the setting of local churches, not seminaries,"[44]

---

42. Weaver, *Becoming Anabaptist*, 20.

43. E.g., Dordrecht Confession, Eighth article, on the church: "This church is to be known by her Scriptural faith, doctrine, love, and godly life" (Koop, ed., *Confessions of Faith*, 300); Prussian Confession, Article IV, on the church: the "signs of the true church" include "life in all goodness, righteousness, and truth, according to the teaching of Christ and his apostles, true faith (Eph. 5:9; Matt. 5:16) in Jesus Christ through obedience to the divine Word (Col. 1:23; John 15:4–7)" (Koop, ed., *Confessions of Faith*, 31).

44. Murray, *Biblical Interpretation*, 11.

and as Koop observes with regard to the writing of confessions of faith, "Without centralized ecclesial authority and without political approval, [Anabaptist] confessional statements depended on congregation assent."[45]

Second, there is an emphasis on the *immediately contemporary* church over the historical church. As Murray observes in *Biblical Interpretation in the Anabaptist Tradition*, "Anabaptists who accepted that the church had a role in biblical interpretation located this role in the present rather than the past, and in local congregations rather than a monolithic structure."[46] He reports that there was in early Anabaptism a "virtual exclusion of the church throughout prior centuries. The focus was," he says, "so sharply on present consensus that little attention was given to past consensus."[47]

Third, the contemporary, local community of Christian faith is an arena, perhaps the most important arena, of *the work of the Holy Spirit*. The confidence Anabaptist leaders placed in the local community of faith was "rooted in their expectancy that the Spirit would operate there in a way he would not in individuals alone.... This was not the church sitting in authority over Scripture but the church as the Spirit's chosen location for interpreting Scripture."[48]

Historical Path of the Church

With a view toward more directly considering the relationship between Anabaptist ecclesiology and the role of tradition, it is important to have some understanding of the sixteenth-century Anabaptist view of the actual historical path of the church. In brief, the visible church—which is not synonymous with the true church—fell, fell early, and fell far. In the Anabaptist view of history, the church became severely distorted and corrupted, to the point of no longer being the true church; and the dominant, highly visible "church" of the sixteenth century existed in this condition. As one Anabaptist scholar has observed, "The Anabaptists' view of the fall of humanity was generally less radical than that of the Reformers, but their view of the fall of the church was more radical and discouraged exploration of earlier writings."[49] Near the beginning of his retrospective look, around

---

45. Koop, "Introduction," 10.

46. Murray, *Biblical Interpretation*, 158.

47. Murray, *Biblical Interpretation*, 180. He goes on to say, citing Balke (*Calvin and the Anabaptist Radicals*, 327), that "This was one of Calvin's major criticisms."

48. Murray, *Biblical Interpretation*, 176; also 58, 97, 145, and 146.

49. Murray, *Biblical Interpretation*, 180.

1560, Obbe Philips says, "In the first place, we must with all understanding concede and confess that the first church of Christ and the apostles was destroyed and ruined in early times by Antichrist."[50] Thus, the fall of the church occurred centuries before the time period that comes to be known as the medieval period.

One of the images sometimes used to describe the eventual form of this fallen church is *Christenheit*, "Christendom," which is, wrote John Denck in 1526, "full of adulterers, misers, drunkards, and more of the same."[51] It is not surprising, then, that whereas Calvin thought it important to identify wherever possible the continuity between his work and that of the early church, including the early church fathers, Anabaptists were generally less interested in such continuity. Indeed, their default, if you will, was to assume *discontinuity* with the post-apostolic church, discontinuity with the visibly prominent church as its history unfolded. If there was a continuity to be sought it was to be, above all else, continuity with Jesus.[52] The corrupted, fallen state of the predominantly visible forms of the church rendered historical continuity a very complicated and off-putting notion for sixteenth-century Anabaptists.

Conclusion: Anabaptists and Tradition

With the above background in view, some summary observations about early Anabaptist views of and practices with respect to tradition can be made.

Scripture

Sixteenth-century Anabaptists had a very high view of scripture. From their perspective, they more clearly saw and more consistently and fully put this principle into practice than did the Magisterial reformers. Anabaptists sought to let scripture lead them wherever it wanted, without the misdirection or restraints of tradition. Thus, Conrad Grebel counseled, "Do not act, teach, or establish anything according to human opinion, your own or that of others, and abolish what has been so established; but establish and teach only the clear word and practices of God."[53]

---

50. Philips, "A Confession," 207.

51. Denck, "Whether God Is the Cause of Evil," 106.

52. Cf. Koop, "Introduction," 12.

53. Grebel et al., "Letters to Thomas Müntzer," 85. These practices included, for example, church discipline, "unadulterated baptism," and "unadulterated Supper."

The Reformation

The Church

The church is a spiritual fellowship that exists first and foremost in the present local fellowship of baptized believers in Jesus Christ. Among other functions of these fellowships—such as living obedient holy lives, exercising proper discipline, and serving one another—they are to function as Spirit-led interpretive communities. They are to be shaped by the teachings of scripture as those teachings are discerned in the particular, present local community of scriptural belief and life. It does not seem unreasonable to suggest that, to a considerably greater degree than the Magisterial reformers, the posture of Anabaptist churches was not one that included "looking back" but rather was one of "looking around."

History

This observation about "looking around" and not devoting much attention to "looking back" reflects not only an Anabaptist view of the church but also the closely related matter of their understanding of the actual historical path of the church. That view of history is one of a particular kind of discontinuity, more than continuity.[54] The history of the church is one of discontinuity in the sense that, as noted above, the church profoundly fell very early in its history. In this regard, then, that history is one which is discontinuous with the history of the predominantly visible churches, first the Roman Catholic Church and then also the churches of the Magisterial reformers. There was, however, a sense of continuity with Jesus and the apostles and with the pre-Constantinian church, but this was a continuity that was most significantly spiritual, and only in the margins of history.

Tradition

Given these understandings of the role of scripture, the nature of the church, and the actual history of the church, it is not surprising that the early Anabaptists had very little regard for and thus gave comparatively little attention to "tradition" as this is usually understood. The Bible was held in high regard—indeed, one can say the highest regard. Moreover, given the fallen character of so much of the historical legacy of the church,

---

54. Cf. Michael Cartwright observes, "[John Howard] Yoder thought that at any given time in human history, God's Holy Spirit could constitute a community of faith around the Word of God read and proclaimed, but Yoder's conception of tradition simply did not permit diachronic continuity" ("Sharing the House of God: Learning to Read Scripture with Anabaptists," 161).

the Bible needed to be, in a sense, protected from the corrupting influence of the dominant interpretive and theological traditions of the church. Stated more positively, the Word of God, accompanied by the Spirit of God, needed to be free to be heard and applied by contemporary, local communities without the distorting constraints of tradition. There was a sense of history, but it was a history that did not bear the weight of authoritative theological tradition.[55] It was not a history conveyed as tradition, in the form of biblical commentaries and creedal statements and theological treatises handed-down through the predominant churches, whether Roman Catholic or Protestant. It was a history of faithful belief and, equally if not more important, faithful, non-violent living—living, and sometimes dying, on the margins.

CONCLUSION

Having briefly surveyed two Reformation-era perspectives on the nature and role of tradition in Christian thought and life, we will conclude by offering seven brief observations—suggestions and questions—under three headings. As will likely be evident, these observations, suggestions and questions do not constitute linear development of a single thought, but are offered as a cluster of interrelated considerations.

Function and Role of Tradition

INEVITABILITY

Whatever one's stated principles of ecclesiastical authority and theological method are, the influence of tradition, of some sort, is inevitable. In the case of the present study, early Anabaptism in particular provides a reminder of this inevitability. While formally, in principle, tradition had little if any role in early Anabaptist biblical interpretation and theology, as a number of Anabaptist scholars have observed, "it is not possible to read the Bible in the absence of some tradition.... The reading of Scripture and the reality of tradition are interconnected and inextricably tied together."[56]

---

55. See Weaver, *Becoming Anabaptist*, where he describes the Anabaptist posture as one which is different from one which has regard for "authoritative tradition" (172).

56. Koop, "Contours and Possibilities for an Anabaptist Theology," 9. Following the work of Koop, it should be noted here that over time a significant role for confessional theology developed within Anabaptism.

The Reformation

Explicit and Tacit

Recognizing that tradition *will* play a role in our reading of the Bible and formulation of applications, the question then arises as to whether this role is and should be explicit or tacit. Relatively speaking, for Calvin the role of tradition was more self-conscious, more explicit; for the Anabaptists it was, particularly in their earliest decades, more tacit and more localized—less lowercase "c" catholic. As with most aspects of Christian life and faith, all things being equal, self-awareness and intentionality will likely bring about better results than unreflective or assumed practices. As have been observed by many, the most powerful kinds of tradition, for good or ill, are traditions that go unacknowledged, and therefore unregulated in any intentional way. It is always worthwhile for both churches and individual Christians to ask, "What is the role of tradition here, both explicit and tacit?"

"Weight," Authority

Again, given that tradition will play a role, what ought that role be? Or, another way to put this is to ask what "weight" or authority tradition ought to have. The larger catholic tradition carried more weight for Calvin than it did for the Anabaptists; and their respective views of the nature of tradition were such that it carried less weight for both of them, and other Protestant reformers, than it did in the Roman Catholic Church. The particular weight that tradition does or does not carry will be informed by some of the matters yet to follow here.

Nature and Character of Tradition

Beliefs vs. "Living"

One must always be careful when working with the distinction—and note the word "distinction," not "separation"—between "belief" and "life" (or "living"). However, it seems reasonable to suggest that for Calvin the nature or substance of tradition was doctrinal, while for Anabaptists it was equally, if not more, existential. By "existential" is meant that it had to do with life, with living, with concrete behaviors. The tradition of which Anabaptists were perhaps most mindful was the tradition of the faithful living, and dying, the tradition of a holy remnant true followers of Jesus over the centuries.

Terminology—"Theological" or "Biblical"?

When tradition is spoken of it is often referred to with terms such as "ecclesial tradition" or "church tradition." This study prompts a question as to whether these descriptors are the best ways to refer to "tradition" as understood by Calvin, the early Anabaptists, and many other sixteenth-century reformers. Instead, a more accurate descriptor might be "biblical tradition,"[57] because for both Calvin and the Anabaptists it was above all else the Bible, more than "the church," to which they turned to determine whether or not to embrace a particular tradition.

Christianity, History, and the Church

Importance of the Church—and Our View of It

The church and our view of it matter. They matter, not least, for our understanding of and drawing-upon (or not drawing upon) tradition. Calvin was comparatively more concerned to be in accord with the church catholic, while the early Anabaptists' greatest concerns were more singularly focused on the present-day, local church. These differing views informed their differing understandings of and use of tradition. So, a very important question to consider when thinking about tradition is, "What is our understanding of the church?"

Importance of History—and Our Understandings of It

Our understanding of the church, particularly as it relates to tradition, will be significantly informed by our understanding of the church *as an historical reality*. Calvin believed that the church slowly, gradually became distorted and corrupted, but was not without voices of biblical and theological wisdom to be heeded along the way. In the view of early Anabaptists, this was far less the case, and what wisdom there had been was lived-wisdom, lives worthy of emulation. If the understanding of the nature and role of

---

57. This thought is prompted in part by the following observation by Irena Backus about Calvin: " he does not hesitate to criticize the fathers on points of doctrine that differ from his own. However, he is fully cognizant of putting together collections of authorities, especially patristics authorities, to show his religious adversaries that it is he, thus not they, who has the weight of theological tradition behind him" (Backus, "Calvin and the Church Fathers," 128). At the same time, in making this terminological suggestion I do not want to reinforce the not uncommon tendency in many Protestant circles to underestimate the importance of the church and of ecclesiological understandings.

tradition is to be advanced, we need to ask ourselves questions such as, "Do we believe that the church 'fell' into profound distortion and corruption at some point in history? If so, how and when?" Whatever one's responses are to those questions, does it matter? What is, and is not, our relationship to the church of past centuries? What, if any, weight ought the beliefs and practices of the church of the past have on us today? For those who are interested, the thought and life of sixteenth-century reformers can be a rich resource when exploring these questions.

BIBLIOGRAPHY

Backus, Irena. "Calvin and the Church Fathers." In *The Calvin Handbook*, edited by Herman J. Selderhuis, 125–37. Translated by Henry J. Baron et al. Grand Rapids: Eerdmans, 2009.

Balke, Willem. *Calvin and the Anabaptist Radicals*. Translated by William Heynen. Grand Rapids: Eerdmans, 1981.

———. "Calvin and the Anabaptists." In *The Calvin Handbook*, edited by Herman J. Selderhuis, 146–55. Translated by Henry J. Baron et al. Grand Rapids: Eerdmans, 2009.

Calvin, John. *Institutes of the Christian Religion*, edited by John T. McNeill. Translated by Ford Lewis Battles. 2 vols. Philadelphia: Westminster, 1960.

———. "Reply to Sadolet." In *Calvin: Theological Treatises*, edited and translated by J. K. S. Reid, 219–56. Philadelphia: Westminster, 1954.

Cartwright, Michael. "Sharing the House of God: Learning to Read Scripture with Anabaptists." In *Engaging Anabaptism: Conversations with a Radical Tradition*, edited by John D. Roth, 145–82. Scottdale, PA: Herald, 2001.

Denck, John. "Whether God Is the Cause of Evil." In *Spiritual and Anabaptist Writers*, edited by George H. Williams and Angel M. Mergal, 86–111. Philadelphia: Westminster, 1957.

Gordon, Bruce. *Calvin*. New Haven: Yale University Press, 2009.

Grebel, Conrad. et al., "Letters to Thomas Müntzer by Conrad Grebel and Friends, Zurich, September 5, 1524." In *Spiritual and Anabaptist Writers*, edited by George H. Williams and Angel M. Mergal, 71–85. Philadelphia: Westminster, 1957.

Headley, John M. *Luther's View of Church History*. New Haven: Yale University Press, 1963.

Holder, R. Ward. "Tradition and Renewal." In *The Calvin Handbook*, edited by Herman J. Selderhuis, 384–95. Translated by Henry J. Baron et al. Grand Rapids: Eerdmans, 2009.

Junghans, Helmar. "Leipzig Disputation." In *The Oxford Encyclopedia of the Reformation*, edited by Hans J. Hillerbrand, 2:417–18. Translated by Susan M. Sisler. 5 vols. Oxford: Oxford University Press, 1996.

Klaassen, Walter. *Anabaptism: Neither Catholic nor Protestant*. Waterloo, ON: Conrad, 1973.

Koop, Karl. *Anabaptist-Mennonite Confessions of Faith: The Development of a Tradition*. Kitchener, ON: Pandora, 2004.

———. "Contours and Possibilities for an Anabaptist Theology." Paper presented at "Anabaptist Theology: Methods and Practices" conference, Trinity Western University, Langley, BC, 7–9 June 2017.

———. "Introduction." In *Confessions of Faith in the Anabaptist Tradition, 1527–1660*, edited by Karl Koop. Translated by Cornelius J. Dyk, et al., 1–16. Kitchener, ON: Pandora, 2006.

Koop, Karl, ed. *Confessions of Faith in the Anabaptist Tradition, 1527–1660*. Translated by Conrnelius J. Dyk et al. Kitchener, ON: Pandora, 2006.

Lane, Anthony N. S. *John Calvin: Student of the Church Fathers*. Grand Rapids: Baker, 1999.

Mouw, Richard J. "Reflections on My Encounter with the Anabaptist-Mennonite Tradition." In *Engaging Anabaptism: Conversations with a Radical Tradition*, edited by John D. Roth, 117–24. Scottdale, PA: Herald, 2001.

Murray, Stuart. "Anabaptism as a Conversation Partner." In *Engaging Anabaptism: Conversations with a Radical Tradition*, edited by John D. Roth, 97–104. Scottdale, PA: Herald, 2001.

———. *Biblical Interpretation in the Anabaptist Tradition*. Kitchener, ON: Pandora, 2000.

Olin, John C., ed., *A Reformation Debate: Sadoleto's Letter to the Genevans and Calvin's Reply*. Grand Rapids: Baker, 1976.

Philips, Obbe. "A Confession." In *Spiritual and Anabaptist Writers*, edited by George H. Williams and Angel M. Mergal, 204–25. Philadelphia: Westminster, 1957.

Torrance, T. F. *The Hermeneutics of John Calvin*. Edinburgh: Scottish Academic, 1988.

Weaver, J. Denny. *Becoming Anabaptist: The Origin and Significance of Sixteenth-Century Anabaptism*. 2nd ed. Scottdale, PA: Herald, 2005.

6

Anti-Semitism in the Reformation Era

Victor A. Shepherd

It is not the case that the Protestant Reformers tragically reflected an extraordinarily virulent anti-Semitism. In truth they were no worse than Gentile Christians have customarily been in the latter's hostility to the "apple of God's eye,"[1] that people to whom God has pledged himself irrevocably in a covenant that can no more be rescinded than circumcision can be undone. The tragedy, rather, is that despite the Reformers' acknowledgement of scripture's normativity, they were no better. In this regard they exemplified the anti-Semitism that appears relentlessly in every era of the church.[2]

Not surprisingly, then, a towering Reformer expostulated, "I have had much conversation with many Jews: I have never seen either a drop of piety or a grain of truth or ingenuousness—nay, I have never found common sense in any Jew."[3] Jews are "profane unholy sacrilegious dogs."[4] "Now the Jews are cut off like rotten limbs. We have taken their place." "They [the Jews] renounced the one through whom they could rule over the world, our Lord Jesus Christ, and placed themselves under the tyranny of

---

1. Deut 32:10.

2. For a judicious assessment of the nature and extent of Christian anti-Semitism see Stark, *Bearing False Witness*.

3. Calvin, *Commentary* on Dan 2:44.

4. Calvin, *Sermon* on Gal 1:6–8.

Satan."[5] Who uttered the foregoing? Everyone wants to point the accusing finger at Martin Luther, because Luther's anti-Jewish pronouncements are common knowledge.[6] My earliest New Testament professor at Emmanuel College, University of Toronto, told me, in 1967, that while the Shoah arose on Lutheran soil, it could not have arisen on Reformed. Alas, John Calvin is the author of the statements above. "I have never found common sense in any Jew," Calvin announced. How many Jews had Calvin met in Geneva? Calvin went to Geneva in September 1536. He lived there until he died in 1564 (apart from his sojourn in Strasbourg, 1538–1541). The last Jew was expelled from Geneva in 1491.[7] When Calvin came to the city there had not been a Jewish person in it for 45 years.

Let us look at another thinker. This one insists that Jews not be allowed to build synagogues in his city. Jews are to be barred from the trades. Jews are to be policed rigorously so as to minimise their "blaspheming Christ." They are to be engaged in "the humblest, most arduous and most trying tasks," namely, sweeping chimneys, cleaning sewers, and disposing of deadstock. Their being assigned such tasks will be a "deterrent and a corrective."[8] The Talmud must be banned. If Jew and Christian are found living together, both must be executed. The man who insisted on such harsh treatment of the Jewish people admitted Torah to be salvific (Jesus Christ, after all, is Torah incarnate); he also emphasized the critical role of the Old Testament in Christianizing the social order of his city. The city is Strasbourg; the Reformer is Martin Bucer, whose irenic demeanor was rivalled only by that of Philip Melanchthon. And yet Luther is blamed for all things anti-Jewish, and, in popular parlance, blamed exclusively.

Reformation-era theologians appear to be inherently anti-Semitic, but did Jewish people receive better treatment at the hands of Renaissance humanists? Since humanism magnifies magnanimity as surely as the Reformers appear to shrink it, could refuge be sought in humanism? This chapter looks at two representative humanists, Reuchlin and Erasmus.

---

5. Calvin, *Sermon* on Isa 14:2.

6. See especially Gritsch, *Martin Luther's Anti-Semitism* and his *Toxic Spiritualty*. Oberman's *The Roots of Anti-Semitism* documents anti-Semitism in the Renaissance more virulent than that of the Reformers. For an exposition of the ubiquitous anti-Semitism Middle Ages see Trachtenberg, *The Devil and the Jews*.

7. Ravenswaay, "Calvin and the Jews," 143–46.

8. Greschat, *Martin Bucer*, 156–58.

The Reformation

Johann Reuchlin (1455–1522) was fully conversant with Greek, Latin, and Hebrew.[9] Hugely learned, he condemned the indiscriminate destruction of Talmudic texts. Nevertheless, he soon advertised himself to be no friend of the Jewish people. He wanted the Talmud preserved only because he had enormous respect for a language of antiquity. In the second place, he insisted on a cabalistic interpretation of the Talmud, and strenuously maintained that knowledge of Hebrew was essential to penetrating cabalistic mysteries. His idiosyncratic cabalistic hermeneutics was exemplified, for instance, in his insistence that the Hebrew letters for "El Shaddai" ("The Almighty One") added up to or otherwise subtly spelt out "Jesuch" (Jesus). Since Jewish readers would not admit this "truth," it was plain that the Talmud stood between Jews and their conversion.

In Reuchlin there is no suggestion that the Talmud is related to Torah, the salvific covenant-forging Word and Act of God. In Reuchlin, a hugely learned Hebraist, there is no suggestion that Hebrew is the language of that people to whom God has bound himself irrevocably; no suggestion that Hebrew is the language apart from which the New Testament is incomprehensible.

Reuchlin maintained that Jewish misery, undeniable throughout the pre-Christian and Christian eras alike, was God-ordained punishment. Jews could escape such punishment only by converting. The Jews in Reuchlin's day were fellow-citizens of the Holy Roman Empire. They remained, on the other hand, adversaries of the Kingdom of God. If they refused to embrace Christ and refused to refrain from money-lending (the one occupation the church had permitted and assigned them), they would cease to be fellow-citizens of the Empire, and would be expelled.

The second thinker we shall probe is the Crown Prince of humanists, Desiderius Erasmus (1466–1536). Erasmus was marvelously learned in Greek and Latin.[10] Fluent in half-a-dozen vernacular languages as well, he did not know a word of Hebrew, claiming his research agenda left him no time to learn the language. I fear, however, that he knew no Hebrew because he did not want to learn any, virulently contemptuous as he was of the Jewish people.[11]

---

9. For the discussion on Reuchlin, see Oberman, *The Roots of Anti-Semitism*, 11–12, 32.

10. Quoted in Oberman, *The Roots of Anti-Semitism*, 18–23, 38–40.

11. It must not be thought that the Humanists among the Reformers were any less toxic. Chillingly Erasmus wanted to see a Europe that Hitler, centuries later, would attempt to deliver; namely, a Europe that was completely *Judenrein*. Bernard Lohse notes

Adept in French, Erasmus relished visiting France. France, he said, was the "purest blossom of Christianity, since she alone is uninfested with heretics, Bohemian schismatics [Hussites], with Jews, and with half-Jewish *marranos* [pigs]."[12] The *marranos*, of course, were Spanish Jews who had forcibly been converted to the church under the reign of Ferdinand and Isabella. A baptized Jew, Erasmus maintained, never really becomes a Christian; he or she remains a half-Jew. Concerning Johannes Pfefferkorn, a Jewish convert to Roman Catholicism, Erasmus announced, "If one were to operate on him, six hundred Jews would spring out."[13] Between 1507 and 1521 Pfefferkorn wrote more vitriolic pamphlets concerning the Jewish people than anyone else in the Renaissance and Reformation.[14] And yet so very ingrained was Erasmus' anti-Semitism that he refused to recognize Pfefferkorn, now a Jewish convert, as a Christian. To sum up the matter, Erasmus wrote, "if to hate the Jews is the proof of genuine Christians, then we are all excellent Christians."[15]

But what about Anabaptists? Balthasar Hubmaier, living in Regensburg, spoke of the Jews as idle, lecherous, and greedy. They are a plague, he contended.[16] (We should note the metaphorical force of "plague" in view of the fact that the Black Death killed 40 percent to 50 percent of Europe in fourteenth century Europe.) These pestilential people should be expelled. Hubmaier incited city authorities to do just this. In 1519 Hubmaier complained of the (supposed) Jewish defamation of Mary. Immediately the synagogue in Regensburg was torched, and a chapel honoring Mary erected in its place.[17]

While these may appear as the nadir of Christian contempt for and mistreatment of the Jewish people, it is not. Pride of place must be accorded Johann Eck, Luther's formidable Catholic opponent at Leipzig (1519), at Worms (1521), and at Augsburg (1530). Eck's anti-Semitic toxicity, said Heiko Oberman (a Renaissance and Reformation scholar without peer in

---

that for Erasmus, "There would be no place for the Jews." Lohse, *Martin Luther's Theology*, 337.

12. Quoted in Oberman, *The Roots of Anti-Semitism*, 38.
13. Quoted in Oberman, *The Roots of Ant-Semitism*, 38.
14. Oberman, *The Roots of Anti-Semitism*, 32–37.
15. Quoted in Oberman, *The Roots of Anti-Semitism*, 40.
16. Oberman, *The Roots of Anti-Semitism*, 7, 77–88, 101.
17. Oberman, *The Roots of Anti-Semitism*, 84.

his day), outstripped anything the Reformers wrote "in crudity, spleen, and slander."[18]

Throughout the Middle Ages the Jewish people had been vilified by the "blood myth"; namely, that Jews needed the blood of a Christian child in order to atone for their having slain Jesus; Jews put children's blood into matzo, the unleavened bread used at Passover; Jewish men menstruated, and were therefore monstrous; Jews desecrated the Eucharistic elements, thereby hexing them so that bread and wine, so far from being Christic, were now Satanic.[19] Eck upheld the medieval blood-myth concerning the Jewish people, and Eck fulminated against Luther since Luther denied the blood-myth.

The accusation that Jewish males menstruated is crucial, for it pronounced Jews to be more than unbelieving, more than Christ-killers, more than murderers; Jews were nothing less than monstrous. After all, a male that menstruates is not human; it is monstrous. Jews, in short, are sub-human: lethal, abhorrent freaks. Eck upheld this notion; he faulted Luther because Luther did not—at that time.

Luther is central to this discussion. He is deemed the *bête noire* where a Christian approach to the Jewish people is concerned. (As noted, however, there were many who were no better, and some who were far worse.) Luther penned six anti-Judaistic tracts, haunted as he was by the Jewish presence in Europe and what he saw as its intractability. Luther had assumed that Jewish people were held off embracing Jesus Christ and entering the church on account of ethical and institutional abuses in the latter. As soon as these abuses were remedied, Luther assumed, Jews would flock to the church. Jews, however, were no more attracted to the church of the Reformation than they had been to the church of Rome. Puzzled at first, Luther eventually became hostile.

The difference in attitude can be seen readily in two major tracts he wrote twenty years apart, *That Jesus Christ was Born a Jew* (1523) and *On the Jews and Their Lies* (1543). In 1523 Luther wrote, "If the apostles who were also Jews had dealt with us Gentiles as we Gentiles have dealt with Jews, no Christians would ever have emerged from among the Gentiles."[20] Johann Eck, Luther's formidable opponent, riposted, "right now there is

---

18. Oberman, *The Roots of Anti-Semitism*, 36.

19. For an exposition of the "blood myth" and its consequences for medieval Jewry, see de Corneille, *Christians and Jews*, 16–35.

20. Luther, "That Jesus Christ was Born a Jew," 200.

this superficially learned children's preacher [Luther] with a hoof of the golden calf in his flank, who presumes to defend the bloodthirsty Jews, saying it is not true and not plausible that they murder Christian children."[21] In his earlier tract, *That Jesus Christ was Born a Jew*, Luther recognizes the Jewishness of Jesus; in addition, he is attempting to correct those who do not. He hopes thereby that "we might convert some of them."[22]

Luther acknowledges the centuries-old mistreatment of the Jewish people, and clearly believes that his own attitude towards them is qualitatively different:

> They have dealt with the Jews as if they were dogs rather than human beings. They have done little else than deride them and seize their property.... When the Jews see that Judaism has such strong support in Scripture and that Christianity has become a mere babble without reliance on Scripture, how can they possibly compose themselves and become right good Christians?[23]

In the same tract he will claim that the scriptural support for Judaism in the Old Testament has been superseded by the addition of the New Testament. He does not say that the Old Testament *itself* has been superseded; he will say, however, that the New Testament, having revealed the true meaning of the Old Testament, has rendered the synagogue obsolete and the Jewish community's adherence to it a political threat. Luther's benign regard for the Jews, seemingly genuine, invariably serves the agenda of conversion.

Yet the Jews did not convert in any significant number. When Luther reflected on this matter his vivid apocalyptic sense became more vivid still. Luther had long regarded the world as beset with apocalyptic conflict. Jewish intransigence was nothing less than collaboration with apocalyptic powers, for which collaboration divine punishment would entail blindness and dispersal. Since the Old Testament was an integral part of Christian scripture, Luther wanted to wrest it out of Jewish hands if only because the Jews persistently and consistently misinterpreted it and thereby threatened the church and the state. His motivation, in other words, was the elimination of falsehood and the protection of Christians.

Unquestionably, the older Luther believed Jewish intransigence to threaten the survival of the gospel. His most virulent statements arose from

---

21. Eck, *Ains Judenbuechlins Verlegung*, 1542 fol. A IV; quoted in Oberman, *The Roots of Anti-Semitism*, 17.

22. Luther, "That Jesus Christ was Born a Jew," 201.

23. Luther, "That Jesus Christ was Born a Jew," 200.

this notion, and for them he has been vilified ever since. Such statements cannot be ignored, nor their baneful aftermath denied. For example:

> Why, even today they [the Jews] cannot refrain from their nonsensical, insane boasting that they are God's people, although they have been cast out, dispersed and utterly rejected for almost fifteen hundred years." (1543)[24]

> "If someone wanted to talk with Jews, it is enough to remind them of the fifteen hundred years as the people forgotten by God." "[Y]ou have no more bitter, venomous, and vehement foe than a real Jew who earnestly seeks to be a Jew."[25]

By 1546 Luther had reversed his earlier position and embraced the medieval blood myth: "Therefore the history books often accuse them of contaminating wells, of kidnapping and piercing children. . . . Whether it is true or not, I do know that they do not lack the complete, full and ready will to do such things either secretly or openly where possible."[26] The Jews traffic in witchcraft, continued Luther; and for this "they should be hanged on the gallows seven times higher than other thieves."[27] Luther proposed shockingly severe treatment for Jews. His final directive was chilling: "We are at fault for not slaying them."[28] To reinforce his point, Luther insisted that all pastors should support the government in such an undertaking. By now Luther had advertised himself as no better than Johann Eck.

There are aspects of Reformation thought that one could expect to mitigate any proclivity to anti-Judaism (defamation of Jewish religion) or anti-Semitism (defamation of Jewish persons). Here we need only recall the Reformers' grasp of the Old Testament, their appreciation of its logic, and their insistence on its being necessary for faith in Christ. Nowhere in the Reformers is there a hint of Marcionism, the notion that Jesus Christ has rendered Genesis-through-Malachi obsolete, or even an impediment. All the Reformers insist, *contra* Marcion, that to disregard the Old Testament is to render Jesus a wax figure whom we can mold as we wish, thereby fashioning a deity in our image.

---

24. *LW* 47:174.

25. *WA* 51:196,16. Quoted in Oberman, *The Roots of Anti-Semitism*, 113.

26. *LW* 47:265.

27. For the seven-item catena of Luther's recommendations for abusive treatment of Jews, their synagogues, and their homes see *LW* 47:268–72.

28. *LW* 47:92.

Luther's first publication was his *Lectures on the Psalms*. He found the *gospel*, no less, everywhere in the OT. His last major publication he spent ten years preparing (1535–1545); namely, his eight-volume *Lectures on Genesis*. Calvin wrote twice as much on the Old Testament as on the New. While we might expect Calvin to say that all of scripture is a comment on the gospel, he maintains that all of scripture is a comment on the *law*[29]— and can expound this without inconsistency just because Calvin insists that the gospel is the content of the law; Jesus Christ is the content of the Torah; which is to say, Jesus Christ is the substance of both testaments.[30] Calvin frequently reminds his readers that while the gospel as attested by the NT may be "plainer," the NT adds *nothing* essentially to that gospel attested throughout the Old Testament.

Both Luther and Calvin insist that God can be known only in Jesus Christ. Calvin avers that apart from Christ *nothing* can be known of God.[31] Luther, as early as the Heidelberg Disputation (1518), declares uncompromisingly that apart from Christ, God is indistinguishable from the devil.[32] The Reformers, hearing and heeding the apostles, agreed that there is only one Mediator by whom anyone may be saved. Yet the Patriarchs were certainly possessed of saving faith. They were saved by the Nazarene *prospectively* as surely as the church today is saved *retrospectively*. Jacob encountered the Mediator as surely as did Peter.

Then what happened to put the Reformers on the trajectory of the anti-Judaism if not anti-Semitism outlined in the first part of this chapter? Specifically, why does Calvin insist that Israel's sons and daughters were saved through a Torah whose Incarnation was yet to occur, while *denying* that *contemporary* Jews can be saved through a Torah whose Incarnation has already occurred?[33] Why is it that when Calvin speaks of Deborah and Miriam he extols them, but when he refers to contemporary Jews he denounces them? The Reformers speak as they do on account of contemporary Jewry's rejection of Jesus Christ. This notion, coupled with a "replacement" theology, legitimizes, in their own understanding at least, their vehement, vitriolic denunciation of Jews.

---

29. Calvin, *Commentary* on Ps 1:2.
30. Calvin, *Institutes of the Christian Religion*, 2.7 and 2.9.
31. Calvin, *Commentary on the Acts of the Apostles* (Acts 7:30).
32. See Forde, *The Captivation of the Will*, 45.
33. Calvin makes this point emphatically in *Institutes*, 4.16.12.

We should acknowledge that the "replacement" theology on which the Reformers went wrong is not peculiar to them; it has always found a ready home in the church, and it remains the operative understanding today of most of the church's view of the synagogue. Several features of it stand out.[34]

Firstly, replacement theology denies that God's covenant with Israel is eternal. It affirms that the church has replaced Israel: "We have taken their place," Calvin insists.[35] Israel proved unfaithful; Israel failed. It assumes, it should be noted, that the church has always exemplified covenant-faithfulness; whereas Israel failed, the church has remained a howling success.

Secondly, replacement theology presupposes that covenant-membership depends on the quality of one's obedience. Disobedience entails God's rejection and abandonment of covenant-violators. Herein the church, albeit left-handedly and perhaps unwittingly, advertises its confidence in its achievement. Since the church keeps covenant, it no longer has to confess "There is no health in us."[36] Grace, God's faithfulness to his covenant with his people, has disappeared; grace has been replaced by merit. Covenant has been replaced with contract, the notion that failure on the part of one party releases the other party from any commitment—a notion that covenant denies.

Thirdly, replacement theology contradicts the apostles' understanding of Jesus Christ. The apostles insist that God's covenant with Israel (ultimately for the sake of all humankind) is fulfilled in Jesus of Nazareth. Jesus is *the* Torah-keeping, covenant-keeping Jew. More to the point, in light of the Incarnation, the apostles confess that humankind's covenant with God is kept by God *as* human. Kept by God himself (albeit by God *as* human),

---

34. Replacement theology is unbiblical; it has proved lethal repeatedly in the history of the church. While organizations such as the World Council of Churches have addressed it through assorted sub-units on Christian-Jewish Dialogue, etc., such undertakings appear rarely to affect local congregations. If replacement theology is to be overturned, it must be dealt with in the course of congregational life. My own congregation in Mississauga "paired" itself with Solel, the closest synagogue to us. We introduced youth groups to each other; we exchanged pulpits; we developed con-jointly Mississauga's first food bank (it now distributes food with an annual market value of $12 million); we provided the leadership for two major affordable housing developments ($15 million and $19 million respectively). I, a Christian pastor, was invited to speak at all the major developments in synagogue life; e.g., the rabbi's twenty-fifth anniversary as spiritual leader, the dedication of a new Torah scroll, or a service commemorating the victims of the Shoah. It is only as people meet that prejudices evaporate and recognition of one's fellow-sufferers occurs.

35. Calvin, *Sermon* on 2 Sam 24:24.

36. Anglican Church of Canada, *Book of Common Prayer (Canada)*, 4.

humankind's covenant with God can now never be undone, its fulfilment never denied.

Fourthly, replacement theology reads past Rom 9:4–5, where Paul declares, in the present tense, " to them *belong* the sonship, the glory, the covenants, the giving of the law, the worship and the promises; to them *belong* the patriarchs."[37] The present tense obviates any suggestion of past tense: "there used to belong to them" or "there once belonged to them." In Rom 11:29 Paul states bluntly, "For the gifts and the call of God are irrevocable."

Fifthly, replacement theology ignores Rom 9–11, the single most sustained exposition of Israel in the New Testament. (1) Paul would give everything (here he's deploying the vocabulary of Moses) to see his people embrace Jesus as Messiah of Israel. (2) Still, God's covenant with Israel remains operative. (3) Israel's non-acknowledgement of Jesus as Messiah of Israel (with the exception of relatively few Jews, such as Paul), however, is God-ordained, and ordained for the sake of gathering the Gentiles into the people of God. Exactly how Jewish non-acknowledgement of Jesus is essential to Gentile acknowledgement Paul never specifies. He speaks of this development as a mystery, not as a secret. (4) When the "full number" of the Gentiles has been admitted, Israel's non-acknowledgement of the Messiah will be rescinded.

Sixthly, replacement theology repudiates the Messiah. The Messiah is always and everywhere the Messiah *of Israel*. Weaker translations of 1 Sam 16:13 state that David, the Messianic prolepsis, was anointed "from among his brothers." More accurate translations state "in the midst of his brothers." The difference is crucial. According to Hebrew logic, the Messiah always includes his people with him. In other words, Christians can claim proximity to Christ only as they claim proximity to his people, Israel, the synagogue. Conversely, if Christians distance themselves from the Jewish people they distance themselves from Christ.

Seventhly, replacement theology supports the theological aberration that liberal theology is. Liberal theology, while posturing as tolerant, inclusive, humane, among other things, can be pervasively and perniciously anti-Judaistic.[38] With its cosmopolitan view of the human, liberal theology

---

37. NRSV, emphasis added.

38. It should be noted that The United Church of Canada, the nation's most liberal Protestant denomination, has acquired a reputation for a one-sided criticism of the state of Israel. In the Christmas issue of *The Observer*, the denomination's magazine, the article depicting Arab families as humane while Jews remain cruel climaxed argumentation that characterized eighteen consecutive issues. Both the United Church of Canada and the

cannot tolerate Jewish particularity. For instance, Friedrich Schleiermacher, the progenitor of liberal theology, appeared 250 years after the Reformation. Nevertheless, it is not anachronistic to speak of him in the context of Reformation-era anti-Semitism, because the Reformation era, in its caricature of Jews, anticipated liberal theology *with respect to this issue* even as the Reformers disagreed with humanist dilutions of the faith that would reappear in the liberal era. In his 1799 *Address on Religion to its Cultured Despisers*, Schleiermacher averred that Judaism had long been dead, and that "those who at present still bear its colours are actually sitting and mourning beside the undecaying mummy and weeping over its demise and sad legacy."[39] Liberal theology regards the faith of Israel as obsolete and now antiquated, attended by those with a penchant for curating museum-pieces. Schleiermacher regarded the Jewish community as a corpse that does not have sense enough to decompose. The Reformers, tragically, were supersessionists; meaning, they believed that the church had superseded Israel, thereby rendering Israel both obsolete and antiquated. Herein the Reformers failed to read the apostle Paul attentively, despite their veneration for the man.

Finally, replacement theology renders God not worth believing in. For a God who violates his covenant with his people on the grounds that they have violated theirs with him is a God who cannot help them. Who needs or wants a God who quits on those who falter before him?

Challenges to the church today remain. For instance, the church tends to ignore the *only* physical description of Jesus that the apostles give us: he was circumcised. In other words, it means *everything* to our faith that Jesus is a son of Israel. (What we call "New Year's Day," January 1, in the church calendar is the Feast of the Circumcision of Jesus. Why does the church make so very much of December 25 and nothing at all of January 1?)

Again, Christians tend to speak of a "new covenant" in the sense of opposed to "old," forgetting that there can only be *one* covenant. If there were more than one covenant, God would suffer from a Dissociative Identity Disorder (what used to be called a Multiple Personality Disorder). While God's covenant with humankind has always remained fulfilled, humankind's covenant with God has now been kept definitively by God as human, on behalf of all humankind.

Presbyterian Church USA, a major liberal denomination in the United States, have formally urged members to boycott goods made in Israel.

39. Quoted in Fackenheim, "Assault on Abraham," 11–16.

The Reformers contended that the church was the beneficiary of God's act under the economy of the gospel, while Israel was the beneficiary of the same under the economy of the Torah, the gospel being the substance of the Torah. Yet when the Christian community arises, the Reformers deny that Jewish people can savingly encounter the Holy One of Israel as surely as the patriarchs could. Why the denial?

I am not denying that the church must bear witness to the synagogue (just as the synagogue bears witness to the church, pre-eminently concerning the faithfulness of God). I am also not denying that it is appropriate for the Jew to become a Christian. (To say anything else would eliminate the apostles.) I am, however, haunted by the Reformers' denial. More to the point, I am haunted that their denial renders impossible the denial that the Reformers contributed prodigiously to the Holocaust—which disaster, say our Jewish friends, is the single largest catastrophe to befall the synagogue; and which disaster, said Dietrich Bonhoeffer, is the single largest catastrophe to befall the church.[40]

BIBLIOGRAPHY

Anglican Church of Canada. *Book of Common Prayer*. Toronto: Anglican Book Centre, 1959.

Bethge, Eberhard. *Dietrich Bonhoeffer*. Translated by Eric Mosbacher. New York: Harper and Rowe, 1977.

Calvin, John. *Commentary on the Acts of the Apostles*. Vol. 1. Translated by John W. Fraser and W. J. G. McDonald. Grand Rapids: Eerdmans, 1965.

———. *Commentary on the Book of Psalms*. Translated by David C. Searle. London: Banner of Truth, 2009.

———. *Commentary on Daniel*. Vol. 1. Translated by T. H. L. Parker. Grand Rapids: Eerdmans, 1993.

———. *Institutes of the Christian Religion*, edited by John T. McNeill. Translated by Ford Lewis Battles. Philadelphia: Westminster, 1960.

———. *Sermons on Galatians*. Translated by Kathy Childress. London: Banner of Truth, 1997.

———. *Sermons on Isaiah*. Translated by T. H. L. Parker. London: Lutterworth, 2002.

———. *Sermons on 2 Samuel*. Translated by Douglas Kelly. London: Banner of Truth, 2002.

de Corneille, Roland. *Christians and Jews: The Tragic Past and the Hopeful Future*. New York: Harper, 1966.

---

40. In his biography of Dietrich Bohonhoeffer, Eberhard Bethge points out that in one Lutheran parish, 1937, only three of fifteen candidates attended the second confirmation class inasmuch as mention had been made of the Old Testament prophets, and these prophets were Jews. Bethge, *Dietrich Bonhoeffer*, 453.

Fackenheim, Emil. "Assault on Abraham: Thoughts After Fifty Years." *Toronto Journal of Theology* 17 (2001) 11–16.
Forde, Gerhard O. *The Captivation of the Will*. Grand Rapids: Eerdmans, 2005.
Greschat, Martin. *Martin Bucer: A Reformer and His Times*. Translated by Stephen E. Buckwalter. Louisville: John Knox, 2004.
Gritsch, Eric. *Martin Luther's Anti-Semitism: Against His Better Judgment*. Grand Rapids: Eerdmans, 2012.
———. *Toxic Spirituality: Four Enduring Temptations of Christian Faith*. Minneapolis: Fortress, 2009.
Luther, Martin. "That Jesus Christ was Born a Jew." In *Luther's Works*, 45:195–299. Translated by Walter I. Brandt. Philadelphia: Fortress, 1962.
———. "On the Jews and their Lies." In *Luther's Works*, 47:268–271. Translated by Martin H. Bertram. Philadelphia: Fortress, 1971.
Oberman, Heiko A. *The Roots of Anti-Semitism in the Age of Renaissance and Reformation*. Translated by James I. Porter. Philadelphia: Fortress, 1984.
Ravenswaay, J. Marius J. Lange van. "Calvin and the Jews." In *The Calvin Handbook*, edited by Herman J. Selderhuis, 143–46. Translated by Judith J. Guder. Grand Rapids: Eerdmans, 2009.
Stark, Rodney. *Bearing False Witness: Debunking Centuries of Anti-Catholic History*. West Conshohocken, PA: Templeton, 2016.
Trachtenberg, Joshua. *The Devil and the Jews: The Mediaeval Conception of the Jew and Its Relation to Modern Anti-Semitism*. New York: Oxford University Press, 1966.

7

Appropriating Reformation Tradition(s) Today

Should We Put the Past Behind Us?[1]

W. DAVID BUSCHART

IN HER 2013 BOOK *The Spiritual Practice of Remembering*, historian Margaret Bendroth observes, "The past tense is essential to our language of faith; without it our conversation is limited and thin—and growing thinner all the time."[2] Is Bendroth correct? Is it true that without the "past tense" our conversations are doomed to be limited and thin? And, is it true that today our conversations are growing thinner all the time? This essay offers some responses to these and several closely related questions relevant to considering the relevance of the Reformation in a post-Christian world.

The appropriation of traditions of sixteenth-century Protestant reformations is but one instance of a larger and perpetual question for Christians of all eras and all traditions: "Should we put the past behind us?" We will consider this question in Part One, offering some general observations about Christianity and history. Protestant Christians who stand in the heritage of the Reformation share some existential and historical commonalities with Christians of all ecclesio-theological traditions and with the

---

1. I am indebted throughout this essay to collaborative work with Dr. Kent Eilers. Much of that collaborative work is presented in Buschart and Eilers, *Theology as Retrieval*, which from time to time will be cited here.

2. Bendroth, *The Spiritual Practice of Remembering*, 6.

history of Christianity in general. In Part Two, we will focus more specifically on contemporary appropriation of Reformation tradition(s). We will think together about some of the topics frequently discussed during the 500th anniversary year of the Reformation, particularly those topics being discussed among Protestants.

SHOULD WE PUT THE PAST BEHIND US? CHRISTIANITY AND HISTORY

Some, perhaps most, of what is said here will constitute a form of stating the obvious, or perhaps making explicit and conscious that which might otherwise remain implicit or unconscious. Thus, there might not be anything "new" here, but there will be, I suggest, matters important to bear in mind if we are to think wisely about the Protestant Reformations in our contemporary contexts of both church and world.

Christianity is Radically Historical

Christianity is radically historical. The inclusion of the adjective "radical" may seem a bit odd. It is included to underscore how fundamental, how important—and too often underestimated—this fact is. Christianity is radically historical. But what is meant by this? While there are many potential angles of approach, four will be identified here.

"The Beginning"

The conditions and raw material for history came into existence "in the beginning," with God's creative origination of all things celebrated in the opening chapter of the Bible. Christians believe that God made all that is, invisible and visible, spirit and matter. He made all creatures, great and small. He made human beings in His image. And, He made human beings as embodied persons who live in space and time, which He also created. All that flows from this, from "the beginning," unfolds, at least for creatures, in space and time. In history.

The Gospel

The heart of Christian proclamation and life is the gospel. And, the gospel is, in both substance and form, historical. Human beings fell into sin in space and time. The good news of the gospel is that God responded, and continued to respond, by acting redemptively in space and time. God the

Father sent His Son to live, die, rise, and ascend in space and time. In 1 Cor 15, the apostle Paul takes pains to remind us that if this has not actually happened—if these are not actual historical events—then those who entrust themselves to Jesus Christ are people who are most to be pitied, exercising faith in vain and futility. However, faith in Christ is not in vain or futile. The culmination of history under the lordship of Christ will take place in history. Jesus will come again, bodily, to space-time earth, and, according to the New Testament, in ways beyond our complete comprehension now, He will assert and manifest His Lordship in the realm of space and time and history in which we live.[3] The gospel is historical.

The Church

The church exists in history and has a history. This is not to deny that as a spiritual reality the church also transcends history; rather, in keeping with present purposes this is simply to underscore that the church also, and inescapably, exists in history. People who today count themselves blessed to be members of the Body of Christ *follow* millions upon millions of others, other members of the Body of Christ, who have lived across the centuries in the same space-time continuum in which we today live and breathe. The church exists in history and has a history.

The Lives of Christians

Correspondingly, the Christian life is lived-out within history. Again, as with the church, this is not to deny the transcendent dimensions of our lives but simply for present purposes to unambiguously state that we live out our lives on the stage of history, the stage of God's creation.

Christians ought to be this-worldly people. Christians ought not be *only* this-worldly people. The lives of Christians in this world ought always be grounded in and framed by our knowledge of and worship of the transcendent triune God. However, among the most egregious critiques that can be made of Christians—and all the more egregious when Christians provide bases for the critique—is that they are so heavenly minded that they are no earthly good. And, one of the best deterrents to thinking and living in ways that provide grounds for this critique is to never forget that

---

3. I am not here asserting one particular eschatological vision, nor am I presuming to engage the question as to whether or not time itself will be a dimension of eschatological reality. Whatever one's thoughts are on these matters, the basic point being made here holds.

the lives of Christians—"the Christian life"—is a this-worldly life. Christianity is radically historical.

History Is a Realm of Divine Action[4]

History is a realm of divine action. Whether or not one thinks that "Redemption history" is synonymous with "history," Christians believe that God is at work in and through history. Whether one is Pentecostal with a strong sense of the immanence of God or a Presbyterian with a pervasive awareness of the transcendence of God, a Christian view of history is a view of history under the sovereign, engaged lordship of the triune God. Modernity had the effect of largely removing God from the realm of history. But authentic Christianity affirms that the Creator is also the Sustainer, that the God of Genesis is also the God of Revelation, and of every moment in between. Thus, history is not merely the domain of human, creaturely activity but the space in which God's providential care and preservation—indeed, ultimately, his will—is carried out.[5]

This belief in divine action in history includes the work of God in and through His church, and this work is of particular significance for retrieval. In uniquely redemptive ways, the church's history is the realm of divine operation. This is not a baptism with approval of all developments, of all theology, of all actions in every chapter of the church's history; it is not a denial of missteps, error, and sin. It is, however, a belief that the church, the Body of Christ, is birthed, knit-together, sustained, equipped and empowered by the Spirit, in spite of human frailties and sin. History—not least, the history of the church—is a realm of divine action. And, because of this there is good reason to think that looking back can be of value for moving forward.

This affirmation of history as a realm of divine action is not without an affirmation of transcendence. God's actions within history are conjoined with his existence beyond and freedom from time and space. However, this transcendent perspective is of significance in part because of the immanental claims that accompany it. We believe that *history, our history, our time and space* is an arena of divine activity. So, what observations can we make about the *structure* of divine activity in this realm, in this time-and-space that we call "history"? Within the time and space allotted here, I will highlight one.

---

4. Also see Buschart and Eilers, *Theology as Retrieval*, 22–24 and 30–31.

5. For a recent survey and analysis of Christian views of history, see Green, *Christian Historiography*.

History Is Always Characterized by Both Continuity and Change

History is always characterized by *both* continuity and change.[6] There has been one and only one transition in or development of reality marked by pure change: "the beginning." Creation *ex nihilo* was a unique event (or events), the only one of its kind. And, part of its uniqueness consists in the fact that it can be said to be characterized by pure change, with no continuity. There is, of course, one continuity which transcends the change that was creation *ex nihilo*: that continuity consists in the fact that God was, and was unchanged, both "before" and "after" creation *ex nihilo*. In this sense, and an important sense it is, there was continuity even in creation *ex nihilo*. However, the point here is that, apart from God's continuity before, during and since the creation event(s), creation *ex nihilo* was in every other respect the only instance of pure change. Since creation *ex nihilo*, all of history in both its macro and micro incarnations is characterized by both continuity and change. All of history—including the history of the church and Christianity—is characterized by both continuity and change.

The assertion that the advance of history—whether one is describing nations or churches, and their doctrines—is characterized by both change and continuity is not capable of precisely quantifiable verification or, for that matter, rejection. However, if we pause to consider the suggestion, it will intuitively, experientially appear to be in fact the case.

History is always characterized by *both* continuity *and* change

	"revolution" "break-through" "transformation"		"stability" "equilibrium" "permanence"	
Pure Change		*Both – change – and – continuity*		**Pure Continuity**
●━━●				
Creation *ex nihilo*				Absolute stasis

Consider for the moment a spectrum with pure change (e.g., creation *ex nihilo* or creation *de novo*) at one end and pure continuity—complete stasis

---

6. While he is not the only scholar to observe this dimension of history in relationship to the history of Christianity, I am indebted to the work of Jaroslav Pelikan for first impressing this fact upon my theological and historical consciousness. It is a fact which is not often enough kept in view. See, for example, Pelikan, *Development of Christian Doctrine*; Pelikan, *Historical Theology*; and Pelikan, *The Mystery of Continuity*.

with no change whatsoever—at the other end. Every other point along the spectrum consists of some combination of continuity and change. When, comparatively speaking, an event or development is characterized by a higher degree of *change* and lower degree of continuity, we use words like "revolution" or "break-through" or "transformation" to describe it. When, comparatively speaking, there is a higher degree of *continuity* and lower degree of change, we use words like "stability" or "equilibrium" or even "permanence" to describe the state of affairs.

It would be possible to rehearse a wide-range of nuanced terms to further portray the range of points along this spectrum between pure change and pure continuity. However, that level of precision or detail is not needed in order to grasp the simple and basic, but frequently neglected, fact: the entire progress of history, on both macro- and micro-levels consists in a combination, a mixture, of both continuity and change. And all the while, God is, as He has been and will be, Creator, Sustainer, and Redeemer.

The Phenomena of Traditions of Christianity

As the conclusion of Part One approaches, we will begin to turn from more general considerations of history to a particular form of historical phenomena, namely traditions of Christianity as these traditions exist in and across time.

BOTH CHANGE AND CONTINUITY

The observations just made regarding history as consisting in a combination of continuity and change applies to the realm of traditions of Christianity, just as it does to other historical phenomena. Traditions change. If there were literally no change in, for example, the Reformed-Calvinist tradition, people like Oliver Crisp would not be writing—and other people would not be reading—books like Crisp's *Deviant Calvinism* and *Saving Calvinism*.[7] Calvinists would simply continue to read Calvin's *Institutes of the Christian Religion* only—with *only* being the key word here—and they would continue to order their services after the Genevan book of worship only—again, with *only* being the key word here. Or, J. Denny Weaver would not likely have written *Anabaptist Theology in Face of Postmodernity*,[8] and he and other Mennonite Christians would simply continue to read and

---

7. Crisp, *Deviant Calvinism* and Crisp, *Saving Calvinism*.
8. Weaver, *Anabaptist Theology in Face of Postmodernity*.

read only Balthasar Hubmaier's *A Christian Catechism* or Menno Simons' *Foundation of Christian Doctrine*. The fact is that having listened to Calvin and others, people like Oliver Crisp help us think about Reformed Christian faith with particular attention to our contemporary context, as Denny Weaver does via Mennonite thought. Traditions change.

At the same time, there is continuity in traditions. That is at the heart of what constitutes them as traditions—a handing-on of that which has been received. This is not always a literal, verbatim repetition (though sometimes it is), but there is enough continuity, enough similarity, enough likeness that we use words like "tradition" to describe the *abiding legacy* of Martin Luther or John Calvin or Menno Simons. Traditions consist in both change and continuity.

The Chorus, Not Just the Soloists

The historian of Christian doctrine Jaroslav Pelikan wisely suggests that we need to "concentrate on the chorus rather than on the soloists."[9] We may cultivate a distorted, incomplete and inaccurate understanding of history if we focus too narrowly on only a very few select figures. This is true of both attempts to study the church catholic as well as efforts to rightly understand specific traditions of Christianity. By all means, listen to Luther and Calvin and Simons and Cranmer, listen to Thomas Aquinas and Karl Barth, to John Wesley and Dietrich Bonhoeffer. But never do so in a de-contextualized way; and here the "context" in question is the larger Christian tradition and the larger theological traditions in which figures such as Luther and Wesley and Barth stand. Listen to them, but do not let them prevent you from hearing the chorus, from hearing the choirs.[10]

History, Especially Early

There are at least two dimensions of any tradition of Christianity that one must study if one is going to truly understand, if one is going to "get inside," a tradition.[11] The first of these two dimensions is history, the history of the

---

9. Pelikan articulates this value and this principle in both the first and last volumes of his five-volume *The Christian Tradition*, 1:122 and 5:6, 7.

10. For a varied sampling of scholars employing this principle, see for example Pelikan, *The Christian Tradition*; Sanders, *The Deep Things of God*; and García and Nunes, *Wittenberg Meets the World*.

11. For further discussion of these two dimensions and for examples of their application to a variety of traditions of Protestant Christianity, see Buschart, *Exploring Protestant Traditions*.

tradition. And, one ought to give particular attention to the founding and earliest chapters of this history. There is usually a particular "DNA" that becomes embedded early in the development of traditions; and, recalling my comments a few moments ago about continuity, in the case of traditions of Christianity that "DNA" usually informs the shape and substance of the tradition for centuries. Thus, while one must not overlook the distinctively contemporary expressions of, for example, Lutheranism, part of what renders it an expression of Lutheranism is certain affinities with, for example, Luther, Melanchthon, and other contributors to *The Book of Concord*. Anyone acquainted with the history of Lutheranism is keenly aware of the many differences and divergences within Lutheranism (even differences between, for example, Luther and Melanchthon). However, when one reads Robert Jenson's *Systematic Theology* or Robert Kolb and Charles Arand's *The Genius of Luther's Theology: A Wittenberg Way of Thinking for the Contemporary Church*, one encounters traces of the DNA of first- and second-generation Lutherans.[12]

Theological Method, Including the Interpretation of Scripture

In addition to the history of a tradition, particularly the early history, a second dimension which must be in some measure understood if one is to "get inside" a tradition is the theological method or principles, including the principles for interpreting the Bible, that are employed. *How* one goes about pursuing theological understanding has quite a bit to do with *what* one concludes. And, of particular, though not exclusive, significance in this regard are the approach to and the principle of interpretation applied to the book of Christianity, the Bible.

Combining these two observations, I suggest the following: once one has an understanding of the history of a tradition of Christianity, particularly the earliest history, and has a basic grasp of the theological method and the biblical hermeneutic which predominates in that tradition, one can likely discern quite a bit about the *internal logic* of the tradition. The term *internal logic* is here not an evaluative term but a descriptive one. This "internal logic" may be right or wrong. Outside observers may or may not (in perhaps most cases, not) agree with it. It may or may not always be consciously employed by those within the tradition. However, the outcomes, the characteristic or distinctive beliefs of traditions of Christianity, are

---

12. Jenson, *Systematic Theology*; and Kolb and Arand, *The Genius of Luther's Theology*.

generally *congruent—and in this sense, "logical"—with* the *history* and the *theological method* which predominates in each tradition.

Conclusion to Part One

In light of what has been said thus far, the response to the question posed in the title of this chapter—"Should we put the past behind us?"—is, in a word, *No*. We should not put the past behind us. Indeed, we cannot do so, and so seeking to do so is both naïve and, at the very least, counterproductive. However, our conversations will not grow thicker simply by declaring the importance and value of history, or by attempting to relive or replicate the past *verbatim*. Rather, we must *retrieve*. That is, we must look back, discerningly. Then, having learned from the past, Christians must be shrewd servants and stewards of "the faith once delivered" (Jude 1:3) by incarnating faithful thought and life today . . . in our time, in our place.[13]

And in this regard, there are numerous signs of hope. To adopt Margaret Bendroth's terminology, there are Christians who are creating *"thicker"—historically shaped and filled—*readings of scripture and spirituality, thicker theology and corporate worship, thicker community and engagement with culture. And, these thicker, deeper, and, Lord willing, wiser expressions of Christian faith are being realized by reclaiming the "past tense." It is to this practice of retrieval, specifically retrieval within Protestant Christianity and retrieval from the Reformations of the sixteenth century, to which we now turn.

PROTESTANT CHRISTIANITY AND REFORMATION TRADITIONS TODAY

As we now narrow our focus more particularly to Protestantism, and more specifically still to the Reformations of the sixteenth century, we will here offer an approach to Protestant and Reformation traditions today that is in keeping—sometimes explicitly, sometimes implicitly—with the observations and principles set forth thus far. We will begin with the last word in the title of this second part of the chapter: *today*.

---

13. On receiving and transmitting "the deposit of faith," see Buschart and Eilers, *Theology as Retrieval*, 15–22.

The Reformation
"Today"

"Today" Changes from Era to Era

Anniversary celebrations of historic events always reflect their context, the historical circumstances in which the celebration takes place. And, the celebrations of and scholarly reflections on 1517 and subsequent Reformation developments are no exception. From the topics that celebrants and scholars choose to note and study (and choose not to note or study) to the methods and angles-of-approach taken in the celebrations and examinations, someone looking back at the Reformation events of 2017 from the perspective of history-yet-to-come will likely discern, in the way that we are engaging 1517, characteristics distinctive of this place and time.

Such contextual shaping is not in principle wrong. Indeed, in keeping with the observations and suggestions made in the first part of this chapter, such contextualization occurs because we are, by God's creation-design, historically embedded creatures. So, it is important to draw attention to the fact that our Reformation reflections today will be informed by our present time and place *not* as a way of dismissing their validity or value, but simply so that we might be self-aware and wisely discern how *our approach to* the Reformations of the sixteenth century may shape what we find and retrieve, and inform the ways in which we do and do not bring the Reformation heritage to bear in our context. This dynamic can be illustrated by identifying and briefly describing just three of the contours of *today* that inform today's looking back and retrieval from the Reformation—three contours, one "global" and two North American, of the time and place *from which we look back* to the sixteenth century.[14]

Global Christianity

Few of us can go too many days without being reminded in some fashion that the centre of gravity of Christianity has shifted from the Euro-American sphere to the Global South. Interestingly, a number of observers have likened this change to the Reformation, suggesting that it is of a magnitude equal to, perhaps greater than, that of the changes that gave

---

14. The three developments identified here are by no means exhaustive in describing "today," and the brief descriptions offered here are by no means comprehensive. These particular developments are cited here because they are among those of particular relevance to the pursuit of retrieval.

birth to Protestantism in the sixteenth century.[15] The lands of European Christendom in which the traditions of Protestant Christianity originated are no longer lands of Christendom, and they are no longer the centre of gravity for mass, popular Christianity in the way they were when *previous generations of* Protestants celebrated the anniversaries of Luther's *Ninety-Five Theses*.[16] And, there appears to be an analogous decline of the broader cultural capital of Christianity in North America.

North American Christianity—Diversification

Second, the North American religious landscape has become far more diverse, some suggest to the point of fragmentation. The religious landscape has and continues to become increasingly diverse, and in diverse ways—theologically, racially, ecclesiologically, demographically, and more. There is today more, and increasing, religious diversity—or at the very minimum, the diversity is visibly, palpably more evident—in North America, and more diversity *within* Christianity and *within* Protestantism, than there was just a few decades ago.

North American Christianity—Detraditionalization

Third, in the second half of the twentieth century many local churches, educational institutions, and parachurch organizations took new steps to connect with and receive as many people as possible. Toward this end one of the steps that many took was to marginalize or retreat from denomination-specific or tradition-specific identities. One of the more common expressions this strategy is the renaming of local church congregations, such as First Baptist Church becoming Journey Fellowship or The Mission. This retreat from tradition-specific identities is a form of detraditionalization.[17] And, because these churches are Protestant, the traditions that they have set to the side are often Reformation or post-Reformation traditions. Furthermore, the effort to increase the scope of reach—that is, to connect with a wider range of people—has often been accompanied by a corresponding

---

15. Among the many students of this phenomenon, perhaps the most widely known is Philip Jenkins. For a summary of his work on this topic see Jenkins, *The Next Christendom*.

16. For an insightful study of ways that the Reformation has been remembered and celebrated see Howard, *Remembering the Reformation*.

17. For a foundational collection of studies of this cultural phenomenon see Heelas et al., eds., *Detraditionalization*.

thinning of Reformation-rooted doctrinal depth. On the surface "the math" is simple: the less that is said theologically, the more people can potentially identify and be drawn-in.

Retrieval and Sixteenth-Century Protestant Reformations

In addition to many conferences and celebrations of the Reformation, a flurry, even a blizzard, of books and other publications preceded and continues to unfold around the quincentennial anniversary year. Some of these books look back to the sixteenth century in an effort to see and understand it more fully, more truly. Others also explicitly seek to think wisely about the twenty-first century in light of the sixteenth—particularly about the state of Protestant Christianity today. The 500-year anniversary has prompted scholars to ask significant questions about the Protestant project, to look back at the path that Protestantism has taken and its current location on the landscape of Christianity and the world.

In 2015, Michael Allen and Scott Swain published *Reformed Catholicity: The Promise of Retrieval for Theology and Biblical Interpretation*.[18] While identifying the distinctively Reformed character of their own work, they identify themselves with numbers of other scholars in the assessment that "modern theology, in [both] more conservative and progressive forms, has exhausted itself as a mode of theological inquiry and that the path toward theological renewal lies in retrieving resources from the Christian tradition."[19] More specifically—and in this lies some of the distinctive character of their contributions—they believe "that classical Reformed thought, both in the era of the Reformation and beyond in the era of Reformed Orthodoxy, provides numerous *examples* of thoughtful appropriation of the catholic tradition and, moreover, that the *principles* of classical Reformed orthodox prolegomena, as well as the principles of classical Reformed ecclesiology, provide a salutary framework within which a Reformed dogmatics of retrieval might be developed."[20]

In 2016, Peter Leithart published a thought-provoking challenge to Protestants, *The End of Protestantism: Pursuing Unity in a Fragmented Church*.[21] Leithart argues for what he refers to as "an interim ecclesiology"

---

18. Allen and Swain, *Reformed Catholicity*.
19. Allen and Swain, *Reformed Catholicity*, 4 (emphasis original).
20. Allen and Swain, *Reformed Catholicity*, 13 (emphasis original).
21. Leithart, *End of Protestantism*.

under the rubric of "Reformational Catholicity."[22] In his chapter titled "A Reformed Church" he offers the following observation: "The Reformation was an effort to *restore* the visibility of a social form that had been nearly buried under what the Reformers considered the rubble of Roman error. The Reformation was a *retrieval*, not a rejection, of catholicity."[23] Leithart devotes the majority of this chapter to a consideration of sixteenth century Reformational theology and developments—both good and, for Leithart, not so good.

Shortly after, theologian Kevin Vanhoozer published *Biblical Authority after Babel: Retrieving the* Solas *in the Spirit of Mere Protestant Christianity*. In his introduction Vanhoozer writes that "the Reformation was a *retrieval*, first and foremost of the biblical gospel, particularly the Pauline articulation, but also, secondarily, of the [early] church fathers. The Reformers were engaged in theology as retrieval long before it became trendy." And a few sentences later he says, "Sometimes viewing the past from our present situation makes the past (and the present) come alive in new ways."[24] "I have written this book," reports Vanhoozer, "not to bury or even repent of the [Reformation] *solas* but rather to sing their praise."[25]

Books and quotations along this line could be multiplied many times. But, with these illustrative soundings, I will here offer the following brief observations. First, these books and others like them depict thoughtful people looking at the *contemporary* theological and ecclesiastical landscape and identifying challenges to be faced. This look at the contemporary scene prompts them to conclude that contemporary resources *alone* are not sufficient for addressing the challenges to be faced.[26] Second, having conducted this look at the present they then look to the past for wisdom—wisdom both formal (that is, related to methods) and material (that is, theological substance). Third, all three of these projects seek to advance a more catholic Protestantism. As is the case with many who employ retrieval, and not just retrieval related to the Reformation, each of them wants to develop *a broader, more inclusive* Protestantism—a Protestantism that is broader and more inclusive both historically and across ecclesio-theological traditions.

---

22. Leithart, *End of Protestantism*, 5 and 6.
23. Leithart, *End of Protestantism*, 41 (emphasis original).
24. Vanhoozer, *Biblical Authority after Babel*, 22–23 (emphasis original).
25. Vanhoozer, *Biblical Authority after Babel*, 26.
26. For more on the role of contemporary analysis in prompting retrieval, see Buschart and Eilers, *Theology as Retrieval*, 28–30.

There is a fourth observation to be made, but before turning to that it is worth noting the following. The theological modality of retrieval is *currently flourishing*. Many Christians—both scholars and practitioners—are looking back, historically, in order to move forward. Retrieval is being employed in studies and proposals for biblical hermeneutics, pastoral ministry, social justice, spirituality, corporate worship, and forms of Christian community.[27] Retrieval is being employed across the eras of the history of Christianity, from the early and medieval periods to the sixteenth century and modern eras. And, the same three phenomena observed in the works by Allen and Swain, Leithart, and Vanhoozer are evident in retrieval projects in these other arenas and time periods. *Having looked around at the contemporary scene and found it wanting and in need, Christians are turning to the past for resources for a richly historical and a theologically more catholic Protestant faith and life.*

Against this broader backdrop of the flourishing of retrieval more broadly, there is a final observation to be made about the three books identified above, an observation of particular relevance to a volume devoted to the Reformation in a post-Christian world. Each of these books—by Allen and Swain, Leithart, and Vanhoozer—is interested, to varying degrees and in different ways, in the sixteenth century Protestant Reformation and its legacy. They are not alone in this interest. For but a thimble-sized sampling, consider the following. Beginning in 2011, IVP Academic launched its ambitious 28-volume *Reformation Commentary on Scripture*, under general editor Timothy George. Numbers of publishers have published or are publishing series of books devoted to the *solas* of the Reformation.[28] Matthew Barrett edited *Reformation Theology: A Systematic Summary*.[29] In recent years Oliver Crisp, of Fuller Theological Seminary, has published books titled *Retrieving Doctrine: Essays in Reformed Theology* and *Deviant Calvinisim: Broadening Reformed Theology*.[30] A student of global Christianity, Dale Irvin edited *The Protestant Reformation and World Christianity: Global Perspectives*.[31] And, there was, of course, a near blizzard of books

---

27. For an introduction to six arenas of retrieval see Buschart and Eilers, *Theology as Retrieval*, 43–255.

28. For example, Zondervan's "The 5 Solas Series," edited by Matthew Barrett.

29. Barrett, *Reformation Theology*.

30. Crisp, *Retrieving Doctrine* and Crisp, *Deviant Calvinism*.

31. Irvin, ed., *The Protestant Reformation and World Christianity*.

about Martin Luther that were and continue to be released in the 500th anniversary year.

As observed above, retrieval—looking back in order to move forward—is currently flourishing. And, when retrieval is done well, Protestant Christianity is the richer and wiser for it. This said, there is a deficiency in some efforts at retrieval—be they retrieval from the fourth or thirteenth or sixteenth century. Where this deficiency exists, retrieval efforts focusing specifically on the Protestant Reformations and their legacies can serve as important correctives and resources.

This deficiency exists when Protestants who employ retrieval *leapfrog over* the traditions of Protestantism before seriously exploring them, and become enamored, perhaps even in a proprietary way, with, for example, Orthodox or Catholic traditions. One cannot but help in this regard to paraphrase and apply G. K. Chesterton's observation about Christianity in general, namely, that it is not the case that it has been tried and found wanting but that it has been found difficult and not genuinely tried. Tom Schwanda, an astute student of Christian spirituality, reports that in the course of his study of spirituality and interaction with fellow Protestants, many of them "were not interested or equipped to search for the treasures of their respective Protestant tradition."[32] It is very important here to stress that this is *not* a suggestion that Protestants should not engage in appreciative inquiry into and learning from Orthodoxy and Catholicism. Rather, these observations are focused on and limited to the specific topic of consideration in view: retrieval from Protestant reformations of the sixteenth century. The caution being noted here is *not* to isolate oneself from Orthodox or Catholic traditions of Christianity, but rather, as Schwanda encourages, to not overlook or bypass the traditions of Protestant Christianity when exploring other traditions of Christianity. Perhaps the essays gathered in this volume can provide just a whetting of the appetite to mine the treasures of Reformation traditions.

CONCLUSION:
OUR POSTURE AND THE GIFTS OF RETRIEVAL

The posture of retrieval can be a bit awkward. (Think about it physically, bodily . . . looking backward as you walk forward.) So, it is important to describe both the posture that is needed for retrieval to be of benefit and

---

32. Schwanda, *Soul Recreation*, xv. Also see Buschart and Eilers, *Theology as Retrieval*, 161–62.

to describe some of the gifts that potentially can be ours as we take a fresh look for today at the Protestant Reformations of the sixteenth century. Doing retrieval well entails having one's eyes and ears, one's heart and mind, open to the possibility that one or more of these gifts of retrieval may be realized. And, note that these gifts are not mutually exclusive of each other. A single endeavor of retrieval, well done, may realize in some measure several of these gifts.

Correction

People both within and beyond our churches are looking for signs of humility on the part of Christians. Looking back can result in the *correction* of beliefs and practices currently held. Retrieval requires humility and openness, and correction is one of the places where that rubber meets the road. One of the prominent themes in current engagements with the sixteenth century is catholicity. Protestants are, rightly, asking themselves how we ought to think about and respond to the divisions (and diversity) that exist within Protestantism.[33] A number of the books already discussed here, for example those by Leithart and Vanhoozer, are committed to wrestling with this continuing challenge for Protestant Christianity.

Another example, with a more narrow focus, is the recent book by W. David O. Taylor, *The Theater of God's Glory: Calvin, Creation, and the Liturgical Arts*. In this book, Taylor examines "Calvin's Trinitarian theology as it intersects his theology of materiality in order to argue for a positive theological account of the liturgical arts."[34] In the process Taylor *reads* Calvin deeply and carefully, and learns from him; *and* at various points Taylor modifies or rejects Calvin's thought; *and* in the process of this, he corrects what he views as misunderstandings and misconstruals of Calvin's theology of physicality and the material, minconstruals by readers of Calvin from both outside and within the Reformed tradition.

Adapting the wisdom of Prov 27:6, one can say that in retrieval there is the opportunity for corrective humbling brought about by "the wounds of a friend." When correction takes place individuals and communities move forward with a fuller measure of God's truth and wisdom.

---

33. Not all differences, including theological and ecclesiastical, are best described as "divisions." A cultural context in which "diversity" is so highly prized needs to be discerning in this regard.

34. Taylor, *The Theater of God's Glory*, 5.

Reaffirmation

Looking back can result in a *reaffirmation* of beliefs already held and practices already employed. Retrieval will be corrupted and corrupting if the sole agenda is correction, if the only reason for looking back is in order to "set the present straight." In addition to correction retrieval can give the gift of reaffirmation. When this occurs there is a deepening of conviction, a new measure of confidence. When reaffirmation is realized, individuals and communities move forward with greater confidence in the beliefs and practices that they embody. Thus, there are Lutherans who entered the year 2018 more appreciative of their Lutheran heritage as a result of the celebrations of 2017. And for members of other Protestant traditions for whom the "Year of the Reformation" provided an occasion to revisit their own sixteenth-century roots—be they Anglican or Anabaptist or Presbyterian—perhaps some of them entered 2018 as more appreciative Anglicans or Anabaptists or Presbyterians.

Reimagining

Reimagining entails elements of both correction and reaffirmation, but is distinctive and merits its own acknowledgment. Alberto García and John Nunes employ this term and the posture indicated by it in their book *Wittenberg Meets the World: Reimagining the Reformation at the Margins*. They describe themselves as "dually situated," being both "rooted deliberately in a Lutheran tradition" and "in postcolonial critique."[35] Their work is, as a result, a "reimagining" of Lutheran Christianity with a view toward seeing not primarily Martin Luther but "Christ alone, the *solus Christus*, incarnationally present" not in the sixteenth century but "in this time and place."[36]

Enrichment

Looking back can result in the *enrichment* of current beliefs and practices. This can be a companion to correction, reaffirmation or reimagining. There is a developmental dimension in enrichment, a deepening or, recalling our opening quotation of Margaret Bendroth, a thickening of beliefs and practices. When enrichment occurs individuals and communities move forward with *more*—more depth, more breadth, more of the richness of the Christian tradition being handed on to those who follow us.

---

35. García and Nunes, *Wittenberg Meets the World*, xiv.
36. García and Nunes, *Wittenberg Meets the World*, xvii.

The Reformation

Reconciliation

Looking back can result in a measure of *reconciliation*. As has been noted several times, retrieval is often accompanied by a greater catholicity, a kind of ecumenical spirit. Sometimes the pursuit of greater catholicity is a prompt to retrieval, and sometimes it is an unanticipated benefit. Those who look back often include in their field of vision beliefs and practices outside of their own tradition. They are becoming acquainted with streams of Christianity in which they do not usually swim. And, while this broader gaze must be taken in with appropriate discernment, every time we find a treasure from ground outside of our own tradition we are blessed with a new opportunity to celebrate the oneness of the body of Christ, the oneness shared by everyone who is reconciled to God in Christ. When even a small token of commonality is unearthed, individuals and communities can move forward in an enlarged company of Christ-followers.

In this regard you may wish to take a look at the *Reforming Catholic Confession*, issued with the commemoration of the Reformation in view, and accompanied by a thoughtful historical and theological essay.[37] Though not an attempt to unite Protestant Christianity with Orthodox and Catholic churches, it is a robust theological confession collaboratively written by Protestants from a diverse range of confessional traditions—Lutheran and Baptist, Anglican and Pentecostal, Presbyterian and Methodist—and offered as a positive theological statement of catholic Protestant beliefs. In the accompanying essay the authors write the following:

> That Protestants are divided is . . . obvious and, given our Lord's prayer for unity ("that they may be one"—John 17:11), even more grievous. While we regret the divisions that have followed in its wake, we acknowledge the need for the sixteenth-century Reformation, even as we recognize the hopeful possibilities of the present twenty-first century moment. . . . We dare hope that the unity to which the Reformers aspired may be increasingly realized as today's "mere" Protestants, like Richard Baxter's and C. S. Lewis's "mere Christians," joyfully join together to bear united witness to the gospel of Jesus Christ and to its length, depth, breadth, and width—in a word, its catholicity. We therefore aim to celebrate the catholic impulse that lies at the heart of the earlier Reformation

---

37. For complete text of both the confession and the historical-theological essay, see "Explanation: A Historical and Theological Perspective," n.p.

even as we hope and pray for ever greater displays of our substantial unity in years to come.[38]

As the authors and signatories recognized, the *Reforming Catholic Confession* is not the last word. And there are, of course, Protestants who do not wish to sign because it is not adequately expressive of their beliefs. Nonetheless, perhaps the confession—and equally important, the spirit in which it was created and offered—can be a constructive example of *both* an appreciative reaffirmation of the sixteenth century Reformation *and* a pointer toward greater Protestant catholicity. May the conversation, both past and present, continue. And, in response to any good gifts that are received by way of retrieval, may we say what we say in response to any good gift, *Thanks be to God.*

BIBLIOGRAPHY

Allen, Michael, and Scott Swain. *Reformed Catholicity: The Promise of Retrieval for Theology and Biblical Interpretation*. Grand Rapids: Baker, 2015.

Barrett, Matthew. *Reformation Theology: A Systematic Summary*. Wheaton, IL: Crossway, 2017.

Bendroth, Margaret. *The Spiritual Practice of Remembering*. Grand Rapids: Eerdmans, 2013.

Buschart, W. David. *Exploring Protestant Traditions: An Invitation to Theological Hospitality*. Downers Grove, IL: IVP, 2006.

Buschart, W. David, and Kent D. Eilers. *Theology as Retrieval: Receiving the Past and Renewing the Church*. Downers Grove, IL: IVP, 2015.

Crisp, Oliver. *Deviant Calvinism: Broadening Reformed Theology*. Minneapolis: Fortress, 2014.

———. *Retrieving Doctrine: Essays in Reformed Theology*. Downers Grove, IL: IVP, 2010.

———. *Saving Calvinism: Expanding the Reformed Tradition*. Downers Grove, IL: IVP, 2016.

García, Alberto L., and John A. Nunes. *Wittenberg Meets the World: Reimagining the Reformation at the Margins*. Grand Rapids: Eerdmans, 2017.

Green, Jay D. *Christian Historiography: Five Rival Views*. Waco, TX: Baylor University Press, 2015.

Heelas, Paul, et al., eds. *Detraditionalization*. Malden, MA: Wiley-Blackwell, 1996.

Howard, Thomas Albert. *Remembering the Reformation: An Inquiry into the Meanings of Protestantism*. Oxford: Oxford University Press, 2016.

Irvin, Dale T., ed. *The Protestant Reformation and World Christianity*. Grand Rapids: Eerdmans, 2017.

Jenkins, Philip. *The Next Christendom: The Coming of Global Christianity*. 3rd ed. Oxford: Oxford University Press, 2011.

Jenson, Robert W. *Systematic Theology*. 2 Vols. Oxford: Oxford University Press, 1997–1999.

---

38. "Explanation: A Historical and Theological Perspective," n.p.

Kolb, Robert, and Charles P. Arand. *The Genius of Luther's Theology: A Wittenberg Way of Thinking for the Contemporary Church*. Grand Rapids: Baker, 2008.

Leithart, Peter. *The End of Protestantism: Pursuing Unity in a Fragmented Church*. Grand Rapids: Brazos, 2016.

Pelikan, Jaroslav. *The Christian Tradition: A History of the Development of Doctrine*. 5 vols. Chicago: University of Chicago Press, 1971–1989.

———. *Development of Christian Doctrine: Some Historical Prolegomena*. New Haven, CT: Yale University Press, 1969.

———. *Historical Theology: Continuity and Change in Christian Doctrine*. Philadelphia: Westminster, 1971.

———. *The Mystery of Continuity: Time and History, Memory and Eternity in the Thought of Saint Augustine*. Charlottesville: University Press of Virginia, 1986.

Reforming Catholic Confession. "Explanation: A Historical and Theological Perspective." *Reforming Catholic Confession*, 2017. Online: https://reformingcatholicconfession.com/explanation/

Sanders, Fred. *The Deep Things of God: How the Trinity Changes Everything*. 2nd ed. Wheaton, IL: Crossway, 2017.

Schwanda, Tom. *Soul Recreation: The Contemplative-Mystical Piety of Puritanism*. Eugene, OR: Pickwick, 2012.

Taylor, W. David O. *The Theater of God's Glory: Calvin, Creation, and the Liturgical Arts*. Grand Rapids: Eerdmans, 2017.

Vanhoozer, Kevin J. *Biblical Authority after Babel: Retrieving the Solas in the Spirit of Mere Protestant Christianity*. Grand Rapids: Brazos, 2016.

Weaver, J. Denny. *Anabaptist Theology in Face of Postmodernity*. Telford, PA: Pandora, 2000.

8

More "Unintended Consequences"

How the Reformation (Mis)Shaped the Church for Mission in North America

David Fitch

MUCH HAS BEEN MADE in recent years of the "unintended consequences" of the Reformation. I speak of course of Brad Gregory's writing on the "unintended consequences of the Reformation," which describes how the Reformation led to a rampant pluralism in the interpretation of scripture, consumer capitalism, and even secularism. Gregory describes all of this as the "unintended reformation" in a book with those words as its title.[1] In a similar vein, Charles Taylor argues (among other things) that the Reformation's rejection of sacramentalism led to an evacuation of the presence of the sacred in the world resulting in the beginnings of a modern naturalism.[2] John Milbank and a host of others blame the Reformation for its alignment with the nominalism of Duns Scotus and the metaphysics of Univocity of Being.[3] Hence we now have the privatization of the sacred and the sociological world has been left to nature, and human life to sheer autonomy and the exercise of power. Scholars as diverse as Peter Leithart

---

1. Gregory, *Unintended Reformation*.

2. This is just one of the themes Charles Taylor is narrating in his magnus opus *A Secular Age*. On this theme, see pp. 72–80.

3. See John Milbank's summary of this issue in his preface to *Theology and Social Theory*, xxiv–xxvi. For an overview and defense of the Radical Orthodoxy view on Duns Scotus, see Pickstock, "Duns Scotus," 543–74.

and Ephraim Radner attribute certain divisions, antagonisms, and the excesses of denominationalism in today's church to the miscalculations of the Reformation.[4] All of these accounts have been much disputed. But, on its 500-year anniversary, I would like to throw in (or pile on) yet one more "unintended consequence" of the Reformation: I want to explore how the Reformation, once transported overseas to North America, specifically Canada and the United States, malformed the Protestant church for mission in North America.

The Reformation dominated the shaping of church life and culture in the United States and Canada once it arrived on its shores four centuries ago. Acknowledging the presence of Roman Catholicism in Quebec, Mexico and elsewhere, and the Church of England in many eastern parts of the Canada and the United States, Reformed Protestantism has still shaped large parts of Christianity in North America via the Puritans, the Presbyterians, the Lutherans, the Wesleyans, the Dutch Calvinists and others. I want to suggest that this theology of the Reformation, once transported across the ocean, left the churches most influenced by it lacking in an ecclesiology with which to engage a post-Christianized North America just a few centuries later. Reformation theology, which once worked so well given the backdrop of Medieval Euro Roman Catholicism, would later fail to sustain an ecclesiology in Canada and the United States sufficient to weather the storms of its post-Christianization. The seeds of current day North American Protestantism's failure in mission, in other words, were sown in the Reformed theology from four hundred years ago.

As a result, this chapter suggests the future of the church in mission in North America—a continent in various phases of being de-Christianized—is not more Reformed theology. Instead it is in the drawing on the wisdom, theology, and ecclesiology of the Radical Reformation and what some now name the Neo-Anabaptist stream of theology. This stream can offer the North American church resources for an ecclesiology that can flourish in its exilic existence via the birthing of communities that witness to the gospel amidst the shifting turf of post-Christendom.

BONHOEFFER'S OBSERVATION

Famed German Lutheran theologian Dietrich Bonhoeffer once described the church in the United States as "Protestantism Without the

---

4. See Radner, *A Brutal Unity* and Leithart, *End of Protestantism*.

Reformation," in an essay entitled as such.[5] In this piece, he argued that Protestantism, in coming to America, a land devoid of the cultural habits of Catholic Christendom, had (mal)formed into a church of the individual. Devoid of the state-church synthesis, no longer tied to reforming the "one true church" and without the backdrop of a singular creedal confession, the Reformation church in essence would lose its original reason for being. With the Reformation having landed across the ocean, each Christian had the freedom to choose his or her church, or to even reject church, and the ability to believe whatever he/she chose to believe. There no longer existed a theological social foundation for engaging and/or resisting the culture. And so, in Canada and the United States, the movement that we call the Reformation would be tested as to whether it had the theology sufficient to form a church that could impact the world, not merely appeal to it.

Bonhoeffer himself was limited in his own theological options at the time. The essay itself reflects that Bonhoeffer was comfortable within the state church alignments in Europe; and we know how fraught with problems this form of church would be in just a few short years in Germany. In addition, Bonhoeffer did not approve of the historical Anabaptists, sometimes speaking of them as enthusiasts and anarchists.[6] But in writing *Life Together*, or in starting the Fincklewalde seminary in response to the Deutsche Christen movement, people like myself (and Stanley Hauerwas[7] and Mark Theissen Nation[8]) see in Bonhoeffer his own leaning toward some very Anabaptist themes in the face of the Reformation church's failure to face Nazism in Germany.

In keeping then with Bonhoeffer's caricature of the American church as "Protestantism without the Reformation," I want to outline three examples of Reformed theology that worked in Europe 500 years ago but, when left without the background of the Catholic church to reform, backfired here in Canada and United States. Three malformations then emerged from these theologies, leaving us incapable of engaging a post-Christianized society. After outlining each malformations, I offer a few comments as to

---

5. This was the title of a piece he wrote after his first visit to the United States in 1930. See Bonhoeffer, *No Rusty Swords*, 92–118.

6. DeYonge, *Bonhoeffer's Reception of Luther*, 159–60.

7. Hauerwas, *Performing the Faith*.

8. Nation et al., *Bonhoeffer the Assassin?*

how the Neo-Anabaptist theological stream offers some resources to move forward.[9]

THE VISIBLE/INVISIBLE CHURCH DISTINCTION: THE MALFORMATION OF AN INVISIBLE CHURCH

The Reformation placed a new emphasis on the distinction between the visible/invisible church. This solved one problem for the Reformation—how can I be a Christian when excommunicated from the one 'corrupt' institutional church? But 500 years later, now transported overseas, this distinction has created a new problem because it presents the conditions for allows a lack of a visible social witness amidst a post-Christianized culture.

The Reformation cannot be blamed entirely for the origin of the visible/invisible church. Augustine in *City of God*, famously said, "there are many sheep without and many wolves within." He makes a distinction between the true body of Christ, which consists of the elect children of God from the beginning, and the mixed body of Christ, which comprehends all the baptized.[10] Yet Augustine never actually used the "visible-invisible church" distinction. Rather it *was the Reformation, in particular Luther, Zwingli, Wycliffe, and even Calvin who put forth this distinction as a necessary development within the Reformation.*[11]

One hundred years after the Reformation, the influential *Westminster Confession of Faith* stated: "The Church, which is *invisible*, consists of the whole number of the elect.... The *visible* Church, (which is... not confined to one nation, as before under the law), consists of all those throughout the world that profess the true religion and of their children." In this confession, the visible church of Christ has been given the ministry, oracles, and

---

9. I use the term Neo-Anabaptist to refer to the numerous writings that follow Hauerwas, Yoder, and other Anabaptist writers, who work out of the streams of post-liberalism, post structuralism, post-linguistic turn, and otherwise post-Enlightenment understandings of culture, epistemology, and language. I see within these writers the influence of historic Anabaptism. By using this term, I also hope to include historic Anabaptist influences, but see the extension of many of the historic Anabaptist themes into current socio-cultural and philosophical discussions as most promising.

10. As cited by Schaff, *History of the Christian Church*, 8:457.

11. Wycliffe used the distinction in order to critique the hierarchy. With Wycliffe, "visible" carried the connotations of "ostentatious" and "fleshly." The earliest use of the terminology itself is in Zwingli around 1530. Leithart on this in his "Augustine on 'Visible-Invisible Church.'" Brad Gregory states Luther originated this idea apart from Wycliffe, Zwingli, etc. See Gregory, *Rebel in the Ranks*, 67.

ordinances of God, for the gathering and perfecting of the saints. And then there is the additional qualifier to the visible churches of purity: "The purest Churches under heaven are subject both to mixture and error; and some have so degenerated, as to become no Churches of Christ, but synagogues of Satan."[12]

In confessions like Westminster, the reformers wanted to communicate that there may be false Christians within the church and many true Christians outside of the church. Indeed, in the early versions of Westminster, the Pope was called the Antichrist and identified as an example of a false Christian in the *visible* church.[13] Westminster identified the Protestants excommunicated by Rome during the Reformation as "true Christians" that were not part of the only *visible* church at that time and place.

In this way, the push for visible/invisible church distinction served the Reformers as a corrective to the Roman doctrine of the Middle Ages (from Cyprian): *Extra ecclesiam nulla salus* (No salvation outside the church). Instead of the church as the only way to salvation, Luther asserted *Sola Christus*, salvation is through Jesus only. In Luther's words "What I am telling you is that it is easier for us humans to believe and trust in everything else other than in the name of Christ, who alone is all in all, and more difficult for us to rely on him in whom and through whom we possess all things."[14] According to Luther, the Roman Catholic Church had clouded the gospel by adding assistants and helpers into the mix of a person's salvation. Rome preached a gospel of "*Jesus and* . . . ": Jesus and Mary, Jesus and purgatory, Jesus and the saints, Jesus and works of charity. Luther and the Reformers cleared the fog by ridding the church of these helpers of salvation. *Sola Christus*!

But, hearkening to Bonhoeffer, the invisible/visible church distinction is fine when the backdrop of the Reformation is one monolithic Christianized culture out of which the church is established. Here the Reformed distinction of the visible/invisible church may now make it possible to call people who have become comfortable in their status as a member of the church and culture to a more faithful discipleship. But separated from this Christianized culture, it has the reverse effect when it moves overseas. It now makes it possible to be a Christian without the church. Five hundred years later in the multi-plural and the divided world of the secularized West

---

12. *Westminster Confession of Faith*, XXV.VI.I–II.
13. *Westminster Confession of Faith*, XXV.VI.
14. Luther, *The Complete Sermons of Martin Luther*, 79.

of the twenty-first century, this malforms the church for witness in at least two ways.

First, we no longer have a visible way of life by which our witness to the world can be located and seen by a watching world. By de-emphasizing the participation in the body politic of the church as the definer of being a Christian, we lose the social reality of the church as witness. In a post-Christianized, secular and a pluralized world, we cannot argue our way to witness. There is no single rationality.[15] The gospel therefore must be displayed in a compelling way of life through visible social bodies in order for there to be witness. In Stanley Hauerwas's words, "The gospel is . . . a seeing of a communion between people the world cannot otherwise know."[16] The malformation of the invisible/visible church distinction therefore leaves us without witness in a post-Christianized society.

Second, without the church as a viable social body we no longer have a way of life in which our language can make sense in the pluralist post-Christianized parts of North America. Truth, in a non-hegemonous world, with no dominant cultural narrative, where meanings and language can no longer be assumed, must have a community within which the words are used, and can be made sense of. Whereas the capacity to be freed from church institution and social embodiment was a positive in the Euro-Christendom Reformation, it is now a hardship in post-Christian society, because we increasingly find ourselves in a world that no longer understands our words like "sin," "salvation," "justice," and "Jesus as Lord." And we have no social world called church from and in which to use these words and from which they can make sense to an onlooking world.

Surely this is an exaggeration. Nonetheless, I contend that the invisible/visible church distinction has injured our ability to display what words mean via a practiced way of life in a pluralist world. In the words of Hauerwas, "Protestant churches in America (who have) lost the ability to maintain the disciplines necessary to sustain a people capable of being an alternative to the world."[17] In a post-Christianized world, where we can no longer assume cultural habits sufficient to shape Christians, where the church's practices have become diminished and consumerized, we by default are

---

15. MacIntyre, *Whose Justice? Which Rationality?*

16. Hauerwas, "Beyond the Boundaries," 68. In the same vein, Anaan Baan argues that Hauerwas correlates what Wittgenstein means by "showing" to witness. *The Necessity of Witness*, 85–86.

17. Hauerwas, "The End of American Protestantism."

now individuals being formed by the practices of a post-Christianized culture. The loss of such a set of practices we call church has left us without a formation for witness. We just blend in. This I suggest is an unintended consequence of the Reformation's emphasis on the invisible/visible church distinction some five hundred years later.

The Neo-Anabaptist trajectory counters this lack. It starts with the assumption that Christians are a minority in the post Christendom world. They believe that alignment with nation-state and/or cultural power is not the way God works to redeem the world. Therefore, Christians must locate their own cultural identity and way of life in a political alternative: the church. It is church, as a visible way of life, that makes possible witness in the world to the way God works. The first task of the church, therefore, is to be the church, a contrast visible community as witness to the world.[18]

Thus, Neo-Anabaptists have traditionally focused ecclesiology on practices.[19] Practices, not separated from beliefs but in conjunction with beliefs, become the starting point for shaping a community that is formed around and in mutual submission to the presence of Christ. Contra the Reformation, which so often founded their churches on Confessions and written catechisms, the Anabaptist stream starts with practices into which we live what we believe and shape how we articulate it anew. More than a confession or belief statement, these practices form a way of life by which we reconcile conflict, read the Bible together, disciple one another, and exercise leadership within the gifted community. These include thick practices of life together such as the way we eat, share economics, discern life together, recognize leaders, and engage the world through resistance and cooperation. All of this generates a way of life that gives witness to Jesus as Lord and His victory over sin, death, and evil. This kind of ecclesiology can be a resource for reinvigorating the visible church as the foundation for witness in the new post-Christendoms of North America.

---

18. Hauerwas's famous line in this regard is "The first task of the Church is not to make the world more just but to make the world more the world." It can be found in numerous places. See his discussion of it in Hauerwas, *The Work of Theology*, 26.

19. A good example of this is John Howard Yoder's *Body Politics*. See also Fitch, *Faithful Presence*.

The Reformation

JUSTIFICATION BY FAITH ALONE: THE MALFORMATION OF A SPLIT—OR INTERIORIZED—SALVATION

The Reformation pushed the individual's justification before God to the forefront of the European consciousness. Salvation now would no longer be mediated via the Roman church by works (according to the Reformers) but directly to each believer by faith in Christ alone. This overcame the immediate problem of a corrupt church, a church which sold indulgences, but it also opened the door to malforming Christians for mission five hundred years later in North America.

Martin Luther pronounced at the first *Proceedings at Augsburg* "no one can be justified except by faith . . . through no works will you be prepared for the sacrament, but through faith alone, for only faith in the word of Christ justifies, makes a person alive, worthy and well prepared."[20] This reversed the Medieval Roman view of salvation, which was once something to be received as a reward at the end of life. Now it was received as something to begin life with Christ.[21] The Christian is now liberated from the impossibility of meeting God's standards and is free to serve God out of the abundance of grace as the overflowing expression of your faith. This is how Luther saw it.

Whether he ever meant to do this, Luther nonetheless, now in some sense, separated works and salvation. In his Galatians commentary ten years later, he clarified the difference between justification and sanctification and his metaphors for justification developed more towards the forensic direction (under the influence of Melanchthon). So now, even though Luther himself talked in much deeper terms of justification (in theosis terms), as did Calvin, the Reformation as a whole was swerving towards understanding justification in forensic terms: that by faith the believer is imputed with righteousness for the forgiveness of sins. By the time of the Formula of Concord of 1577, or the Belgic Confession written in the 1560s or the Westminster Confession of the 1600s, justification had become more narrowed to the forensic understanding and split from sanctification.

Add on to this, that Luther had already started to split the interior salvation of the soul from the transformation of the socio-political realm beginning with the German Peasants' Revolt. Historian Brad Gregory makes the case that this is where Luther reconfigured external works of the body

---

20. Luther, *The Annotated Luther*, 143.
21. This argument is made by Gregory, *Rebel in the Ranks*, 80.

away from inner workings of the soul (sanctification from justification). Here Luther overtly rejects the peasants' claim that salvation meant external change of social conditions.²² Instead, he is convinced that the gospel, faith, and salvation are not to be combined with politics, social realities, or the economy. Works of mercy result from your salvation, they don't contribute to it. And so, Luther again interiorizes salvation.²³

Luther's split is also on display in his two kingdoms theology via his writings in *On Secular Authority*.²⁴ God has ordained two governments, he outlines, the spiritual by which the Holy Spirit produces Christians and righteousness and the temporal, which restrains the wicked.²⁵ Catholic political theologian C. C. Pecknold in his book *Christianity and Politics: A Short History* narrates how this led to a radical democratization of society where this idealized, individualized, interiorized ecclesiology drives a wedge between the individual and his/her social community.²⁶ All of this, I contend, led to the conditions for a Christian malformation for mission 500 years later in North American Protestantism.

This distancing of Christ's work in the individual soul from his work in the socio-political realm took place from within the Reformation frame of the magisterial reformation. Here the Reformers had confidence in the magistrates, and their respective governing authorities, to lead the culture according to and in harmony with Christian principles and the church. But when transferred across the ocean, once the established church was done away with, a whole new series of developments were set off.

In terms articulated by Bonhoeffer, in the essay previously mentioned, "God granted American Christianity no reformation. He gave them revivalist preachers, churchman, theologians, but no reformation by the Word of God." The Protestantism that thus took shape in America "stands in

---

22. Instead, in his 1525 *On the Robbing and Murdering Hordes of Peasants*, he writes, "It is just when one must kill a mad dog; if you do not strike him, he will strike you." See *LW* 50.

23. Gregory, *Rebel in the Ranks*, 111.

24. Luther wrote *On Secular Authority* (1523) before his Galatians Commentary (1535). Here he said that "Secular government has laws that extend no further than the body, goods, and outward earthly matters . . . but where the soul is concerned, God neither can nor will allow anyone but himself to rule . . . [for] by what right does secular authority, in its folly, presume to judge a thing as secret, spiritual, hidden as faith?" See Luther and Calvin, *Luther and Calvin on Secular Authority*, 23, 25.

25. Gregory, *Rebel in the Ranks*, 93.

26. Pecknold, *Christianity and Politics*.

conscious seclusion and detachment from the general life of the church."[27] It becomes essentially a private "religion and ethics."

Whereas in Christendom medieval Europe, Christians could once lazily assume their cultural systems were Christian (even though today we see their miserable failings), once across the ocean, several hundred years later, we can assume no such thing. And with now an interiorized faith, Christians are essentially left alone to their own individual status with God, quite separate from what is happening in culture, economics, and politics. As a result, we have been able to see ourselves as souls going to heaven when we die and managing our earthly lives as best we can in the meantime. In this process, Christians become people who live pious lives in a convenient indifference to the unjust social systems as long as they are working to their own advantage.[28] And so, transported overseas, Reformed forensic soteriology separates our status of justification in Christ from the sanctification of our bodies in the world, extracting ourselves from God's mission of justice in and among cultures.[29]

The effects of all this on our formation for mission, some five hundred years later, is daunting. It shapes Christians to be passive to the injustices in the world, and to manage them, ala Luther in the Peasants' Revolt, for pragmatic outcomes. We give up both participation in our witness and God's work for His justice in the world. We appear duplicitous and dispassionate. This I believe has happened in the culture of the Moral Majority in

---

27. Bonhoeffer, *No Rusty Swords*, 117.

28. This explains the evangelical indifference to Trump's amoral ethos, all the while many evangelicals in the US voted for him.

29. NYC pastor Tim Keller has sought to overcome this (what I have called) malformation of Reformed theology for mission by making the individual's experience of being justified by faith the conduit through which God's grace flows to show love, mercy, and charity to the hurting. Keller says the individual, fully forgiven in Christ, naturally is moved to see victims of injustice differently. In that Christians have received of the grace and forgiveness of God's love, we cannot help but give the same generously to those who are hurting and in need among us. Much like Luther, Keller sees the works of justice flowing though the saved individual and the transformation that springs forth in each person out of gratitude and love for God. The problem however is that Keller's approach makes justice the after effect of salvation. Justice is the consequence of God's kingdom instead of the very reality that God does in and through his reign. It becomes something we do instead something God does as his reign restructures the way we live in the world. Our good works now become suspect. They become just what Luther feared, our attempts to do good to prove something. This too, in its own way, undermines witness. See Keller, *Generous Justice*.

the 1980s up to the various evangelical voting blocks voting in the Trump presidency since 2016.

Theologian Willie Jennings describes this kind of malformation via the experience of Westernized forensic salvation of the African Olaudah Equiano being "saved" on a British slave ship in the eighteenth century. He says, "His vision of salvation touches the ground, but it cannot do anything about the ground it touches. . . . If the social order and the processes of commodification are not transformed in relation to the body through salvation, then salvation becomes hyperlocalized to a single relationship: God and the one being saved."[30] And so Christianity gets absorbed into the evil systems of slavery and inducts Equiano into slavery as part of the process. Salvation becomes a status extrinsic to the injustices we participate in the world. And we lose our witness, nevermind God's justice in the world.

Jennings describes viscerally the social dynamic that occurs via a soteriology that extracts the individual's salvation from the world into an individualized isolated relationship with God. It is powerless to "do anything about the ground that it touches." This individualization, which started in Reformation Europe, could be ignored as long as there was the backdrop of an assumed Christian society and social institutions. But, when transferred across the ocean, this soteriology becomes the means by which our witness is undermined. It separates salvation from the salvation God is working in the world to make the world right in Jesus Christ. It separates us from mission. In so doing we are malformed to make space for God's work in the world, to become witnesses/participants to his work of justice in the world.

The Neo-Anabaptist starts from a different place in its soteriology. Its understanding of salvation starts with the whole discipleship of the person into the whole of Christ's kingdom in a local space and time. This discipleship looks not only to Christ's atoning death, resurrection, and victory, for an understanding salvation. It looks to his ascension, reign over the world, and bringing of his kingdom until he returns. The cross is not only the defining moment by which we have been redeemed (past tense) from the chains of sin, it is the sign of the way God works in the world and shall bring in his kingdom.

In the same way, Neo-Anabaptist discipleship focuses on Jesus' life and his ascension as key understandings that lead us into a discipleship that follows Jesus into the renewal of all things. Jesus now rules from the right hand of the Father bringing in his kingdom. For "he must reign until all

---

30. Jennings, *The Christian Imagination*, 196.

enemies have been made subject" (1 Cor 15:25, my translation). Following Jesus then is more than a personal moral journey, it is becoming a subject of his rule and extending his rule into space and time through his presence wherever he may be received. Being justified and forgiven is the entry into his kingdom. By entering his very presence, we become a participant in his mission. Salvation is not about forgiveness of sin *only*. It is about bringing all things—personal and social—under the Lordship of Christ.[31] This unites justification and sanctification and mission in the world into one. Herein lies the resources for those Christians in Canada and the United States who have individualized salvation through appropriating Reformed forensic notions of soteriology.

SOLA SCRIPTURA: THE MALFORMATION OF INDIVIDUALIZED SCRIPTURAL HERMENEUTIC

The Reformation in Europe placed a new emphasis on the authority of scripture standing as the corrective to a corrupt church. This solved one problem for the Reformation (how can a corrupt church be called to faithfulness?), but it left Christians across the ocean with a new problem 500 years later: how do we interpret scripture faithfully when it has been separated from an authoritative community's teaching office? In a now pluralist and vastly post-Christianized culture, where we must navigate new moral issues not confronted previously, the church is faced with pluriform interpretations of multiple texts on each issue. Some versions of evangelical Protestantism solved this problem with a hardened propositional view of scripture locked into modernist frames unable to engage meaningfully with post-Christendom cultures on truth and epistemology. As a result, these churches are caught up in a kind of enlightenment paralysis incapable of engaging our cultures for mission.

When Luther is summoned, as a heretic, before the Diet of Worms by Charles V, he responds famously to the demand to recant some of his writings by saying, "I have been subdued by the Scriptures . . . my conscience is held captive to the Word of God, as a result. . . . I cannot and will not recant anything, because to act against my conscience is burdensome, injurious

---

31. For a deeper understanding of discipleship as following Christ in the way of nonviolence, suffering, and his kingdom, read Snyder, *Following in the Footsteps of Jesus*. Here through the eyes of historic Anabaptism we find the roots of Neo-Anabaptist engagements with culture through communal discipleship.

and dangerous. God help me! Amen."[32] Luther thereby defies the Emperor and the Pope. Shortly thereafter he translates the Bible into German. Thus, one of the central tenets of the Reformation is born. The scriptures themselves shall stand above the church's authority and shall (eventually) be made available to individuals apart from the mediation of the church.

John Calvin used words like "infallible rule of faith and practice" and "*final* authority on Christian doctrine and practice" to articulate this new authority of scripture.[33] Yet over time, this doctrine of scripture would require additional clarity on what this would mean in terms of practice within the Reformation. Many years later, the Westminster Confession will articulate *Sola Scriptura* with phrases like: "Scripture is sufficient," "contains therein all that is necessary for faith and practice," "nothing need be added," "Scripture is final in authority, infallible," "whereas the Pope, the fathers, etc. even the Councils are still fallible . . . Scripture is perspicuous." These ideas, all contained in the Westminster Confession, shaped a new understanding of scripture's authority over the church.[34]

Within the bounds of unified Euro Christendom, this shook Roman Catholicism and brought much change. It renewed a commitment to the study of the Bible and to seeking a new faithfulness to the apostles' teaching. But as this doctrine traveled across the ocean, having been melded together with an enlightenment epistemology, it would soon provide an opening for several new understandings of scriptural authority including a hardened view of inerrancy, verbal inspiration, and, with the aid of the Spirit's immediate illumination, perspicuity. In each case, the center of one church as arbiter of interpretation of scriptures was diminished. The interpretation of scripture became multiple, among the many churches, and all Christians were now freed to choose between them. This I suggest would later malform the church for mission in North America 500 years later.

It is safe to say that Luther at the Diet of Worms, and Calvin in his writings, had no intention of unleashing *Sola Scriptura* as the "most important historical source of Western hyperpluralism."[35] And yet, it can be argued nonetheless, that the Reformation's new emphasis on scripture

---

32. As quoted in Gregory, *Rebel in the Ranks*, 83–84.

33. Manetsch, "Is the Reformation Over?" 199.

34. *Westminster Confession of Faith*, VI, VII.

35. An admittedly controversial assessment found in Gregory, *Unintended Reformation*, 92.

became a fountain of chaos, albeit a coherent chaos.[36] It is true that there were other forces at work. Yet five hundred years later we still feel the unintended consequences of this doctrine in our inability to navigate the waters of post Christendom.

An example of this malformation is the way our readings of scripture can now be co-opted by the culture. In the words of Hauerwas, we "fail to stand under the Word because the Word has been captured by practices and narratives that are more constitutive of that entity called America than the community we call church." In other words, Christians in Canada and the United States fail to grasp that interpretation is a cultural practice that requires a whole community, not only a single exegetical expert. Hauerwas goes on to say that

> [F]undamentalism and historical criticism are but two sides of the same coin—that is, they are both developments of the Protestant stress on *sola Scriptura* that was transformed into sola text by the printing press. These developments were then given ideological formation through the development of democratic social orders, which created something called the individual citizen that presumed the ability to read the Bible without spiritual formation and moral guidance. As a result, the Bible was separated from the community necessary for it to be read as the word of God—that is, the church.[37]

As a result, we have a scriptural hermeneutic with no bite. On each test, each individual gets to make up his or her own mind, or perhaps even worse, each pastor, as he or she preaches, gets to choose which of the three or four options in his/her commentary to get a message across. We have lost the ability to read and interpret scripture as a practice of the community in shaping our imagination for what God is doing among us and in the world for his mission. Today's Christians, devoid of a communal interpretative practice, default to interpret scriptures to meet the needs of parishioners. This is a recipe for the church losing our witness in the world for his mission. This is a recipe for a lack of imagination for how Christians can participate in his mission in the world.

Here too, the Anabaptists have an alternative way to offer. Even though Anabaptists have often been blamed for pushing *Sola Scripture* to *Solo Scriptura*, they, nonetheless, have historically practiced reading scripture

---

36. As described by Mark Noll in his "Chaotic Coherence."
37. Hauerwas, *Unleashing the Scripture*, 42–43.

together, especially in times of conflict or struggle. J. H. Yoder, for example, in his *Body Politics* calls the church to practice the "Rule of Paul" and traces its heritage to several early radical reformers.[38] The church is called to gather together in reading a text. Then let those recognized as gifted among us teach, those of other gifts, such as pastoral and prophetic gifts, to speak, and allow the whole gathering to come together and be led in mutual consideration. Scholarship is part of the process, but the text is not hardened to the point that we cannot consider what it might mean anew, or how this truth might be extended into this new situation. There is a submission to tradition in this communal interpretative practice, yet the Spirit can extend faithfulness into spaces we have never encountered before.

In this way, reading scripture is political in nature. We read and interpret not only for a personal moral challenge or precept, but to learn who we are and how we are to be and act as a political body in the world. Scripture becomes the source of shaping our witness in the world. Rather than the Bible becoming a proof text to argue over, the Bible becomes God's Story in the world and we become his people who extend his story of mission and redemption into the world as we perform this Grand Drama.[39]

CONCLUSION

The goal of this chapter has been to argue that the Reformation, though it may have started out well in Euro Christendom, became the breeding ground for malforming the church for mission, once it was transported across the ocean. It left the church in Canada and United States, some five hundred years later, lacking the theo-political resources to engage a post Christianized North America. A way forward, I would suggest, is not more *Sola Christus*, *Sola Fide*, and *Sola Scripture*. The way forward is not more Reformation. Instead, I point to the Neo Anabaptist theological trajectory, along with its historic antecedents, as the resource for the renewal of mission in North America. Though I have provided only the briefest of forays into what the Neo-Anabaptist direction might look like, I hope nonetheless these forays offer windows by which to see how the future of mission in North America lies in a renewed local ecclesiology of mission grounded

---

38. Yoder, *Body Politics*, 61. I acknowledge with much grief the abusive behavior of Yoder with women he was teaching in graduate school. Therefore, when using Yoder as a source, I acknowledge doing this with discernment, especially in regard to his teachings and writings on sexuality.

39. Vanhoozer, *The Drama of Doctrine*.

in communal practices, a holistic discipleship, and a reading of scripture grounded in the local church. I believe the Neo-Anabaptists can help us think through these challenges for our time.

BIBLIOGRAPHY

Baan, Anaan. *The Necessity of Witness: Stanley Hauerwas's Contribution to Systematic Theology*. Eugene, OR: Pickwick, 2015.

Bonhoeffer, Dietrich. *No Rusty Swords: Letters, Lectures and Notes, 1928–1936*. New York: Harper and Row, 1965.

DeYonge, Michael P. *Bonhoeffer's Reception of Luther*. Oxford: Oxford University Press, 2017.

Fitch, David. *Faithful Presence: Seven Disciplines That Shape the Church for Mission*. Downers Grove, IL: IVP, 2016.

Gregory, Brad S. *Rebel in the Ranks: Martin Luther, the Reformation, and the Conflicts that Continue to Shape Our World*. New York: HarperOne, 2017.

———. *The Unintended Reformation: How a Religious Revolution Secularized Society*. Cambridge, MA: Harvard University Press, 2015.

Hauerwas, Stanley. "Beyond the Boundaries: The Church is Mission." In *Walk Humbly with the Lord: Church and Mission Engaging Plurality*, edited by Viggo Mortensen and Andreas Østerlund Nielsen, 53–69. Grand Rapids: Eerdmans, 2010.

———. "The End of American Protestantism," *ABC Religion and Ethics*, 2 July 2013 (Updated 2 September 2015), n.p. Online: http://www.abc.net.au/religion/the-end-of-american-protestantism/10099770

———. *Performing the Faith: Bonhoeffer and the Practice of Non-Violence*. Eugene, OR: Wipf & Stock, 2015.

———. *The Work of Theology*. Grand Rapids: Eerdmans, 2015.

———. *Unleashing the Scripture: Freeing the Bible from Captivity to America*. Nashville: Abingdon, 1993.

Jennings, Willie. *The Christian Imagination: Theology and the Origins of Race*. New Haven, CT: Yale University Press, 2011.

Keller, Timothy. *Generous Justice*. London: Hodder and Stoughton, 2010.

Leithart, Peter. "Augustine on 'Visible-Invisible Church,'" *Patheos*, 23 November 2003, n.p. Online: http://www.patheos.com/blogs/leithart/2003/11/augustine-on-visible-invisible-church/#lZ5CQ7whozAOV4K8.99

———. *The End of Protestantism: Pursuing Unity in a Fragmented Church*. Grand Rapids: Brazos, 2016.

Luther, Martin. *Luther's Works*. Vol. 46, edited by Robert C. Schulz. Translated by Robert C. Schulz. Philadelphia: Fortress, 1967.

———. *The Roots of Reform*. Vol 1. of *The Annotated Luther*, edited by Timothy Wengert. Minneapolis: Fortress, 2015.

———. *The Complete Sermons of Martin Luther: 7 Volumes*, edited by Eugene Klug. Grand Rapids: Baker, 2000.

Luther, Martin, and John Calvin. *Luther and Calvin on Secular Authority*, edited by Harro Höpfl. Translated by Harro Höpfl. Cambridge: Cambridge University Press, 1991.

MacIntyre, Alasdair. *Whose Justice? Which Rationality?* Notre Dame: Notre Dame University Press, 1989.

Manetsch, Scott M. "Is the Reformation Over? John Calvin, Roman Catholicism, and Contemporary Ecumenical Conversations." *Themelios* 36.2 (2011) 185–202.

Milbank, John. *Theology and Social Theory*. 2nd ed. Oxford: Wiley-Blackwell, 2006.

Nation, Mark Thiessen, et al. *Bonhoeffer the Assassin? Challenging the Myth, Recovering His Call to Peacemaking*. Grand Rapids: Baker Academic, 2013.

Noll, Mark. "Chaotic Coherence: *Sola Scriptura* and the Twentieth-Century Spread of Christianity." In *Protestantism After 500 Years*, edited by Thomas Albert Howard and Mark Noll, 258–81. New York: Oxford, 2016.

Pickstock, Catherine. "Duns Scotus: His Historical and Contemporary Significance." *Modern Theology* 21 (2005) 543–74.

Pecknold, C. C. *Christianity and Politics: A Brief Guide to the History*. Eugene, OR: Cascade, 2010.

Radner, Ephraim. *A Brutal Unity: The Spiritual Politics of the Christian Church*. Waco, TX: Baylor University Press, 2012.

Schaff, Philip. *Modern Christianity. The Swiss Reformation*. Vol. 7 of *History of the Christian Church*. 3rd ed. Grand Rapids: Eerdmans, 1958.

Snyder, C. Arnold. *Following in the Footsteps of Jesus*. Maryknoll NY: Orbis, 2004.

Taylor, Charles. *A Secular Age*. Cambridge, MA: Harvard University Press, 2007.

Vanhoozer, Kevin. *The Drama of Doctrine*. Philadelphia: John Knox, 2005.

Westminster Confession of Faith (1647).

Yoder, John Howard. *Body Politics: Five Practices of the Christian Community Before the Watching World*. Scottdale, PA: Herald, 2001.

9

William Byrd and the Musical Reshaping of Liturgy in Reformation England

Insights for Worship in a Post-Christian Context

WENDY J. PORTER

WILLIAM BYRD LIVED AND worked as a composer in the chaotic liturgical world of sixteenth-century Reformation England. The Reformation in England seems less well-defined than on the continent and it came with many ambiguities, although Robin Leaver contends that "there was an essential unity in the basic theological concerns and activities that spanned England and the Continent."[1] Leaver cites G. E. Duffield's preface to a facsimile of the first English psalter, who says, "study of the actual documents suggests that the idea of English isolation in the Reformation period, invented at the end of the nineteenth century, is only a myth. The closest contact was maintained between the English Reformers and those on the Continent."[2] However, Chiara Bertoglio aptly notes that for the English there were "several important spiritual leaders instead of a single charismatic figure," and that "the practical implementation of theological theories often depended on the reigning sovereigns (who did have religious authority but seldom could be considered as theological guides)."[3] Whether or not the experience in England mirrored that on the continent,

1. Leaver, *Goostly Psalmes*, 1.
2. Leaver, *Goostly Psalmes*, 1.
3. Bertoglio, *Reforming Music*, 225.

it must have seemed very much like a post-Christian world to those who lived in England in the middle of it, especially those for whom worship was radically disrupted and uprooted.

Byrd lived in a world of worship wars, some of which resulted in fellow believers being put to death.[4] Philip Brett describes Byrd as "a tenacious Catholic in a Protestant country whose governments were increasingly (if unwillingly) committed to punitive action against 'recusants,' those who refused to attend services in the reformed church."[5] Byrd was not willing to betray important theological beliefs even though he had the most significant musical appointment in England, for he worked directly for the Queen of England. He sometimes risked that role by holding to his original liturgical practices and beliefs. At the same time, he provided some of the finest music for worshippers on both sides of this liturgical-theological divide. He created musical expressions of heartfelt worship and beauty for those who worshiped in the Church of England, and he played a major role in musically reshaping the liturgy for this corporate worship that was authorized. However, he also did this for small unauthorized gatherings of worshippers, those who were not in the safe environs of the Church of England. His work, perhaps surprisingly, has relevance for contemporary worship songwriters, leaders, and worshippers in the North American church today.

BYRD'S EARLY YEARS

Byrd was born around 1540,[6] and grew up during the height of King Henry VIII's efforts to wield power and to acquire more land and property. William was born into a devout Catholic home. No effort to destroy monasteries or their art or sacred liturgical books or music manuscripts and hand-copied partbooks of choral music—all of which took place under Henry VIII's direction and watchful eye—would have gone unnoticed in that home. The young Byrd lived in a world that had received word, through

---

4. See, e.g., Williams, *Later Tudors*, 289–91, on the Jesuit, Edmund Campion, who was executed in 1581 for attempting to restore Catholic faith and worship among those who had become Protestant.

5. Brett, "Byrd," 1.

6. For years, scholarly literature represented Byrd's birth year as 1543, but Harley, *William Byrd*, 14, showed how 1540 (or possibly 1539) was a more viable date. Unfortunately, we know little of the young William's childhood or youth, but see Harley, *William Byrd's Modal Practice*, 1. Byrd died in 1623.

The Reformation

The Act of Supremacy of 1534, that the King was "the only supreme head in earth of the Church of England."[7] In Peter le Huray's words,

> One of the most striking manifestations of that new power was to be seen in the whole-sale redistribution of church property, a process that began in 1536 and which continued in various guises for fifty years or more. The first and most spectacular stage was over within the space of four years. During that short time well over eight hundred monastic foundations were dissolved.[8]

The idea that a monastery might be "dissolved" seems so much more innocuous than the physical reality.

A. G. Dickens writes, "The religious, cultural and social issues which [the English Reformation] raised remain to this day both profound and inexhaustible."[9] It is tempting to view the Reformation in England like a series of movie clips that capture the swishing of royal robes of one monarch to the next as they each ascend and then descend the throne—from Henry VIII to Edward VI to Mary to Elizabeth I. With those boldly colored and lavish robes, it is easy to overlook the rustle of dark clerical robes passing by in the background in discreet and nondescript ways, to say nothing of the average churchgoer whispering or perhaps gasping in the background. The sounds of the English Reformation include the violent crash of falling bricks and toppling statues of the so-called dissolving of those monasteries, as well as the echoes of stinging words of conflict over prayers and rubrics and music within the stone walls of a cathedral.

Interestingly, the Dutch Christian humanist, Erasmus, whose life was over before Byrd's began, took notice of the musical practices in England. Clement Miller writes, "While personally acquainted with popes, kings, and princes, and a frequent visitor to their courts and chapels throughout Europe, Erasmus seemed particularly concerned with the music he heard in England."[10] In one of his comments on music, Erasmus wrote,

> In some countries the whole day is now spent in endless singing, yet one worthwhile sermon exciting true piety is hardly heard in six months . . . not to mention the kind of music that has been brought into divine worship, in which not a single word can be

---

7. See a digital reproduction at parliament.uk; and a modern transcription at tudorhistory.org.

8. Le Huray, *Music and the Reformation*, 2.

9. Dickens, *English Reformation*, v.

10. Miller, "Erasmus on Music," 338.

clearly understood. Nor is there a free moment for singers to contemplate what they are singing.[11]

Elsewhere, Erasmus expressed further issues with the nature of music in the churches, including their "meaningless sound" and "a certain elaborate and theatrical music," decrying that people "flock to church as to a theater for aural delight" and bemoaning the fact that "children spend every summer in practicing such warblings." Especially pertaining to English monks, he added, "Their song should be mourned; they think God is pleased with ornamental neighings and agile throats."[12] Miller notes, "In a revealing comment on improvised music in England, Erasmus speaks of a kind of music 'among the English, in which many sing together, but none of the singers produce sounds which the notes on the page indicate.'"[13] Miller thinks it likely that Erasmus heard this improvisational style personally, during one of his stays in England. Truly, England was a place of musical expertise, and improvisation was clearly one area in which they excelled. Contemporary musicians who have developed the skill and expertise of improvisation may find surprising resonance with English church musicians of the early-sixteenth century.

By the time that Byrd was in full form as a musician, there were at least three general perceptions about and approaches to music in the church. Christopher Marsh writes that "England's leading Protestants all agreed on the need to leave behind forever the supposedly obscurantist musical traditions of the late medieval church, but they were permanently divided on the question of what precisely this should entail in practical terms."[14] He describes "moderate Protestants" who shared Luther's view that music was a vital tool of persuasion and should be given a full role in the "service of God," while "Protestants of a hotter sort often looked to continental Calvinism . . . and consequently developed a more suspicious attitude to church music." In a third group "were those on the more radical wing of English Protestantism who denied the validity of virtually all music in the public praise of God."[15] In the wake of the Reformation, both the use of choirs and of organ was under scrutiny, as well as the use of other instruments;

---

11. Miller, "Erasmus on Music," 338, citing Erasmus's *Opera omnia*, VI:73.
12. Miller, "Erasmus on Music," 339.
13. Miller, "Erasmus on Music," 341.
14. Marsh, *Music and Society*, 392.
15. Marsh, *Music and Society*, 392–94.

meanwhile, at the other end of the spectrum was a rise in the practice of vernacular psalm-singing, at least in parish churches.

Dickens, cited above, mentioned kings, prelates, monasteries, and prayer books. There is no question that there is much to notice about the radical rulings of monarchs, the disrupted lives of church dignitaries, the remains of monasteries, and the Prayer Books of Edward's reign that reflected the newly-constructed liturgy and subsequent Prayer Books to come.[16] But Dickens is right to notice the ordinary women and men, in this case, the ones who came to worship God, who longed to worship God, who were the real story when it came to William Byrd's most important music, even if we do not know their personal details or their stories. Byrd's life and work give us glimpses into his heart for God and for the worshipper around him. They also reveal some relevant insights for the church of the twenty-first century church, especially for the contemporary songwriter and worship leader. Byrd shows us what it means to write worship music that is meaningful and connects to diverse worshippers. He shows us what it means to be involved in a small disenfranchised group, both empowering them and participating with them, at great personal risk. Byrd's world must have seemed post-Christian, but his work speaks to the fact that he viewed the Christian part to be very much alive and well.

MUSICAL-LITURGICAL BACKGROUND

Late in the 1400s, prior to the Reformation, there was what came to be known as a "rebirth" of music in England, captured especially well in the music of the Eton Choirbooks.[17] Music at the time was hand-copied and contained either in choirbooks or partbooks. Choirbooks contained all the parts for the entire choir in a single book, but in multiple copies, while partbooks contained the separate voice parts in separate books. This meant

---

16. See the content of the Edwardian 1549 Book of Common Prayer in *The Two Liturgies*, 16–158. Bowers, "Chapel Royal," *passim*, describes Elizabeth's hesitant shift from Edward's Prayer Book of 1549 to a restoration of the 1552 version with additional rubrics in the 1559 Prayer Book. Her Injunctions from that same year also provided some brief guidance on music and worship.

17. See Benham, *Latin Church Music*, 21, and later in the book where he writes, "The Eton choirbook . . . is unquestionably one of the greatest monuments of English music in any age" (58). For a fascinating introduction to the rediscovery of The Eton Choirbook and its music, which was heard first in the early 1950s after a 400-year hiatus, see Harrison, *The Eton Choirbook: I*, as well as discussion in his *Music in Medieval Britain*, 307–28.

that each partbook must be available in order for the work to be performed (for example, one book would contain only the bass part, another would contain only the tenor part, etc.). These books were tremendously valuable to the institutions themselves as well as containing part of the nation's cultural heritage. England's music was considered the height of musical achievement in all the surrounding countries at the time. Hugh Benham describes the music in the Eton Choirbook as having been written on a much broader scale than music of preceding eras. Where earlier works were written for three voice-parts, now they were for five parts, which resulted in music that was far more complex and that required larger and more sophisticated resources. The vocal range of the voices was extended both higher and lower, which placed it well beyond the range of what would have been heard on the continent—and the continent was always the point of comparison. Benham describes the Eton Choirbook music as "complex, elaborate and florid," and how the pieces were known for their very long phrases on a single syllable and for their great rhythmic complexity, such that, "in the words of Erasmus, 'the congregation cannot hear one distinct word.'"[18] But Benham describes the music of the Eton composer as "God-centred, a vehicle for devotion." In his judgment, it aided worship, it was important to worship services, it reflected a divine order, and it was not just for entertainment or merely to display or evoke emotion.[19]

David Wulstan writes that in the early 1500s, "The resplendent and complex style of polyphony developed by British composers . . . [was] without parallel on the Continent."[20] The music of John Taverner, who lived from 1490 to 1545 (just barely overlapping Byrd's life), reflected the complexity and floridity of Eton's music. The musical range of Taverner's vocalists was wide, with parts written for boy sopranos to sing exceptionally high pitches with some frequency. Wulstan has contended for some time that the music would have been sung up to a minor third higher than what the written sources indicate,[21] so both the ability and the expectations for music and musicians was exceptionally high.

The changes that resulted in England's church music after the rise of Lutheranism on the continent were not received well by those who loved

18. Benham, *Latin Church Music*, 3.

19. Benham, *Latin Church Music*, 3–4.

20. Wulstan, "Vocal Colour," 19.

21. See the full range of this discussion in Wulstan, "Vocal Colour," as well as Bowers, "Performing Pitch," "Further Thought," and "Vocal Scoring."

England's church music. Perhaps a hymn like Luther's own "interpretation of Psalm 46, which for subsequent generations has epitomized the essence of the Lutheran Reformation: *Ein feste Burg ist unser Gott*" may have been welcomed,[22] but most of the changes resulted in skilled and talented musicians now being displaced. Benham writes that these changes

> had profound effects on the extent and character of church music. If Erasmus had been alive to visit England in Edward VI's reign or in Elizabeth's he would have been delighted to find a major reduction in musical activity, for like him many Reformers considered that far too much time, talent and money had formerly been spent on church music.[23]

The Chantries Act of 1547 had disbanded many choral foundations, with the result that full choral services were only heard in a few cathedrals and chapels now.[24] Reformers may have thought that this was a good change, but, in retrospect, was that really the case?

Byrd's musical education would have begun early. He may have been a student of the English composer Thomas Tallis, and therefore one of the young choristers with the Chapel Royal, or possibly a chorister at St. Paul's Cathedral, along with two brothers.[25] Either way, his musical education would have been excellent. Following the pattern of the best church or cathedral schools in training young choristers during that era, Byrd would have started with learning to sing chants, first from memory and then from musical notation. Then he would have learned to sing parallel lines around a chant, called "faburden," and then to sing descants, where you improvise a counter-melody above a choral piece. Some young choristers learned to play the "viol," an instrument much like a guitar, but played upright. Some learned to play the virginals, a smaller version of a harpsichord. Some learned the organ. Byrd learned and played them all. Improvising descants, singing parallel lines to a chant, and knowing how to play the instruments were all superb training for the improvisation required in actual musical

---

22. Leaver, *The Whole Church Sings*, 158 and 149. Leaver refers to how the hymn undoubtedly appeared first as a "broadside" in 1529 (see 158), which, along with pamphlets and small booklets, could be "relatively quickly set, printed, and sold cheaply" (82), so it would have been distributed widely. See also Lenti, "Earliest Lutheran Hymn Tradition."

23. Benham, *Latin Church Music*, 6.

24. Benham, *Latin Church Music*, 6.

25. Harley, *William Byrd's Modal Practice*, 1.

composition.[26] These were critical skills for someone who would become the leading Gentleman of the Chapel Royal.[27] The Gentlemen of the Chapel Royal were the monarch's appointed musicians of the royal entourage, the highest musical appointment available.

With this training as his own background, it would be interesting to hear what Byrd would have to say to churches in North America who have distanced themselves from trained and educated musicians and moved more towards those who are untrained or uneducated in an effort to embody "authenticity." It is not that there is no room for the educated and trained musician in the contemporary church, but there seems to be far less room than there was. Byrd would surely protest. After all, he poured his life into creating musical art for worship that was at the highest musical level, work that required the very best of his skill, talent, and effort. As a mentor, he would surely expect something similar from a twenty-first-century protegé or student. He would also certainly argue that there must be a place in the church in which that skill, talent, and effort is cultivated and honored.

This was the context within which Byrd lived and worked, with cataclysmic shifts taking place in the liturgy. He was to write music for an English-language liturgy, instead of Latin, although Latin was still largely the language both of the church and of the academy, which included a musician's training and education. English must have seemed like a foreign language, but the English text was to be transparent and audible, which meant a drastically simplified approach to musical composition.

Thomas Cranmer, Archbishop of Canterbury, created an English Litany in 1544, the first vernacular liturgical book for the public.[28] He followed the principle that he had articulated in a letter to Henry VIII that "in myne opinion, the song that shalbe made thereunto, wolde not be full of notes, but, as nere as may be, for every sillable, a note; so that it may be songe distinctly and devoutly."[29] These instructions actually pertained to monody or chant, not to polyphony as often was mistakenly claimed, but it became a mantra for the rest of the century in one way or another. The often-cited Royal Injunctions of Queen Elizabeth I of 1559, Item 49, was

26. Harley, *William Byrd's Modal Practice*, 1.

27. See, e.g., Le Huray's chapter on the Chapel Royal in *Music and the Reformation*, 57–89.

28. Wulstan, *Tudor Music*, 279–80.

29. *State Papers of King Henry the Eighth*, CXCVI, "Cranmer to King Henry VIII," 760–61.

relaxed from earlier articulations but still adhered to the principle of intelligibility of each word in singing:

> that there be a modest and distinct song, so used in all parts of the Common Prayers in the Church, that the same may be as plainly understood, as if it were read without singing. And yet, nevertheless, for the comforting of such that delight in music, it may be permitted, that in the beginning, or in the end of Common Prayer, either at morning or evening, there may be sung an hymn, or such-like song, to the praise of Almighty God, in the best sort of melody and music that may be conveniently devised, having respect that the sentence of the hymn may be understood and perceived.[30]

For a superb composer such as Byrd, even in his young twenties, this must have seemed restrictive, but although he was not convinced by this approach to liturgy, he approached the challenge with talent and skill and creativity. His work to develop new directions in music for worship is an overlooked area of the impact of the English Reformation on subsequent generations of churches that continue to worship in the English language. While the English-speaking church at large may have known some of the Reformers' music, such as a German hymn from Luther or Psalm-singing in French, it was English-speaking musicians and hymn writers who most directly influenced the development of music and worship in England and, subsequently, in North America. Some of this was through the metrical vernacular psalms developed by those who fled to Switzerland during Mary's brief reign. But it was an English Byrd who implemented approaches to musical worship that still resonate with today's worshippers and whose innovations still have a place in the practices of today.

Byrd's first major position was as organist and master of the choristers at Lincoln Cathedral, at the age of twenty-three. He was the lead musician in a very prestigious cathedral, one that had survived the early days of the Reformation when much to do with music was destroyed, but Lincoln Cathedral's musical resources somehow survived without significant damage. The cathedral still had a choir, consisting of twelve adult singers and nine choristers, young boys.[31] This was an outstanding location to begin a career, to develop as a composer, and to learn the ropes of being the lead worshipper and lead musician. Kerry McCarthy reminds us that we do not really

---

30. Frere and Kennedy, eds., *Visitation Articles and Injunctions*, 3:23.
31. McCarthy, *Byrd*, 22.

know how Byrd spent his apprentice years, but, even at such a young age, "they left him qualified to run a large musical establishment and compose new works for it,"[32] and compose he did. Later in his life he was "a well-educated man, fluent in the humanistic Latin of the Renaissance, a reader and collector of books."[33] We do not know if he studied at a university or traveled abroad in his early years, but there is an educational college with close ties to Lincoln and perhaps Byrd received some of his education in these years.[34]

The prospect of being one of the Gentlemen of the Chapel Royal must have been high in the young Byrd's hopes, and his appointment as one while still in his twenties, while he was the lead musician at Lincoln Cathedral, must have been one of the greatest achievements imaginable for a promising young composer. However, while it would provide opportunities of which few musicians could even dream, it would also provide nearly insurmountable challenges.[35] In that respect, Craig Monson describes the radical changes of music within the Chapel Royal as one monarch followed another, but how it "set the standard for the realm in sacred music."[36] He says, "With the return of the puritan faction after the demise of Mary Tudor, the Chapel Royal remained the most important bastion of elaborate ritual amid the intense and abiding attack on church music by Genevan reformers."[37]

As noted above, Byrd composed at a time when musical composition was at an exceptionally high level, even if there was a major effort to eliminate it from the church or at least reduce its importance. His compositions stood out, even against that backdrop. He was prolific and creative. He was also deeply attuned to the significance of how music embodies the texts that it frames. This was in a period when paying attention to lyrics was not thought to be a high priority, yet Byrd's music shows evidence that he was highly attuned to the words.[38] Today's worship songwriters and leaders are

32. McCarthy, *Byrd*, 23.
33. McCarthy, *Byrd*, 23.
34. McCarthy, *Byrd*, 23.
35. McCarthy, *Byrd*, especially her chapter, "Lincoln Cathedral," 22–37.
36. Monson, "Elizabethan London," 306–7.
37. Monson, "Elizabethan London," 307.
38. Brett, "Word-Setting," 53, writes in reference to Byrd's secular music that Byrd "generally extracts deeper feeling from a poem than composers more dependent for their effects on vivid images or on elaborate parallels."

accustomed to the necessity of paying attention to lyrics, and yet, sometimes either the music or the lyrics, or both, seem to be lackluster, shallow, even trite. Byrd provides a model of paying attention and working diligently and artistically to write, or at least choose, music that emulates this standard of musical and lyrical integrity.

PUBLIC WORSHIP

The Church of England was the authorized form of Christian worship and Byrd wrote music especially for this new theological institution. He set the new English language liturgy in his Short Service,[39] a setting that uses simple and accessible musical resources. He also composed a Great Service,[40] a large complex work that provided the church with a musical setting of the liturgy that had a place for many skilled and talented musicians, effectively giving them a voice.

Some of his individual songs, such as his "Sing Joyfully," were very popular.[41] Although there are no longer any extant sixteenth-century sources of this piece, there are about a hundred printed or manuscript versions of it from the early seventeenth century,[42] which provide clear evidence of its continued use. It is interesting to consider the fact that popularity of certain new worship songs is not a unique phenomenon of the twenty-first-century church, after all. Of course, the evidence of popularity in Byrd's day was not found through the number of times a song is accessed through CCLI,[43] or viewed on YouTube, but through the number of copies that were made—potentially hand-copied—in order to keep it in print and in use.[44] Popularity shows us something about what is included in a church's musical canon, and, while not necessarily a reliable form of evaluation of the quality of a piece, it certainly says something about its use in public worship, both in the sixteenth century and in the twenty-first. This gives us a window into

---

39. Monson, ed., *The Byrd Edition*, 10a. *The English Services.*

40. See the full setting in Monson, ed., *The Byrd Edition*, 10b. *The English Services II: The Great Service.*

41. Monson, ed., *The Byrd Edition*, 11:82–90.

42. See *Oxford Book of Tudor Anthems*, "Sing Joyfully," no. 29, 287–97, with the source notes by John Morehen, 287. The lyrics of the piece are from Ps 81:1–4.

43. Christian Copyright Licensing International, accessible online at: ca.ccli.com.

44. See discussion of the nature of music printing in the Appendix entitled "Elizabethan Music and Music Publishing," in Kerman, *Elizabethan Madrigal*, 257–67.

a congregation's actual musical practice of worship, a glimpse of a congregation at worship.

Meanwhile, developing in the churches of England was a form of metrical vernacular psalm singing, an influence from the continent. Beth Quitslund writes that the "Prayer Book congregations of the Marian diaspora adopted metrical psalmody as a part of their confessional identity... English writers in Geneva created a hymnal that could articulate a range of godly prayers and affirmations."[45] Interestingly, "the Church never officially sanctioned it as part of the liturgy."[46] Nonetheless, as Timothy Duguid writes, although "the psalms' only official place in the Prayer Book was in reading and reciting them in prose, some churches began nonetheless to sing metrical psalms both before and after the sermon."[47] Marsh contends that in understanding the Reformation's success in forging new personal identities in England, one of the "most convincing explanations for the transformation will be a musical one."[48] He continues, "Ordinary parishioners may not always have welcomed lengthy sermons, but they loved to sing psalms."[49] Oddly enough, the Queen's Injunctions of 1559 had made room for this, although surely that was not her intention.

Quitslund describes the anomaly of printer John Day's fortune in getting the metrical Psalms into print, "which became the most printed book in England during the early modern period," and asks, "what was everyone doing with all those books? And, as importantly, what did people think about them?"[50] She acknowledges recent studies that emphasize the significance of their popularity and how, in contrast,

> later seventeenth-century criticism of the metrical psalms—as puritan, vulgar, and poetically crude—has continued to color the discussion of their reception in the Elizabethan period. In addition, among literary critics the history of psalm-singing has been influenced by one late Elizabethan and early Jacobean writer who seldom ventures into explicit comments on religion: William Shakespeare. Yet Shakespeare's references to the psalms are

45. Quitslund, *Reformation in Rhyme*, 155.

46. Duguid, *Metrical Psalmody*, n.p. See extended discussion in Zim, *English Metrical Psalms*, and the critical edition of the lyrics and melodies in the two volumes by Quitslund and Temperley, *Whole Book of Psalms*.

47. Duguid, *Metrical Psalmody*, n.p.

48. Marsh, *Music and Society*, 391.

49. Marsh, *Music and Society*, 391–92.

50. Quitslund, *Reformation in Rhyme*, 239.

unusual and potentially quite misleading. What a closer look at Elizabethan sources shows is a book that was embraced by virtually all of the English Church, in marked contrast with its devaluation among the cutting-edge churchmen and literati of the Stuart period.[51]

She estimates that "approximately 220,000 copies had been produced by the end of Elizabeth's reign—more than one for each 18 inhabitants of England and Wales in 1600."[52] This was a major grass roots movement that permeated the church en masse, and for highly accomplished musician-artists, it must have been devastating to have been replaced so easily and quickly by simple tunes for an entire book of psalms with sing-song poetry that sounded much like these first lines of Ps 23: "The Lord is only my support, and he that doth me feed: How can I then lack anything whereof I stand in need? He doth me fold in cotes [sheds] most safe, the tender grass fast by; And after drives me to the streams which run most pleasantly."[53]

Unsurprisingly, Byrd did not favor these "Genevan jigs," a term considered a contemptuous reference by critics, and one known to be shared by Elizabeth herself.[54] Some scholars suggest that early performance style of the metrical psalms may have been at a lively tempo, but most think that the term "purposefully mocked a singing style which was grave and solemn from the outset."[55] Duguid describes the nature of the derogatory and somewhat sarcastic tone of the phrase:

> an English jig was a burlesque that combined drama, music and dance. It joined improvised popular songs from the past with traditional ritual dances... the descriptions of Genevan psalm tunes as "Genevan jigs" refer to their appeal to the peasantry and their use of popular tune styles. Since psalm tunes were to be sung with "weight and majesty" the term was probably also a sarcastic jab at the slower speeds of psalm singing.[56]

---

51. Quitslund, *Reformation in Rhyme*, 239.
52. Quitslund, *Reformation in Rhyme*, 242.
53. Quitslund and Temperley, *Whole Book of Psalms*, 104.
54. See, e.g., Davies, *Worship and Theology*, 377–404 (387).
55. Bertoglio, *Reforming Music*, 356.
56. Duguid, *Metrical Psalmody*, n.p. Nicholas Temperley outlines how they originated with Thomas Sternhold's collection of psalm paraphrases for the young King Edward, how John Hopkins added to them after Sternhold died, and then how this small book was printed as "devotional recreation." He says, "when several thousand English Protestants took refuge in Frankfurt, Geneva, and other Continental centres to escape Mary

It certainly is hard to imagine Byrd, as a master composer, finding something redeemable in these songs, although he did not object to setting the Psalms to be sung in more refined ways. He wrote some fairly expansive five-part settings of psalms for festive occasions, often set as "a simple dialogue between the two sides of the choir," including, for example, "Teach Me O Lord" that made use of solo voices.[57] McCarthy writes that the "underlying aesthetic of his liturgical psalm settings . . . is not unlike that of his earliest secular songs: clarity, decorum, and moments of quiet but distinctive beauty."[58] Bertoglio writes:

> Even among those who, in the Church of England, were closer to the Calvinist positions, music was rarely denied its symbolic dimension and its capacity to move; there was awareness, however that—precisely by virtue of this power—music could be either very useful or potentially very dangerous. The "godly" (i.e. those who fostered a Calvinist orientation in the Anglican Church, frequently in consequence of their experience of Reformed worship during the Marian exile) could sometimes oppose even the chanting of liturgy, let alone the complex polyphony or instrumental music in church, while, of course, metrical psalmody was not only admired but actively encouraged.[59]

There are those in the church of today who have been protesting for years against what they perceive as the equivalent of metrical psalms in contemporary worship. Byrd would urge today's worship songwriter or leader not to waste time on meaningless, frivolous, or mundane songs that do not do justice to the lyrics or the music itself, to say nothing of being worthy of worship to God. He poured himself into developing the very best music possible; he would expect the songwriter of today to do the same. However, a songwriter who does make this investment may not be well-known, and their work can be overlooked in the crowd that is lined up for the next song from songwriters who have become household names in the circles of worship leaders and contemporary worshippers.

Tudor's return to the Roman rite, its texts became the nucleus of a new development of congregational singing on the French model, represented by the first English metrical psalter with tunes, published at Geneva in 1556." See Temperley, Review of *Metrical Psalmody*, 269.

57. McCarthy, *Byrd*, 34.
58. McCarthy, *Byrd*, 34.
59. Bertoglio, *Reforming Music*, 226.

Byrd's work took place in an era when there was huge disruption in worship, cataclysmic shifts in everything from style to the language of worship to whether the music could be complex or, of necessity, must be extremely simple. Perhaps it is not surprising to discover that in later years in his life, he committed a good deal of time and artistic effort in assembling music and his own thoughts and observations about it in his *Gradualia* cycle, reflecting "his commitment to well ordered worship."[60] At the time when he was doing this work, recusant worship, that is, illegal worship of Catholics in a legally-Protestant nation,

> was elaborate in some places, but also, by its very nature, ephemeral; it was something that could physically vanish in moments if discovered or hijacked . . . English Catholics were accustomed to this sort of surprise. It was a realistic possibility every time they met for worship, even at well hidden locations deep in the countryside.[61]

For evangelicals and other Protestants today who may be accustomed to viewing Catholics as the "other" in terms of faithful Christian worship, it may seem surprising to think that someday they could find themselves in similar circumstances in their own nations where Christianity has been an accepted religion, but perhaps will not be the case indefinitely. Ironically, they may find themselves identifying more with recusant Catholics in England than those within their own historical church denominational lines of descent. It is interesting to consider that recusants who were not permitted to worship freely, or even at all, "were eager even for detailed descriptions of elaborate worship, being generally unable to participate in it themselves."[62] Will there come a day of longing to just hear about the opportunity of others to engage in full-voiced, free and open Christian worship?

As a composer, Byrd was willing to take risks in his compositions, even in his instrumental works.[63] But as a composer of songs for worship, he was willing to take even greater risks. Meanwhile, Byrd took a creative approach to the traditions and resources that were available to him. For instance, at Lincoln Cathedral, and elsewhere in Elizabethan England, choirs were divided into two separate choirs, one on each side of the chancel, with almost everything alternating back and forth between the two choirs. (Any

60. McCarthy, *Liturgy and Contemplation*, 71.
61. McCarthy, *Liturgy and Contemplation*, 72.
62. McCarthy, *Liturgy and Contemplation*, 73.
63. McCarthy, *Byrd*, 30–31.

visit to an English cathedral or many of the college chapels today will reveal this same pattern still in evidence.) Byrd used this given as an opportunity to compose some pieces that would add extra parts at some point in the work, and then return to the original number. He would use these antiphonal resources to the highest level in his Great Service, with up to ten parts in various sections of this extensive English-language setting.[64]

To a worship leader and worship songwriter of today, he—and other great composers, such as Bach—would strongly encourage taking pre-existing restrictions and to use them creatively and well. Buildings that provide obstacles, lack of musical resources, inadequate numbers or quality of musicians, all provide an opportunity to be more creative as an artist. Sometimes artists need restrictive challenges to open up new ways of creating and crafting their art, and to give the local church new ways of engaging in worship that are uniquely suited to them.

CONCEALED WORSHIP

Byrd's Latin motets were musical gems, and they captured the heart of Catholic worshippers.[65] Meanwhile, his three Latin Masses are among some of his most important contributions to the worship of the church,[66] not only for their musical value and for their contribution to worship contexts at the time, but also for what they can teach us today. As McCarthy describes it, when Byrd began setting the mass to music in the early 1590s,

> he was doing something that no English composer had done for thirty years. Given the political and cultural risks involved, it is surprising that he managed to do it at all. The 1559 Act of Uniformity strictly forbade the celebration of the old Catholic liturgy in England. Those who went on cultivating it could be punished with fines, imprisonment, or, in exceptional cases, even death. What had taken place daily at every pre-Reformation altar, from the humblest parish church to the greatest cathedral, was now a rare and dangerous luxury.[67]

---

64. McCarthy, *Byrd*, 33.

65. See, e.g., Kerman, "On William Byrd's *Emendemus in melius*," as well as Kerman, "Byrd's Motets."

66. The primary source for this is Kerman, *Masses and Motets*. See also the chapter on the three masses in McCarthy, *Byrd*, 133–50.

67. McCarthy, *Byrd*, 134.

To slip ever so briefly into the musical world of William Byrd at this point, listen to the opening segment of his Mass for Five Voices, the Kyrie.[68] It is a beautiful setting of this eloquent prayer for mercy, set for a small group of believers that would have included some highly skilled musicians, composed by a musician who had the acclaim and authority to write for the Chapel Royal itself, but who dedicated some of his most beautiful work for these tiny enclaves of worship.

While his Latin motets involved some "expressions of Catholic protest and explicit Catholic solidarity," his Latin Masses were designed simply to enable his fellow Catholic worshippers to worship.[69] These were nothing like the extremely simple Mass setting by John Merbecke in 1550, who was modelling how to set the liturgy along the lines of "for every syllable a note."[70] Instead, they were appreciated by private patrons, such as the Petres, who were active Catholics who also loved music, and small communities that grew up around them. Byrd and his family found a safe community with them in later years when Byrd no longer worked for the Queen.[71] However, there were also Protestant patrons, some who were remarkably eclectic and tolerant in this period, "typified by the Queen's own willingness to employ the Catholic Byrd in the Chapel Royal."[72] Elizabeth is known to have been intentionally blind towards Byrd's Catholic affinities and she herself still apparently loved the music, even the liturgy itself.[73] But it was a fine line for Byrd to walk, guessing at how much would be tolerated and when this would no longer be the case.

Later in life, as already noted, Byrd compiled a collection of some of his music in two books called *Gradualia*, carefully constructed to aid Catholic worshippers in the entirety of their worship services. It is remarkable that both books were published, and even reissued in 1610, all during a time when Catholic worship was illegal and those who were in possession of such books were punishable by law.[74] In his preface to the first volume of

68. Listen, for instance, to recordings of the Masses by The Tallis Scholars (thetallisscholars.co.uk) or The Sixteen (thesixteen.com).

69. Kerman, "Byrd's Settings," 410.

70. *The Office of* The Holy Communion *as Set by John Merbecke*, 11.

71. In 1594, Byrd moved to Stondon Massey, where other Catholic worshippers also met within the safety of the Petres' residence.

72. Williams, *Later Tudors*, 402.

73. Williams, *Later Tudors*, 401.

74. Kerman, *Masses and Motets*, 224.

Gradualia, Byrd spoke eloquently of his belief about the value of his art as a composer in setting texts that are used to worship God. He writes, "For even as among artisans it is shameful in a craftsman to make a rude piece of work from some precious metal, so indeed to sacred words in which the praises of God and of the Heavenly host are sung, none but some celestial harmony (so far as our powers avail) will be proper."[75] He addresses "the True Lovers of Music" as "most high-minded and righteous, who delight at times to sing to God in hymns and spiritual songs."[76] In these two volumes, he provided resources so that his fellow worshippers could worship throughout the church year. Even if they were forbidden to meet in churches, they now had the musical and liturgical materials that they needed. North Americans do not know much about this issue (yet), but in some parts of the world, this is a familiar and troubling challenge.

In contemporary church life of the twenty-first century, at least in the evangelical church, the idea of being a "true lover of music" seems to be viewed with some skepticism. Perhaps loving music seems to conflict with loving God. However, for those who truly love music, who find in music great creative and spiritual expression, to say nothing of soul-stirring beauty and a place in which to encounter God's Spirit, for those within whom God has created this capacity, there must be a place for them within the realm of corporate worship, even today.

In the era of Catholic recusant worship, to worship in the manner of a Catholic was dangerous. McCarthy writes, "When recalcitrant English Catholics were jailed or executed, the official charge was treason, claiming the authority of the pope over that of the monarch."[77] It would be tempting to imagine that worship services in these hidden locations with such potential cost would have employed a sparse, bare-bones approach to worship. Interesting details in a recusant commentary by Laurence Vaux, published in 1568, indirectly reveal something of the manner of worship in these secret services. McCarthy notes that "The musical evidence of these passages is slim but compelling."[78] Vaux refers to the gradual and alleluia as "songs," not just allegorically, suggesting that these parts of the service were, indeed, sung. He describes the priest either saying or intoning the Kyrie, as well as the Gloria. He writes, "all the people, or such as supply their place" actually

---

75. Strunk, ed., *Source Readings*, 137–38.
76. Strunk, ed., *Source Readings*, 139.
77. McCarthy, *Liturgical Practice*, 103.
78. McCarthy, *Liturgical Practice*, 77.

sing the Sanctus and Benedictus. Meanwhile, at the point in the service of the Agnus Dei, "Lamb of God," Vaux observes that the faithful are present and pray for mercy and peace to be delivered by the hands of the Lamb of God. McCarthy observes that the kind of polyphonic settings that Byrd wrote for the Latin Mass for this kind of context would be totally at home here.[79]

These details suggest that worship in these hidden locations looked like a full worship service, complete with sung segments, a priest functioning fully in leading the service, the people responding at the right times with prayers and supplications to God. The reason this is an important window on recusant worship is that in a post-Christian world, where Christian worship in the future may not always be welcomed or tolerated, it is interesting to take note of the fact that worshippers did not step back from fully engaging in worship, and that a composer such as Byrd still thought it worthwhile to contribute the best of his craftsmanship, his art, his work, to worship that might only take place in these small discreet locations. In a contemporary culture that thrives on megachurches, and where small churches try to emulate what they think they see in a megachurch environment, the idea of a gifted songwriter or worship leader devoting great effort to creating rich resources in order to facilitate worship expressions for a tiny congregation, perhaps one that meets only in a home, and which may never be uploaded to YouTube for millions of others to watch and copy, may seem like an undesirable scenario. However, with Byrd as a model, this option needs to be weighed seriously. Is a musical or worship contribution only valuable if it can be seen and experienced by large crowds or congregations? What if this small group is really the sum total of the worship experience and exposure? Is there still a willingness to pour one's best work into it? And if not, what does that suggest about who it was for in the first place?

One other detail in some of Byrd's compositions merits mention in light of the controversies of his time and potential controversies in a present post-Christian culture. Certain words were the locus of dispute and dissension; for instance, the word "merit" in relation to a "Catholic doctrine of holiness by individual merit" was "one of the teachings most despised by the Reformers."[80] In one motet,[81] Byrd sets the Latin text of a Christmas

---

79. McCarthy, *Liturgical Practice*, 77.

80. McCarthy, *Liturgical Practice*, 103.

81. See interesting perspectives on the creative process of composers and songwriters of the time, including how someone like Byrd may have composed at either the organ or

song that was well known, though not a biblical text. In his setting, he skips over the actual word for "merit" in the text when it shows up in a part, although he leaves exactly the right number of notes that would correspond to its Latin syllables in the music. Was this a casual mistake or oversight? It seems unlikely, because the music and text are meticulously presented in every other way. What seems more probable is that he intentionally did not include the single word that all the controversy was about,[82] counting on the singers to know exactly what word went there and to sing it regardless of it being printed in the text. Technically, he did not use the "problem" word. Perhaps Christians today in politically sensitive times will find that sometimes they need to be creative at stepping over and around words that could blow up, especially when there are more important things to attend to. Every generation seems to have these touchstones, but they may not be the most important ones to include in songs of worship.

INNOVATION IN WORSHIP

Byrd's music may seem to have no relevance for the contemporary church today. The style is not what a contemporary church uses. Many churchgoers in today's church may not even appreciate a concert of his music, although that perhaps suggests a need for a vastly increased knowledge of and appreciation for great music. Notwithstanding that, Byrd introduced a number of things in his music and into the church that are at least historically relevant.

He developed a kind of choral piece called the "verse anthem," which was designed to have instrumental accompaniment. Liturgical music of the day was choral, so it was designed for a group of skilled singers. It was likely performed without an instrument, or the instrument would have doubled the sung parts. Byrd's "Teach Me, O Lord" is "one of the earliest examples in English church music of the use of a solo voice," not just designed for the whole choir. It also has an independent organ part, not just a doubling of choral lines.[83] So, the piece begins with the organ playing alone, and then a solo voice begins to sing the opening lines, "Teach me, O Lord, the way of thy statutes: and I shall keep it unto the end."[84] Both of these details would

---

with a lute, in Owens, *Craft of Musical Composition*, 73.

82. McCarthy, *Liturgical Practice*, 103.

83. *Oxford Book of Tudor Anthems*, Preface, n.p.

84. *Oxford Book of Tudor Anthems*, "Teach Me, O Lord," no. 30, 298–306; the piece is edited by John Morehen. The Scripture text is from Ps 119:33–38.

surely have made people look up and take notice when they first heard them.

When churches use instrumental accompaniment in songs of worship for the church, as most do for the majority of worship songs today, Byrd had a part in bringing that practice into play. When worship teams use solo voices set apart from the rest of the group, as contemporary worship music—and choral music—frequently does, Byrd had a role in bringing that into church music. These were not part of the familiar mode of the day, so he inaugurated them or rediscovered them and gave them a place in the music of the church. What is now so familiar as to not even merit notice, was at one time, in Byrd's day, innovations in musical worship.

Remember the viol mentioned above? The viol was an instrument for secular music, that is, for consort music. So what did Byrd do? He brought the viol into choral music in the church; that is, he brought an overtly "secular" instrument into a "sacred" place.[85] He made no apologies for this. There was a period in the twentieth century when the saxophone was not considered appropriate for church music. The "sax" was a "secular" instrument, a "sexy" instrument, not suitable for "sacred music." Eventually, it became apparent to many that a sax could make an outstanding contribution to musical worship in the church. Byrd spoke into that sacred-secular dichotomy back in the sixteenth century by selecting an instrument for sacred worship from a range of instruments that were not normally considered appropriate for worship.

Byrd was a prolific composer of instrumental works, although instrumental composition was still a new field. He published very little of his instrumental music, partly because it was very challenging for printers of the day to set it and print it. Besides that, faith was his prime objective, which, writes Oliver Neighbour, "he could serve most directly by setting sacred texts."[86] But his instrumental music is of the highest order. Neighbour describes how Byrd "brought the same intelligence, energy and certainty of purpose to his instrumental music as to the rest of his output; it shows the working of his genius no less clearly, and is no less remarkable for its qualities of personal expression. No composer, whether English or continental, working without the guidance of a sung text, had hitherto encompassed so

---

85. Consider the idea of sacred places in light of John Inge's thoughtful work, *A Christian Theology of Place*.

86. Neighbour, *Consort and Keyboard Music*, 19.

wide a range of character or of structural invention."[87] Byrd did not reserve his talent and energies only for the most acceptable elements of worship, but also for his other compositional work that surely was a form of worship but that would have not have a place in the liturgy and worship of the day.

In many churches of today, there is little space for instrumental music, apart from functional music that acts as a transition or as a filler or background while something else is taking place. There was little place (one could argue, "no" place) in the continental Reformation for such abstract and non-text-based music in the church, and it is doubtful that there was space in the liturgy in Byrd's locale, either, but the fact that he wrote it is worth noting. Must there be a panoply of words for every moment of our worship? Must our time of worship be totally crammed with words, or could there be space for instrumental compositions in the church today that invite quiet reflection and room to simply be in the presence of God? Must the church always be working in order to be a church at worship? Protestant worship practices are grounded in a movement that tried to move away from works-related salvation, and yet, corporate worship often seems to be built upon our "work." What would it be like to have spaces of "rest" in corporate worship? As a rest is what makes sense of spoken sentences, and of musical phrases, perhaps the introduction of "rests" into corporate worship would also bring a greater measure of sense, and of beauty. Perhaps Erasmus's outrage that there is no "free moment for singers to contemplate what they are singing" is relevant for corporate worship today.[88]

One other small off-beat detail worth noting is the impact of the notion of "syncopation," in this case, beginning with more recent generations and then looking at Byrd's day. There were strong opinions in the twentieth century against the introduction of syncopation into music in the church, even in music in general.[89] Syncopation was thought to be a "secular" practice. But, ironically, syncopation had been in use in the church off and on since at least the sixteenth century. Byrd certainly used it in his compositions, including in his sacred works. Even Luther would surely raise an eyebrow over this one, because his early form of "A Mighty Fortress" involves syncopation that still is unsettling to the unwary first-time participant.[90]

87. Neighbour, *Consort and Keyboard Music*, 19.
88. Miller, "Erasmus on Music," 338.
89. See, e.g., Faulkner, "Does Jazz Put the Sin in Syncopation?," a contribution to the *Ladies Home Journal* in 1921, that gives some sense of early-twentieth-century concerns.
90. See discussion about this hymn and images of 1530 and 1533 versions of the

The Reformation

ART AND EMOTION IN THE CHURCH

Byrd lived and worked in an era where art was still valued in the church, at least by his royal patron. Howard Mayer Brown summarizes Byrd's gifts as an artist-composer when he writes that Byrd shared with virtuoso Franco-Flemish composer, Orlanda Lasso,

> the astounding fluency to command every technique and genre of his time, but [Byrd] differs from his great contemporaries in at least two important ways: his music reflects the English independence from developments on the continent; and he . . . stands at the beginning as well as at the end of a period of history, for he not only incorporated into his own music the achievements of his predecessors, but he also ushered in the most brilliant musical era his country had ever known, during the later years of Elizabeth I and the reigns of James I and Charles I.[91]

A contemporary of Byrd's, Thomas Morley, also acknowledged the composer's status as a gifted musician, "whoso can, upon any plainsong whatsoever, make such another way as that of Mr. Byrd . . . may with great reason be termed a great master in music."[92]

For Byrd, the hard work of cultivating and refining his art was still prized. This was not exactly true on the continent at the time or in parish churches in England, and it is not exactly true in the church of today. There is among some a reticence about working hard (or admitting that we have worked hard) to create art at the highest level. It would rather be said that "it was nothing," in the interests of an assumed modesty and a more spiritual-sounding humility. Coupled with this is an ambivalence about, perhaps even outright disregard for, the place of art in the church at all. Byrd understood that he was a musical *artist*, and his work was to create *worship art*. He was educated and trained to do this. He was gifted to do this. He was motivated to do this. And he was employed to do this, which was certainly a bonus. But he also did a lot of this on his own time, especially in later years, without hope of payment or recognition for his artistic works.

Added to the dubious role of the arts in the church is the question about the suitability of emotion in music for worship. Criticism against

---

printed music in Fenner, "*Ein feste Burg ist Unser Gott*," accessible online at: hymnologyarchive.com.

91. Brown, *Music in the Renaissance*, 283.
92. Morley, *Plain & Easy Introduction*, 201.

contemporary musical worship in the church sometimes centres on this issue of emotion, and whether such use of emotions is appropriate (beyond its potentially manipulative use). Interestingly, Byrd wrote music that was emotionally evocative. Some of it is exuberantly joyful, such as "Sing Joyfully," mentioned above. Some of it encompasses deep lament for great losses in the church as he knew it and for the people who were now ostracized and forbidden to worship in public places.[93] Byrd's motets particularly capture this intense degree of emotion. In fact, in some ways, Byrd's motets functioned for the recusant Catholic worshippers in the way that African American spirituals functioned for a people who were stranded somewhere between God and humanity, in a liminal region that was relegated to being sub- or non-human. The music and words of spirituals embodied deep emotion, and a heartfelt call to God. Catholic worshippers in Byrd's time could be captured and killed. They were separated from familiar places and ways to worship God. They understood what it was to be in exile. Byrd gave them a voice, a means to express this sorrow and anger and fear. Byrd's songs were not an effort to manipulate worshippers, but to give them a voice.

Does the contemporary worship song capture the best of this? Perhaps not. Are the lyrics thoughtfully-constructed and well-articulated texts with theological integrity, set to music that eloquently expresses these? Not necessarily, or at least not always. But Byrd might point out that emotion itself is not the problem. I think he would say that the cry has not been matched by the skill to give it voice. In that case, investing in developing the skill and artistry of the artist to do so is well worth pursuing.

Byrd knew the pain of deep loss in his life, loss of beloved forms of worship, loss of artistic freedom in some cases, but, even more, the loss of life of fellow Catholic worshippers. At times, persecution of Catholics was the "fiercest and bloodiest of the century."[94] In 1581, Oxford witnessed the public martyrdom of the Jesuit, St. Edmund Campion and his fellows (Alexander Briant and Ralph Sherwin), out on one of the main streets of the city, not far from the famous pub where C. S. Lewis and his literary companions spent many hours. Byrd used his compositional skills to give voice to the outrage and grief that this caused him and others, including both a consort song (that would have been performed in a secular context

---

93. See, e.g., Kerman, on an earlier motet in "On William Byrd's *Emendemus in melius*."

94. Bertoglio, *Reforming Music*, 528.

such as at the monarch's royal residence) and a motet (that would have been used in private Catholic services but also perhaps elsewhere). For this motet, *Deus, venerunt gentes*, he chose the first verses of Ps 79, the very verses that English martyrs frequently spoke as their final prayer, and also considered the official text to use in prayer to request that Catholic faith be returned to full and free expression in England.[95]

Grief and pain at the situation that Catholic worshippers were experiencing in England gave rise to music that had multiple levels of meaning, both linguistically and musically. As Bertoglio describes it,

> Many of such compositions are of an almost shocking beauty and succeed in blending a touching emotionality with an otherworldly serenity. Though these musicians were suffering themselves for the divisions brought by confessionalisation, and were expressing the pain of the members of their community, their music somehow unites them.[96]

She suggests that grief in music can be shared across denominational and confessional boundaries. She continues,

> It is as if the very fact of suffering for one's faith was actually much more important, crucial and meaningful than which confession they represented and which confession was persecuting them. Suffering for Christ, in short, and expressing this suffering through music was the means by which the persecuted were truly in communion.[97]

In the contemporary context of Christian worship, we could learn much about the value of giving voice to grief and pain, both within our own places of worship, and beyond them. Post-Christian worship could learn a lot from Byrd about giving voice to fellow-believers to cry with the psalmist, "How long, Lord?"

THE BUSINESS OF SONGWRITING AND PUBLISHING

Joseph Kerman describes Byrd as "the first English musician to profit from the printing press."[98] Byrd, along with Thomas Tallis, who was a mentor as well as a colleague to Byrd, approached Queen Elizabeth for a patent

---

95. Bertoglio, *Reforming Music*, 528.
96. Bertoglio, *Reforming Music*, 565–66.
97. Bertoglio, *Reforming Music*, 566.
98. Kerman, "Byrd's Motets," 359.

to print a collection of music, the first of its kind. The patent was granted to them, for more than just this single work. Byrd and Tallis set to work to produce a volume of printed music that included eight of each of their compositions, the collection called *Cantiones Sacrae* or "Sacred Songs."[99] Byrd had to choose the right pieces, prepare music for print, work with a publisher,[100] and he showed that he even understood marketing. Every contemporary church songwriter understands something about this challenge or issue. Regardless of the range of opinion on this aspect of Christian worship songs, that is, whether writing songs of worship should also be about business, most would agree that as a topic, it is pertinent to the church today. Byrd had something to say, for he was at the forefront of it as a practice.[101]

Calvin Miller writes an intentionally provocative piece to describe the troubled intersection of the Reformation and the arts in the evangelical church. I quote him extensively here in the hopes that although his bold style might elicit some smiles, that it also might prompt some thoughtful reflection. He writes,

> the church—particularly the evangelical church—has traditionally been a little schizoid over whether or not the arts are a sanctified way to go about praising God. [On January 1, 1519,] on the eve of the Swiss Reformation, Huldrych Zwingli became the "people's priest" at Grossmünster in Zurich. Incensed over what he considered to be the "pagan icons" of the church, he swept through the building, ripping down the paintings and casting the religious statues to the floor, shattering them.[102]

One might wonder whether Henry VIII took lessons from Zwingli. Miller describes how the Swiss Reformer went on to purge the church of many images, instruments, priestly garments, and so on. In 1531, Zwingli

> was slain in a war for religious liberty. By then, however, he had widely established Reformation sentiments against religious art. . . . [But] Zwingli's dash through the cathedral ended oddly.

---

99. See Milsom, ed., *Thomas Tallis and William Byrd*.

100. See insights into the world of sixteenth-century music publishing in Clulow, "Publication Dates for Byrd's Latin Masses."

101. He also understood the need for outside sources of income, and he invested a lot of time in learning about and actively working towards winning legal disputes over property that could help to fund his artistic work.

102. Miller, *Into the Depths of God*, 64.

> There stands in Zurich a well-sculpted statue of the old statue-smasher, Bible in one hand and a sword in the other. If he were alive today, this statue of himself would be too big for him to push over.[103]

Miller probes contemporary practice when he writes, "Evangelical sermons and sanctuaries have been void both of art and interest.... Our many words produce a dullness of soul, a dead litany of boredom." He suggests that "Art doesn't become idolatry until our praise of God dies and all that is left is our praise for the art form. Idols are born when artists quit worshiping God and begin singing *te deums* to their own genius."[104] There is something in this to ponder for those who are deeply immersed in worship practices in the twenty-first century.

CONCLUSION

Byrd and his fellow Catholic worshippers must have believed that they lived in a post-Christian world. In similar manner, many in the West live in a world where leaders can no longer expect everyone to know the hymns and worship songs being sung or to know or understand the traditions of corporate Christian worship. Perhaps the contemporary context is more like early Christianity.

For Byrd and his fellow-worshippers, their worship became costly. It also became more fervent, more ardent, more intense, and it essentially went underground—or, at least, out of town. They met in secret places and they were at risk in doing so. Were there problems in Catholic understanding of faith and worship that needed to be addressed? Yes. Were there genuine believers and followers of God within this group? Undoubtedly.

Evangelicals still have things to learn from Catholic worshippers. Evangelicals often admit that they do not recall moments of transcendent worship while sitting in the pew of an evangelical service, but they do catch glimpses of such experiences in a Catholic cathedral, where monks might still chant part of the service, where skilled musicians might still sing some of Byrd's motets and masses.

What would Byrd say to those who live and worship today in a post-Christian culture? He would urge Christians to keep bringing their very best to those who are committed worshippers of God. He modelled the

---

103. Miller, *Into the Depths of God*, 64–65.
104. Miller, *Into the Depths of God*, 65.

efforts that he thought were merited to provide worship resources for people to engage in meaningful worship. He would surely push to provide the relevant resources that are needed now to give God's people a voice to participate.[105] He would encourage taking some risks in order to offer the very best works of art and artistry and craftsmanship to God, and to his people, even if the group of people who use and appreciate these is small.

Many of Byrd's motets were musical masterpieces designed for these small gatherings of worshippers, possibly gathered around a kitchen table, with only a few musical manuscripts available and a handful of musicians engaged together in singing the liturgy. Byrd's three Masses are pinnacles of his compositional work, but they were not composed to be used for large congregations in the authorized church, only for small, secret gatherings. The later part of Byrd's life was devoted to shaping and preparing his *Gradualia* as a complex of works with all the detailed parts of the liturgy that were needed by the worshippers but were not available to them otherwise. Byrd designed all this for these secret worshippers.

It was not that Byrd did not know how to make something commercial, marketable, income-generating, and valuable for posterity. It was just that he had something more important to do, to provide the very best musical-liturgical resources for those who met to worship in secret. He cared about these worshippers and their needs, and he cared about offering his best work as his own worship to God. But he also poured energy and creativity into musical worship for the official church of the land, for worshippers who met in public places.

There is much to learn from this master composer who functioned on two sides of a theological divide, but who did not sacrifice his integrity, his faith, or his art. Byrd had a creative hand in reshaping the musical liturgy for his fellow English worshippers in the Church of England. He certainly had a major role to play in reshaping the musical liturgy of his fellow Catholic worshippers who met in places of secrecy and were in danger. Both groups still owe him a debt of gratitude. His music is still sung in churches

---

105. See Kreider and Kreider, *Worship and Mission after Christendom*, 116–18, who speak of a lost understanding of 1 Cor 14 as a model for worship that has been overshadowed by theological disputes that miss the point. What they call "multi-voiced" worship, and which they believe to be a model worthy of emulation, showed up in various ways during the Reformation, in Luther, in the Swiss Brethren, in the Anabaptists, in early Baptists, and especially among Quakers. Kreider and Kreider suggest that it is time to recover that idea of everyone's participation in worship, making space for the variety of gifts and voices that are present in the group, not just professional leaders at the front.

of both traditions. But for those willing to consider it, Byrd has modeled some ways forward for the competing liturgies and practices and values of the North American evangelical church, now also beginning to meet in a post-Christian world.

BIBLIOGRAPHY

Act of Supremacy, Public Act, 26 Henry VIII, c. 1. United Kingdom Parliamentary Archives, HL/PO/PU/1/1534/26H8n1. Accessible online: https://parliament.uk. Modernized spelling accessible at: https://tudorhistory.org.

Benham, Hugh. *Latin Church Music in England c. 1460–1575*. London: Barrie & Jenkins, 1977.

Bertoglio, Chiara. *Reforming Music: Music and the Religious Reformations of the Sixteenth Century*. Berlin: de Gruyter, 2017.

Bowers, Roger. "The Chapel Royal, The First Edwardian Prayer Book, and Elizabeth's Settlement of Religion, 1559." *The Historical Journal* 43 (2000) 317–44.

———. "Further Thought on Early Tudor Pitch." *Early Music* 8 (1980) 368–75.

———. "The Performing Pitch of English 15th-Century Church Polyphony." *Early Music* 8 (1980) 21–28.

———. "The Vocal Scoring, Choral Balance and Performing Pitch of Latin Church Polyphony in England, c. 1500–58." *Journal of the Royal Musical Association* 112 (1986–1987) 38–76.

Brett, Philip, ed. *The Byrd Edition 4: The Masses (1592–1595)*. London: Stainer & Bell, 1981.

———. "Word-Setting in the Songs of Byrd." *Proceedings of the Royal Musical Association* 98 (1971–1972) 47–64.

———. Liner notes. CD Recording: "Byrd: *Missa in tempore paschali*." Recorded by Chanticleer. HMC 905182. Recorded at St. Ignatius Church, San Francisco, 1986. Arles, Germany: Harmonia Mundi, 1987.

Brown, Howard Mayer. *Music in the Renaissance*. Prentice Hall History of Music. Englewood Cliffs, NJ: Prentice-Hall, 1976.

Clulow, Peter. "Publication Dates for Byrd's Latin Masses." *Music and Letters* 47.1 (1966) 1–9.

Davies, Horton. *Worship and Theology in England: From Cranmer to Hooker, 1534–1603*. Book 1. Vol. 1. Grand Rapids: Eerdmans, 1996.

Dickens, A. G. *The English Reformation*. New York: Schocken, 1964.

Duguid, Timothy. *Metrical Psalmody in Print and Practice: English "Singing Psalms" and Scottish "Psalm Buiks," c. 1540–1640*. St Andrews Studies in Reformation History. Burlington, VT: Ashgate, 2014.

Faulkner, Anne Shaw. "Does Jazz Put the Sin in Syncopation?" *Ladies Home Journal* (August 1921) 16–34.

Fenner, Chris. "*Ein feste Burg ist Unser Gott*." Hymnology Archive, October 2018. Accessed at https://www.hymnologyarchive.com/ein-feste-burg.

Frere, Walter Howard, and William P. McClure Kennedy, eds. *Visitation Articles and Injunctions*. Vol. III. *1559–1575*. Alcuin Club Collections 16. London: Longman, Greens, 1910.

Harley, John. *William Byrd: Gentleman of the Chapel Royal.* Aldershot, UK: Ashgate, 1997. Amended reprint, 1999.

———. *William Byrd's Modal Practice.* Aldershot, UK, and Burlington, VT: Ashgate, 2005.

Harrison, Frank Llewellyn, transcriber and ed. *Musica Brittanica: A National Collection of Music.* Vol. X. *The Eton Choirbook: I.* 2nd ed. London: Stainer & Bell, for the Royal Musical Association, 1967.

———. *Music in Medieval Britain.* Studies in the History of Music. London: Routledge and Kegan Paul, 1958.

Kerman, Joseph. "Byrd's Motets: Chronology and Canon." *Journal of the American Musicological Society* 14 (1961) 359–82.

———. "Byrd's Settings of the Ordinary of the Mass." *Journal of the American Musicological Society* 32 (1979) 408–39.

———. "On William Byrd's *Emendemus in melius*." *The Musical Quarterly* 49 (1963) 431–49.

———. *The Elizabethan Madrigal: A Comparative Study.* New York: American Musicological Society, 1962.

———. *The Masses and Motets of William Byrd.* The Music of William Byrd 1. London and Boston: Faber & Faber, 1981.

Kreider, Alan, and Eleanor Kreider. *Worship and Mission after Christendom.* Harrison, VA: Herald, 2011.

Le Huray, Peter. *Music and the Reformation in England, 1549–1660.* Cambridge Studies in Music. Cambridge: Cambridge University Press, 1978.

Leaver, Robin A. *"Goostly Psalmes and Spiritual Songs": English and Dutch Metrical Psalms from Coverdale to Utenhove, 1535–1566.* Oxford: Clarendon, 1991.

———. *The Whole Church Sings: Congregational Singing in Luther's Wittenberg.* Grand Rapids: Eerdmans, 2017.

Lenti, Vincent A. "The Earliest Lutheran Hymn Tradition as Illustrated by Two Classic Sixteenth-Century German Chorales." *The Hymn* 50.2 (1999) 17–25.

Marsh, Christopher. *Music and Society in Early Modern England.* Cambridge: Cambridge University Press, 2010.

McCarthy, Kerry. *Byrd.* Oxford: Oxford University Press, 2013.

———. *Liturgy and Contemplation in Byrd's Gradualia.* New York: Routledge, 2007.

Miller, Calvin. *Into the Depths of God: Where Eyes See the Invisible, Ears Hear the Inaudible, and Minds Conceive the Inconceivable.* Minneapolis: Bethany House, 2000.

Miller, Clement. "Erasmus on Music." *The Musical Quarterly* 52 (1966) 332–49.

Milsom, John, ed. *Thomas Tallis and William Byrd: Cantiones Sacrae 1575.* Early English Church Music, 56. London: Stainer & Bell, 2014.

Monson, Craig. "Elizabethan London." In *The Renaissance: From the 1470s to the End of the 16th Century,* edited by Iain Fenlon, 304–40. Englewood Cliffs, NJ: Prentice Hall, 1989.

———. *The Byrd Edition.* 10b. *The English Services II. The Great Service.* London: Stainer & Bell, 1982.

———. *The Byrd Edition.* 11. *The English Anthems.* London: Stainer & Bell, 1983.

Monson, Craig, ed. *The Byrd Edition.* 10a. *The English Services.* London: Stainer & Bell, 1980.

Morley, Thomas. *A Plain & Easy Introduction to Practical Music (1597).* Edited by R. Alec Harman. New York: Norton, 1952.

The Reformation

Neighbour, Oliver. *The Consort and Keyboard Music of William Byrd*. The Music of William Byrd. Vol. 3. London: Faber & Faber, 1978.

The Office of The Holy Communion *as Set by John Merbecke, 1550*. Edited by Edmund H. Fellowes. London: Geoffrey Cumberlege, Oxford University Press, 1949.

Owens, Jessie Ann. *Composers at Work: The Craft of Musical Composition 1450–1600*. New York: Oxford University Press, 1997.

Oxford Book of Tudor Anthems: 34 Anthems for Mixed Voices. Compiled by Christopher Morris. Preface by David Willcocks. Oxford: Music Department, Oxford University Press, 1978.

Quitslund, Beth. *The Reformation in Rhyme: Sternhold, Hopkins and the English Metrical Psalter, 1547–1603*. Burlington, VT: Ashgate, 2008.

Quitslund, Beth, and Nicholas Temperley. *The Whole Book of Psalms: Collected into English Metre by Thomas Sternhold, John Hopkins, and Others. A Critical Edition of the Texts and Tunes*. 2 vols. Renaissance English Text Society. Temple, AZ: Arizona Center for Medieval & Renaissance Studies, 2018.

State Papers Published under the Authority of His Majesty's Commission. Vol. 1. *King Henry the Eighth*. Parts I and II. N.p.: John Murray, 1831.

Strunk, Oliver, ed. *Source Readings in Music History: The Renaissance*. New York: W. W. Norton, 1965.

Temperley, Nicholas. Review of Timothy Duguid, *Metrical Psalmody in Print and Practice*. *Music & Letters* 96 (2015) 269–71.

The Two Liturgies, A.D. 1549, and A.D. 1552, with Other Documents Set Forth by Authority in the Reign of King Edward VI, edited by Joseph Ketley. The Parker Society. Cambridge, UK: Cambridge University Press, 1844.

Williams, Penry. *The Later Tudors: England 1547–1603*. The New Oxford History of England. Oxford: Clarendon Press, 1995.

Wulstan, David. "Vocal Colour in English Sixteenth-Century Polyphony." *Journal of the Plainsong and Medieval Music* 2 (1979) 19–60.

———. *Tudor Music*. London: J. M. Dent, 1985.

Zim, Rivkah. *English Metrical Psalms: Poetry as Praise and Prayer, 1535–1601*. Cambridge, UK: Cambridge University Press, 1987.

10

Imperishable Seed

A Sermon for the 500th Anniversary of the Reformation

JENNIFER POWELL MCNUTT

Adapted from a Sermon Preached at Philpott Memorial Church in Hamilton, Ontario on 29 October 2017.

SCRIPTURE: MARK 4:1–20

Prayer:

Father God,
In your goodness, may the gathering of believers here today be edified, nurtured, and equipped for service by your holy Word, in the name of your Son, and through the power of your Holy Spirit.
May our hearts be filled with your grace and power, our minds illumined by your truth, and our actions spurred on as we seek to grow in faith and to live faithfully to your glory alone.
In Christ's Name, we pray.
Amen.

MARKING ANNIVERSARIES

YOU CERTAINLY COULD NOT have chosen a better year to celebrate 125 years of ministry! I have been reflecting on your anniversary in preparation for today and thinking about how it is a tribute to your faithfulness to serve the Lord through seasons of both lean and plenty. From a seedling church planted by Salvation Army officer P. W. Philpott in 1892 to joining the Associated Gospel Churches of Canada in 1925,[1] God has been good to sustain you through this time. I am very honored to be with you on this special day and on this Reformation Sunday as we celebrate these two milestones: the milestone of your church and of the Protestant church, as well.

And what a week this is! It is hard to believe that Reformation Sunday 2017 has finally arrived, since I have been speaking about and anticipating this anniversary for five years now. This coming Tuesday, we mark 500 years from when Martin Luther, an Augustinian friar and university professor as well as a parish priest at the Castle Church in Wittenberg, posted 95 concerns about the theology and practice of the Christian life relating to penance and indulgences. The issues with which he was grappling at that time were central to the life of the church. If you look at the very first thesis from his *Ninety-Five Theses*, you can get a sense of what primarily motivated him. He was concerned about the practice of repentance and the lack of confession. There, in that first thesis, Luther defined the whole Christian life as one of "repentance" as commanded by Christ in Matthew 4:17.[2]

Through the printing as well as translation of the *Ninety-Five Theses* from Latin into German—the common language of the people—these concerns rapidly circulated through Germany and opened the door for a broad, theological and biblical conversation that involved the whole church. In the words of today, Luther's post went unexpectedly viral in a time before social media, and that alone was cause for consternation within the hierarchy of the church.

What is fascinating to consider about this event is that there is nothing extraordinary about what Luther did that day. By all accounts, Luther was just an ordinary, unknown monk at a brand-new university in an out-of-the-way town. He had moved to Wittenberg, Saxony in 1511, and he described the town as on "the edge of civilization."[3] As a university professor, he had every right to address theological issues and point out ecclesiastical reform, and he was permitted to fulfill that office in the manner that he did. This was not even the first time that Luther spoke out against the corruptions of indulgences, and many people and even church councils before

---

1. History available at Philpott Memorial Church website: acommunityofgrace.org.
2. Luther, "Disputation for Clarifying the Power of Indulgences," 34.
3. Pettegree, *Brand Luther*, 7.

Luther had raised concerns as well.[4] Indulgences were certificates that people could purchase in order to lessen their time in purgatory, and the innovation that happened in the fifteenth century was that indulgences could be purchased for those who had already passed away.[5] Now you could buy one for yourself *and* for others, even those in the afterlife.

Luther saw this innovation as leading to corruption since the papacy was essentially cutting out the contrite heart from the practice of confession.[6] And so, Luther started a theological debate in an ordinary way but with extraordinary results. Within five years of the *Ninety-Five Theses*, with the support of the printing press, Luther became Europe's most published author ever.[7] On 31 October 1517, Luther planted a seed that has grown today into 560 million Protestants worldwide.[8] Reformation Sunday, then, is a chance to reflect on our heritage as believers and in light of the teachings of scripture in the context of worship.

And so, these past many weeks, I have been regularly traveling and speaking to various groups—to Christians in churches and scholars at conferences—all about the Reformation in anticipation of this anniversary. Through these exchanges, I have been struck by the many different responses. For some, the Reformation anniversary is a source of great joy. In fact, I was at one school speaking in chapel where they broke out into spontaneous applause at the mere mention of the fact that it *was* the 500th anniversary. While for others, the anniversary is a source of frustration as a divisive and fragmenting movement within the church that has so little to offer us today but regret. For some, there is pride, for others pain. In my experience, there is a fair share of misconception circulating as well. At the same time, for some, there is complete indifference over the value of reflecting on the tradition at all as Protestants, and for those outside the church, there is even no recognition at all of the Reformation event.

On Saturday, after my arrival in Hamilton, I engaged in conversation with a woman about the Reformation at the local A&W (my first visit there!). It just so happens to be part of my personality to engage in friendly

---

4. Consider canon 62 of the Fourth Lateran Council of the Church for evidence of the church's pre-Reformation awareness that indulgences were prone to corruption.

5. See Sixtus IV, "Salvator noster," 57.

6. Archbishop Albert of Mainz's commission of indulgence indicated that confession was not required in order to acquire the confessional letter.

7. Pettegree, *Brand Luther*, xi–xii.

8. The Center for the Study of Global Christianity at Gordon-Conwell reports that 41 percent of Protestants are living in Africa. See Johnson et al., "Christianity 2017," 1–12.

conversation with people I do not know, and these conversations about the Reformation have now been regularly happening all over and especially at the airport. I am not actually seeking these conversations out, but there are really very few questions these days that do not lead to the answer of "Martin Luther." Where am I going, and why? What do I do? What am I reading? The woman I met at the A&W certainly did not know what to think, and so, I am apparently and unintentionally exposing random people that I come across to the news of the 500th anniversary.

And what can be said about the Reformation in these encounters? If you had two seconds to sum up the origins of the Protestant tradition and what many consider to be the root of the modern era—how would you do it? What can be said about the Reformation that is understandable and even meaningful to the average person today? I have thought a lot about this, of course, and my answer is the same whether I am talking to scholars, to Christians in the pew, or strangers at the A&W. For the reformers, the *heart* of the Protestant Reformation was to recover the good news of Jesus Christ proclaimed in scripture. To pull that message out from the rocks withering it and out from the thorns choking it in the hopes of restoring what they believed had been stolen from people's hearts and from the life of the church.

And by no means is this challenge peculiar to the Reformation. This is how the Reformation moment relates to our context today and the complexity that we face in this post-Christendom world. This was not a particular challenge for the Reformation since it is the task of *every* generation to faithfully point to the person and work of Jesus Christ our savior in our time and place just as the Reformers did in their time and place.

LUTHER'S GATE OF PARADISE

Nevertheless, during the Reformation, this Protestant recovery of the gospel was particularly disruptive in ways that still reach us today. This does not mean that Luther set out to disrupt the world, even if scripture was dead set on disrupting him. Rather, Luther attributed his transformation to an encounter with scripture when—by the power of the Holy Spirit—God's Word altered his thinking and understanding and consequently transformed his life, and incidentally, the world. For Luther, the book of Romans was critical to that transformation of his understanding of the gospel message. Shaped by the scholastic theology of his day, he had struggled with understanding Rom 1:16–17. At that point, he was reading the New

Testament in Greek, lecturing on Romans at the university, and coming to a new understanding of the process of salvation. Luther grappled with the meaning of this particular passage because he felt like it lifted up a standard that he could not meet. He was doing everything he could to live a holy life, and yet, he still knew that he was unworthy. Maybe you know what that feels like.

There are a lot of stories about Luther in these angst-filled moments (or *anfechtungen*) and the way in which he was mentored by Johannes Staupitz, who was his confessor and superior within the Augustinian Order, to look to the grace offered by Christ on the cross.[9] Nevertheless, Luther still felt deeply the gravity of every sin that separated him from God. This quandary left him reeling, and he would later reflect on how it led him to hate "the righteous God who punishes sinners."[10] Until, in the midst of lecturing on Romans, the passage opened to him in a new and profound way. He saw there, for the very first time, that the righteousness we require in order to be received by God was also provided by God in the righteousness of Christ. That we are justified, not by our own works, but by our faith in the work of Jesus Christ alone according to God's grace alone. For Luther, this was a life changing turning point, which he later described as being "altogether born again and had entered paradise itself through open gates."[11] Through Romans, Luther experienced a dynamic restoration of the gospel message in his life and for his leadership within the church. He discovered the profound truth that the Christian life was rooted not in one's own ability to achieve sufficiency but in Christ's sufficiency alone.

THE BIBLE BOOM

This encounter with Romans is the primary reason why the reformers worked so hard to advance the Bible in their time and space so that each person might have a life-changing encounter with God's Word. Luther believed and would say many times that the Bible had grown increasingly forgotten, unknown, or hidden in the church. This was less of a remark about the number of Bibles available and more about encounters with the *message* that the Bible proclaims. And so, the Reformation advanced scripture as the supreme rule over the person's life and the life of the church.

9. Steinmetz, *Reformers in the Wings*, 15–22.

10. *LW* 34:327–38.

11. Luther's "Preface to the Complete Edition of Luther's Latin Writings" (1545) in *LW* 34:327–38.

Affirming the priesthood of all believers was instrumental in promoting more opportunities for engagement with the life-giving word of scripture in a language that could be understood.[12] Soon after, early modern Europe began to encounter God's Word in multifaceted ways from the church to the taverns and from the household to the street corner. Preaching was occurring. Scripture was being read. Theology was being sung. All this took place in the common languages of the people to the point that scripture was filling not only the liturgical life of the church but also everyday life from the taverns, to the streets, and to the homes.[13]

The Bible in common languages began to take on a new role in the spiritual lives of everyday Christians, both Protestant and Catholic. Luther had translated the New Testament into German in 1522, and by 1534, he published the complete Bible based upon the original languages. Luther's Bible was a fantastic success in the publishing world with around 450 editions in part and whole released over the course of his lifetime and half a million copies circulating by his death.[14] The Bible had never been more accessible as it was during this period thanks to the printing press and the flourishing of everyday language. Luther's opponent Johannes Cochlaeus famously bemoaned the success of Luther's Bible saying that it was read by "tailors and shoemakers, even women and simpletons."[15]

I saw the legacy of the Reformation lived out in a powerful way a few years ago in my own family. We were worshiping at the Maundy Thursday service at our church. My oldest daughter was in second grade at the time, and she was pouring over the pew Bible during the service. At first, I was not sure what she was doing, and I wondered if she was paying attention to the service. Then I realized that she was dutifully looking up each of the passages being read from the Gospel of Mark throughout the service. The joy of discovery marked her face as she poured over her pew Bible and read along with the liturgist, using her finger to trace from word to word. In that moment, watching her, I realized that I simply could not think of a better representation of the Reformation legacy than a little girl pouring over her Bible in order to participate in worship.

---

12. Luther affirmed the priesthood of all believer in his first 1520 treatise: *To the Christian Nobility of the German Nation*, 382.

13. Scribner, "Oral Culture and the Diffusion of Reformation Ideas," 49–69.

14. Pettegree, *Europe in the Sixteenth Century*, 100; Pettegree, *Brand Luther*, 188.

15. Cochlaeus, *Historia Martini Lutheri*, 120 as quoted in Gow, "The Contested History of a Book," 12.

Reformers understood that scripture was for all people, including little girls, and that it was sacred, holy, and not to be taken lightly when encountered. They knew that the Bible was no mere book. It was precious because God revealed himself there. In the reading of it, by the work of the Holy Spirit, you might never be the same. A special bond was forged between believers and Bibles during the Reformation to the point that some would give their lives to see Protestant Bibles circulate.[16] Luther comments on Heb 4:2 saying, "That uniting or combination of the Word and the hearts is reciprocal. For these three—faith, the Word, and the heart—become one. Faith is the glue or the bond. The Word is on one side; the heart is on the other side. But through faith they become one spirit, just as man and wife become 'one flesh' (Gen 2:24)."[17]

I recently read a parody from the Babylon Bee entitled, "Surgeon General's Warning to Be Stamped on All Bibles starting Next Year":

> In an effort to make sure the public is educated about the drastic effects the Word of God may have upon its readers, the FDA has announced that beginning next year, all new Bibles sold in America must be stamped with a warning from the Surgeon General which notifies them that 'Bible Reading Can Cause Belief In Objective Truth, Disagreement With Socially Accepted Values, Faith And Trust In God, And May Forever Change Your Life And Eternity.'[18]

This tongue-in cheek, fake-news article offers some levity even as it highlights the challenge that we face today in communicating the power of scripture to our world. The story of Luther's transformative encounter with the Bible is an important reminder for us today of what can happen when we turn to scripture and dare to meet God there.

And yet, even in that meeting, the reformers did not believe that scripture was always easy to hear or simple to understand. This is a fine distinction, but the reformers taught that clarity of scripture was assured for that which was sufficient to know in order to be saved. They did not believe that we could understand all of scripture perfectly. In practice, the

---

16. Olson, *Calvin and Social Welfare*, 50–69. See also Olson, "The Quest for Anonymity," 33–56.
17. *LW* 29:160 as quoted in Rittgers, ed., *Hebrews, James*, 57.
18. "Surgeon General's Warning," *Babylon Bee*, 30 August 2017.

reformers understood that there were "hard places" that required scripture to interpret scripture.[19] And so, we come to our parable this morning.

THE PARABLE OF THE SOWER & THE REFORMATION

This morning we are exploring the Parable of the Sower from Mark 4:1–20, and it is a challenging passage. Though this is perhaps the most well-known parable of the New Testament, biblical scholars also emphasize its complexity. In the first place, the parable is special because it is found in all three Synoptic Gospels, though with some slight variation. All three accounts indicate that Jesus had the practice of teaching the crowds and then providing further explanation in private. All three accounts reference the words of Isa 6 in some way (Mark 4:12), which indicates that this particular passage is the root of the parable itself. All three Synoptic Gospels echo Ezek 3:27 in declaring, "Let the one who has ears to hear, hear" (Mark 4:9; cf. Luke 8:8; and Matt 13:9).

The Parable of the Sower is the most prominent parable in the Gospel of Mark primarily because Mark does not recount Jesus teaching as many parables as Matthew and Luke. Mark's account has also been described as the harshest version of the three since there is a hardening of the heart that can happen not merely for outsiders but for Jesus' disciples. This is a difficult passage because it seems to indicate that Jesus tells parables *so that* people will not understand him. And yet, by using parables, Jesus was also fulfilling Old Testament prophecy from Ps 78, thereby revealing his identity to the people before communicating the true meaning of the message through his disciples. The medium of parable takes on a veiled quality, but the purpose of it is to confront, to engage, and to promote action according to the work of Klyne Snodgrass.[20] Jesus's words cite Isa 6:9–10 in order to spur the listener to hearing and obedience.

For our purposes, I would like to consider the overarching emphasis in Mark's account on hearing the message of the kingdom of God. In fact, there are thirteen usages of the Greek verb "to hear" from Mark 4:3–33. Mark's account is the only version that preserves Isa 6's emphasis on both hearing and seeing. And yet, this is no simple command. The Parable of the Sower warns us that there are many dangers that lurk in this world that

---

19. Reference to the "hard places" is common in the Geneva Bibles, such as the 1560 edition's title page and the 1599 Geneva Bible preface.

20. Snodgrass, "Hermeneutics of Hearing," 59–79.

threaten to destroy the gift of God's Word to us. That is to keep up from hearing and seeing God.

In the first place, God's Word can be stolen from our path. In Luther's time, he believed that the preaching and selling of indulgences in his region was essentially akin to stealing the good news of Jesus Christ from people's lives. He would stress that only the cross reveals the true character of God, who is hidden in suffering,[21] and only Christ's death on the cross was a sufficient sacrifice for our salvation. To point to anything else as the basis for our assurance was to steal the true story of God's graciousness from all.

And so, the reformers believed that the obfuscation of the gospel was a result of not only the system and practices of the church but the inattention to the Bible itself. In the 1539 Wittenberg edition of Luther's German writings, he declared that "the Bible lies forgotten in the dust under the bench."[22] To bring the seed back to the path, reformers emphasized the necessity of encountering scripture in common languages so that the everyday people of the church could hear and receive the gospel message proclaimed there. The urgency was clear. In the preface to the French Bible, Genevan reformer John Calvin would describe scripture as "the unique pasture for our souls" or the nourishment that we need in order to receive eternal life.[23] Without it, he says, we are left to "graze in the wind."[24] Without it, the sustenance for life with God is stolen beneath our feet.

Secondly, God's Word can wither on the rock without roots. In Luther's time, he regarded the withering of the word in the life of the church as due in part to the church being built on the wrong foundation. The name "Peter" means "stone" in Greek or "Cephas" in Aramaic, and it was common to interpret that the church was built on the rock of Peter according to Matthew 16. This was a very important passage that had to be reinterpreted by the reformers, and so, Luther argued that the only true rock and foundation of the church could be Jesus Christ and that God's Word would wither on any other foundation. The reformers saw the Reformation as a chance to re-center Christ in the hearts of believers and in the life of the church.[25]

21. "Heidelberg Disputation, 1518," 67–119.

22. *LW* 34:283–88.

23. See Calvin's 1546 preface in *La Bible*: "C'est la pasture unique de nos ames, pour les nourrir à la vie éternelle."

24. Calvin's 1546 preface in *La Bible*.

25. Scott Hendrix explains that the underlying intention of reform was re-Christianization. See Hendrix, "Rerooting the Faith," 558–77. See also Hendrix, *Recultivating the Vineyard*.

They were to point to Christ the cornerstone according to Isa 28:16 and the living stone according to 1 Pet 2:4. John Calvin wrote, "First, in him the promises have their firmness; secondly, the salvation of men rests on him alone, and therefore if Christ be taken away, the Church will fall down and be ruined . . . these statements must undoubtedly be referred to Christ, without whom there is no certainty of salvation."[26] And so, Petrine Supremacy was replaced with Solus Christus (Christ alone).

Thirdly, God's Word can be choked by the weeds. During the Reformation, the parable of the workers in the vineyard was an important biblical story used to reflect on their contemporary challenges within the church. In 1556, Lucas Cranach the Younger completed a beautiful painting of the parable, which hangs in St. Mary's Wittenberg. Cranach depicted the passage itself in the lower bottom portion of the painting while an account of the Protestant/Catholic divide took prominence at the center of the painting. And so, there is thick historical, interpretive commentary present in the painting that speaks to the divide faced by the church at that critical juncture. There are two sides of the painting separated by a wall. On one side of the painting, we see unknown Catholic workers of the church hierarchy destroying the vineyard. They are filling the well with stones and throwing vines into the fire. They are depicted as fighting, bickering, drinking, sleeping on the job, and playing cards. They have failed in their job. There is nothing neutral about this painting.

It is important to see how Cranach depicted Luther. Luther stands at the center of the divide, and he is raking the weeds and the undergrowth in order to free the soil. Meanwhile, other reformers are removing the stones and helping him to clear away the underbrush. The gospel is identified with the tilled soil, and so Luther sought first and foremost to clear away all that obstructed the soil in order that growth might finally flourish. As Luther declared in his 1529 foreword written for his colleague and friend, Philip Melanchthon's commentary on Colossians, "I have to dig out the roots and stumps, chop out the thorns and underbrush, and fill in the potholes. Thus I am the rough woodsman, who has to clear and straighten the path."[27]

In fact, it was not that long before, in 1520, that the Pope's bull, *Exsurge Domine*, described Luther as a "wild boar" ravaging the vineyard. According to Cranach, the "wild boar" is portrayed not as the destroyer of the

---

26. Calvin, *Commentary on the Prophet Isaiah*, 291.
27. Luther, "Preface to Philip Melanchthon," 248–50.

vineyard but as the true cultivator since his work is done for the purpose of ensuring the flourishing of God's Word.

RE-ROOTING OUR FAITH TODAY

What is stealing, withering, and choking God's Word from your lives today? What is preventing you and your church from being transformed according to God's Word and to his glory? How can we all re-root our lives in Christ?

There is hope in this passage though the landscape looks bleak. There is seed that falls on good soil. The soil hears God's Word, accepts it, and bears good fruit as a result. Because when something flourishes, it not only grows, but it passes the seed on to the next patch of good soil to grow. For the reformers, this process of flourishing was dependent upon pulling the Bible out of its obscurity and giving it a supreme role in all matters and in all hearts. For the reformers, access to the Bible was access to the gospel message and, therefore, key to becoming good soil. For the reformers, being good soil meant things like faithful attendance at church, faithful reading or listening to scripture, faithful time of prayer and repentance, and faithful community with the body of believers. How does the recovery of the gospel need to happen in our lives? In our churches? In our cultures?

Yet, none of this re-rooting can happen without abiding in Christ, and that is seen as the crux of Luther's thought. The seed that flourishes is rooted in Christ, and despite all the challenges of the world, nothing can overcome that. As scripture declares in 1 Pet 1:23, "You have been born anew, not of perishable but of imperishable seed, through the living and enduring word of God" (NRSV). Christ then is our cornerstone and our assurance, and this is proclaimed in an important way by Scripture's many references to "imperishable seed."

When we trace the use of the terms "imperishable" in the Bible, the fullness of the gospel message is communicated to us. According to Rom 1:23, the God revealed to us through the person of Jesus Christ is proclaimed as imperishable. Because God is imperishable and Jesus Christ is God, he resurrected from the dead, and this defeat of death is the good news of the gospel. Because God is imperishable, the good news of the gospel itself is imperishable, and it promises to us that by living in Christ we will become imperishable as well. Therefore, 1 Cor 15 powerfully proclaims the promise that we will receive incorruptible bodies (1 Cor 15:42), which is a term found in the semantic domain of "imperishable." According to 1 Cor 9:25, this is the incorruptible prize that we receive at the end of the race.

Here is the fullness of the hope that we have in Jesus Christ that is proclaimed to us through his Word, and this is the message that the reformers were seeking to restore for their time and place. It is the job of every generation to communicate that good news to every age as followers of Christ. The reformers pursued this work in their time, and we are tasked to fulfill it in ours. It is our turn to be vigilant against the weeds, thorns, and rocks that seek to prevent us and our churches from being deeply rooting in God's saving Word. In this way, the church lives as both reformed and always being reformed, until the end of the age.

Thanks be to God!
And to the one God, Father, Son, and Holy Spirit.
Amen.

BIBLIOGRAPHY

Babylon Bee. "Surgeon General's Warning to Be Stamped on All Bibles Starting Next Year." 30 August 2017. Online: https://babylonbee.com/news/surgeon-generals-warning-stamped-bibles-starting-next-year/

Calvin, John. *Commentary on the Prophet Isaiah.* Vol. 1. Translated by William Pringle. Grand Rapids: Baker, 2009.

———. "Preface." In *La Bible.* Jehan Girard: Geneva, 1546.

Cochlaeus, Johannes. *Historia Martini Lutheri.* Ingolstadt, 1582.

Gow, Andrew C. "The Contested History of a Book: The German Bible of the Later Middle Ages and Reformation in Legend, Ideology, and Scholarship." *Journal of Hebrew Scriptures* 9 (2009) 2–37.

"Heidelberg Disputation, 1518." In *The Annotated Luther: The Roots of Reform.* Vol. 1, edited by Timothy J. Wengert, 67–119. Translated by Dennis Bielfeldt. Minneapolis: Fortress, 2015.

Hendrix, Scott. *Recultivating the Vineyard: The Reformation Agendas of Christianization.* Louisville, KY: Westminster John Knox, 2004.

———. "Rerooting the Faith: The Reformation as Re-Christianization." *Church History* 69 (2000) 558–77.

Johnson, Todd M., et al. "Christianity 2017: Five Hundred Years of Protestant Christianity." *International Bulletin of Mission Research* 40 (2016) 1–12.

Luther, Martin. "Disputation for Clarifying the Power of Indulgences." In *The Annotated Luther: The Roots of Reform,* edited by Timothy J. Wengert, 1:13–46. Minneapolis: Fortress, 2015.

———. "Preface to the Complete Edition of Luther's Latin Writings." In *LW* 34:327–38.

———. "Preface to Philip Melanchthon, *Exposition of Colossians, Translated into German by Justus Jonas* (1529)." In *Luther's Works: Prefaces,* 1:248–250. Translated and edited by Timothy J. Wengert. St. Louis: Concordia, 2009.

———. *To the Christian Nobility of the German Nation*, edited by James M. Estes. In *The Annotated Luther*, edited by Timothy J. Wengert, 1:369–465. Minneapolis: Fortress, 2016.

Olson, Jeannine. *Calvin and Social Welfare: Deacons and the Bourse Française*. Plainsboro, NJ: Associated University Presses, 1989.

———. "The Quest for Anonymity: Laurent de Normandie, His Colporteurs, and the Expansion of Reformed Communities through Worship." In *Semper Reformanda: John Calvin, Worship, and Reformed Traditions*, edited by Barbara Pitkin, 33–56. Göttigen: Vandenhoeck and Ruprecht, 2018.

Pettegree, Andrew. *Brand Luther: 1517, Printing, and the Making of the Reformation*. New York: Penguin, 2015.

———. *Europe in the Sixteenth Century*. Oxford: Blackwell, 2002.

Philpott Memorial Church Website. Online: acommunityofgrace.org.

Rittgers, Ronald K., ed. *Hebrews, James*. Reformation Commentary on Scripture 13. Downers Grove, IL: IVP Academic, 2017.

Scribner, R. W. "Oral Culture and the Diffusion of Reformation Ideas." In *Popular Culture and Popular Movements in Reformation Germany*, 49–69. Oxford: Clarendon, 1994.

Sixtus IV. "Salvator noster." In *A Reformation Reader*, edited by Denis R. Janz, 57. 2nd ed. Minneapolis: Fortress, 2008.

Snodgrass, Klyne. "A Hermeneutics of Hearing Informed by the Parables with Special Reference to Mark 4." *Bulletin for Biblical Research* 14 (2004) 59–79.

Steinmetz, David. *Reformers in the Wings: From Geiler von Kaysersberg to Theodore Beza*. 2nd ed. Oxford: Oxford University Press, 2001.

Index of Names

Adrian VI, 31
Albrecht of Mainz, 17–18, 19, 21, 37, 38, 41, 44, 45, 49, 50, 185
Alesius, Alexander, 68
Allen, Michael, 126, 128
Apostle Paul, 111, 112
Aquinas, Thomas, 34, 52, 121
Arand, Charles, 122
Aristotle, 13
Augustine, 24, 138

Baan, Anaan, 140
Backus, Irena, 99
Barth, Karl, 121
Barrett, Matthew, 128
Bender, Harold S., 93
Bendroth, Margaret, 115, 123, 131
Benham, Hugh, 157, 158
Bertoglio, Chiara, 152, 165, 176
Bethge, Eberhard, 113
Biel, Gabriel, 15, 52
Bonhoeffer, Dietrich, 113, 121, 136–38, 139
Brett, Philip, 153
Briant, Alexander, 175
Brown, Howard Mayer, 174
Bucer, Martin, 75, 103
Bugenhagen, Johann, 25
Byrd, William, 152–80

Cajetan, Thomas, 51

Calvin, John, 3, 13, 75, 82–100, 103, 109, 110, 121, 130, 138, 142, 147, 191, 192
Campion, Edmund, 153, 175
Charles V, 17, 146
Chesterton, G. K., 129
Chrysostom, John, 70
Clopton, John, 59, 62, 65, 66, 71
Clopton, Richard, 76
Cordell, William, 66
Cranmer, Thomas, 58–80, 121, 159
Crisp, Oliver, 120, 128
Cromwell, Thomas, 64, 69
Cyprian, 24

Day, John, 163
Dickens, A. G., 154, 156
Duffield, G. E., 152
Duffy, Eamon, 58
Duguid, Timothy, 163, 164

Eck, Johannes, 53–54, 87n20, 105–106
Edward VI, 59, 72–73, 76, 154, 156, 158, 164, 174
Edward the Confessor, 59
Eilers, Kent, 115
Elizabeth I, 59, 66, 78, 154, 159, 164, 168, 174, 176
Erasmus, Desiderius, 16–17, 64, 103, 104–105, 154–55, 158, 173

Foxe, John, 72, 77
Francis I, 88

Index of Names

Frederick the Wise, 32

García, Alberto, 131
George, Timothy, 128
Gordon, Bruce, 85, 89
Grebel, Conrad, 91, 95
Gregory, Brad S., 2–3, 135, 138, 142–43
Grey, Jane, 78–79
Grey, Thomas, 78

Hauerwas, Stanley, 137, 138, 140, 141, 148
Hendrix, Scott, 191
Henry VIII, 59, 63, 64, 66, 68, 71–72, 73, 79, 153–54
Holder, R. Ward, 90
Hubmaier, Balthasar, 105, 121

Irvin, Dale, 128

James I, 59, 174
Jenkins, Philip, 2, 125
Jennings, Willie, 145
Jenson, Robert, 122
Jerome, 24, 25
John Paul II, 21n25, 25

Keller, Tim, 144
Kerman, Joseph, 176
Klaassen, Walter, 92
Kolb, Robert, 122
Koop, Karl, 90–91, 94, 97

Lasso, Orlanda, 174
Leithart, Peter, 126, 128, 130, 135–36
Leo X, 21, 37–38, 49, 51, 55
Lewis, C. S., 175
Luther, Martin, 1–2, 3, 11–27, 29–56, 86, 87, 90, 103, 106–109, 121, 122, 125, 129, 131, 138, 139, 142, 143, 146, 155, 158, 160, 179n, 184–85, 186, 188, 189, 191, 192
Lydgate, John, 60

MacCulloch, Diarmaid, 72
Marsh, Christopher, 155
Martyn, Roger, 58–80
Marquart, K., 48

Mary I, 59, 64–65, 66, 77, 154
Mary Magdalene, 60
Mary, Mother of Jesus, 61, 62, 80, 105
McCarthy, Kerry, 160–61, 165, 167, 169
Melanchthon, Philip, 13, 103, 122, 142, 192
Merbecke, John, 168
Milbank, John, 135
Miller, Calvin, 177
Miller, Clement, 154–55
Monson, Craig, 161
More, Thomas, 64, 66
Morung, Dietrich, 18
Mouw, Richard, 83
Murray, Stuart, 83, 90, 92, 94

Nation, Mark Theissen, 137
Neighbour, Oliver, 172
Nunes, John, 131

Osiander, Andreas, 64

Pecknold, C. C., 143
Pelikan, Jaroslav, 119, 121
Pfefferkorn, Johannes, 105
Philips, Obbe, 95
Philpott, P. W., 184

Quitslund, Beth, 163

Radner, Ephraim, 136
Raimudi, Peraudi, 18
Reuchlin, Johann, 103–104

Sadoleto, James, 82, 85, 87–88
Schleiermacher, Friedrich, 112
Shakespeare, William, 163
Sherwin, Ralph, 175
Simons, Menno, 121
Sixtus IV, 35–36
Snodgrass, Klyne, 190
Spalatin, Georg, 26
Staupitz, Johannes, 187
Sternhold, Thomas, 164
Swain, Scott, 126, 128

Tallis, Thomas, 158, 176–77

Index of Names

Taverner, John, 157
Taylor, Charles, 135
Taylor, W. David O., 130
Temperley, Nicholas, 164
Tetzel, Johann, 17, 21, 37, 38–40, 44, 45
Torrance, T. F., 85
Trump, Donald, 145
Tyndale, William, 68

Vanhoozer, Kevin, 127, 128, 130
Vaux, Laurence, 169
Von Bora, Katherina ("Katie"), 25–26, 27

Weaver, J. Denny, 93, 120
Wesley, John, 121
William of Ockham, 52
Wulstan, David, 157
Wycliffe, John, 138

Yoder, John Howard, 96, 138, 149
Young, Frances, 79

Zwingli, Ulrich, 3, 13, 86, 90, 138, 177

Index of Subjects

"A Mighty Fortress," 173
A Sermon on Indulgences and Grace
    (Marin Luther), 21
Act of Supremacy, 67
Address to the Nobility of the German
    Nation (Martin Luther), 22
Anabaptists, 82–100, 179
Anglicanism, 80
Anfechtungen, 187
Anti-semitism, 102–13
Apocalyptic, 107
Associated Gospel Churches of
    Canada, 184
Augsburg Confession, 29
Augustinian Monks, 13, 14

Babylon Bee, 189
Belgic Confession, 142
"Blood myth," 106, 108
Boleyn, Anne, 66, 78
Book of Common Prayer, 74–76, 78, 80
Book of Martyrs, 72
Bubonic Plague, 12, 105

Cambridge, University of, 64
Center for the Study of Global Christianity, 185
Chantries Act (1547), 158
Christendom, 2, 52, 95, 125, 137, 140,
    144, 147
Clement VI, 35
Clerical celibacy, 23, 25
Clerical marriage, 24–25, 67

Communion (Holy Communion;
    Eucharist; the Lord's Supper), 24,
    67, 106
Council of Trent, 2, 30, 52
Creation, 116, 119

Deutsche Christen movement, 137
Diet of Augsburg, 105
Diet of Nuremberg, 31
Diet of Worms, 16, 105, 146
Discipleship, 139, 145

Ecclesiology, 94, 117, 138–41
Ecumenism, 29–57
English Bible, 68–70
English Reformation, 58–80, 152–80
Erfurt University, 13
Eschatology, 117
Eton Choirbooks, 156, 157

Fourth Lateran Council, 185
Formula of Concord, 142
Fuggers, 19, 37–38
Fundamentalism, 148

Geneva, 85, 88, 103
Global south, 2, 124
Gospel (good news), 20, 42, 116–17
Gradualia, 168–69, 179

Heidelberg Disputation, 109
Holocaust, 113
Holy Roman Empire, 2, 11, 18

Index of Subjects

Holy Spirit, 34, 189
Humanism, 13, 103, 161

Indulgences, 17, 20–22, 30–40
Institutes of Christian Religion, 84, 86, 88, 109

Justification, 15–16, 19, 142, 144

Katherine of Aragon, 64
Kingdom of God, 25
Koppe, Leonhard, 25

Leipzig Dispitation, 87, 105
Liberal theology, 111–12

Magisterial Reformation, 85, 90, 91, 96, 143
Martyrdom, 92
Mass, 167–68, 170
Missions, 135–50
Moral Majority, 144–45
Music, 152–80

Neo-Anabaptists, 137–38, 141, 145–46, 149
New Testament, 107, 109, 117
Ninety-Five Theses, 1, 17, 18, 21, 22, 26, 29–56, 125, 184, 185
Nominalism, 15

Oath of Supremacy, 64–65
Old Testament, 24, 107, 109
Orthodox, 129, 132

Peasants' Revolt, 144
Pentecostalism, 118
Philpott Memorial Church, 184
Pope, 17, 43, 45, 47, 52, 71, 139
Presbyterianism, 118
Priesthood of all Believers, 188
Printing Press, 20

Radical Reformation, 136
Renaissance, 103
Righteousness, 15–16
Rome, 14, 17, 19, 32, 88

Sacerdotalism, 23–24
Saints, 76
Sanctification, 142
Schleitheim Confession, 82
Scholasticism, 53
Scripture, 15, 183–94
Simony, 18
Sola Christus, 149, 192
Sola Fide, 84, 149
Sola Gratia, 84
Sola Scriptura, 83, 84–85, 146–49
Soli Deo Gloria, 84
Soteriology, 73
St. Peter's basilica, 37–38
Stotternheim, 12
Suffolk, 58
Swiss Brethren, 179

The Bablyonian Captivity of the Church (Martin Luther), 22
The Freedom of the Christian (Martin Luther), 22
Transubstantiation, 67, 76
Two Kinds of Righteousness (Martin Luther), 15, 19

University of Wittenberg, 40
United Church of Canada, 111

Wars of the Roses, 59
Wartburg, 18
Westminster Confession of Faith, 139
White Horse Tavern, 64
Wittenberg, 1, 17, 18, 33, 184, 191
World Council of Churches, 110

Zurich, 177

www.ingramcontent.com/pod-product-compliance
Lightning Source LLC
Chambersburg PA
CBHW070327230426
43663CB00011B/2242